Tales of a Theatrical Guru

Tales of
a Theatrical

Danny Newman

Foreword by Studs Terkel

UNIVERSITY OF ILLINOIS PRESS

Urbana and Chicago

Music in American Life

*A list of books in the
series appears at the end of this book.*

Guru

Caricature of Danny Newman by
Al Hirschfeld © Al Hirschfeld.
Reproduced by arrangement with
Hirschfeld's exclusive representative,
The Margo Feiden Galleries Ltd.,
New York, at www.alhirschfeld.com

Caricature of Danny Newman in 1951
by Xavier Cugat. (Author's collection)

Library of Congress Cataloging-in-Publication
Data

Newman, Danny.
Tales of a theatrical guru / Danny Newman ;
foreword by Studs Terkel.
p.   cm. — (Music in American life)
Includes index.
ISBN-13: 978-0-252-03164-9 (cloth : alk. paper)
ISBN-10: 0-252-03164-4 (cloth : alk. paper)
1. Entertainers—Anecdotes.
2. Singers—Anecdotes.
I. Title. II. Series.
PN1583.N49   2006
791.0922—dc22   2006006966

Contents

Foreword

STUDS TERKEL

Danny Newman is the last of an American species, vanishing fast—the press agent. Long before the bloodless robotic phrase-makers, public relations (PR) practitioners distinguished our lingo and provided our celebrities with faceless, voiceless beings who held coats, there was Danny Newman.

Dick Christiansen, long-time drama critic of the *Chicago Tribune*, said it all: "Danny Newman continues to spread the gospel and wave his banner high. . . . some kind of warrior-priest in the arena of the arts, ever the man in motion. . . . both battling and exulting, sounding the charge, trumpeting his victories, covering every front . . . the world's foremost exponent of subscription ticket sales for performing arts institutions . . . a more interesting character than many of the stars he has promoted."

Being a press agent was his calling ever since he was fourteen, some seventy years ago. In listening to him speak (never, perish forbid, sotto voce) he declaims, proclaims to the world, in superlatives, of course—seldom heard these days—the virtues of the artiste (never a mere artist) or the company he represents.

How can anyone, how *dare* anyone, resist his W. C. Fieldsian, his Barnumesque sales pitch? Let Claudia Cassidy, Chicago's most prestigious music and theater critic for many years, say it: "If Mr. Newman were a critic, producers would buy billboards or maybe blimps to quote him . . . when he says, 'Subscribe Now!'—people do. If someone tells you that *The Tempest* is 'one of the bard's most scintillating works of genius, offering a quicksilver profusion of frolicking goddesses, clown fairies, sprites and spirits, weaving mythically and magically through the tangled, tropical jungle of our subconscious'—wouldn't you?"

No matter what the milieu—grand opera, symphony, burlesque, wild west show, ballet, circus, theater, pageant, whatnot—Danny Newman has been there, a Joshua blowing his trumpet, and all the walls of resistance invariably came tumbling down.

There is also Till Eulenspiegel in him, the imp who causes an occasional ruckus (that, of course, makes page one of the metropolitan newspapers). Consider the case of Maria Callas during her appearance as Chicago Lyric Opera's Madame Butterfly. She, in her dressing room, still in her kimono as the delicate Cio-Cio-San, is served with a subpoena for some breach of contract. The hapless process server, one Stanley Pringle, fedora perched gingerly on head, is given a good going-over by the diva, her lips curled in a furious snarl. "How dare you? I am a goddess!" It was, naturally, the talk of the town. Yes, it was Danny Newman who arranged to have a platoon of photographers on the spot. The boy has a touch of clairvoyance, too.

Need I say more? He has, with the idea of group subscription, saved theater, opera, dance, and symphonic companies in all parts of the world. Al Hirschfeld honored him with not one but two caricatures, for Danny is as famed as those artists he has celebrated.

One incident may be all that needs be said. During World War II, when trains were still the prime means of cross-country travel, Danny was in a crowd awaiting the arrival of the Twentieth Century Limited. He was there to greet his new client, Jimmy Durante. As the comic stepped onto the platform, he immediately spotted Danny, whom he had never seen before. He sprang toward him. "How did you know it was me?" asked Danny. Jimmy replied, "I knew you was a press agent 'cause you had dat *worried* look!" You see, Danny Newman has always had a face; a rarity among PR boys and girls of today.

Acknowledgments

This book is dedicated to Alyce Newman, my wonderful wife, who inspires me with her love and her goodness.

I am honored to have been powerfully motivated to write this book by Saul Bellow—my fellow octogenarian (he was only three and a half years my senior) and dear friend who promised that he would refuse to die until I had written it!

I'm grateful to Studs Terkel, my multitalented pal of the past half century, who paused—in his still-burgeoning literary activities—to dash off a splendid foreword.

Thank you Susan Mathieson Mayer, my brilliant, beautiful colleague, for all manner of encouragement and assistance in this ambitious project.

I acknowledge the patient persistence of my opera-loving friends and admirers, Ben and Natalie Heineman, who have so long awaited this volume's publication. My gratitude to Pete Ciecka for painstakingly transcribing my two-fingered, manually typed manuscript into orderliness.

I greatly appreciate the understanding and kindly guidance of Judith McCulloh, executive director of the University of Illinois Press, who understands that in writing this account I have found some repetition and duplication to be of essential importance and have not sought to avoid it.

I deeply regret that my late wife, the actress Dina Halpern, and my late sister and mentor, Marcella Marks, did not live to read my "insider insights."

Tales of a Theatrical Guru

Introduction to a Whip-Cracking American Showman's Memory Montage— Covering More than Seventy Years of Backstage and Onstage Involvements!

Do I possess a musical or theatrical heritage? The answer is no. Yes, my wonderful father (of blessed memory) did provide me with weekly piano lessons when I was a motherless little boy, and I did learn to play "Bob-O-Link, Spink, Spank, Spink!" I lacked the basic talent, however, and soon gave up. Neither of my Lithuanian-born parents had any arts background. Yet even though I began with no family show biz–performing arts connections, as the years progressed I seemed to develop a slew of them. The Newmans arrived in Chicago, USA, in 1888. My father Jacob Newman, then fifteen, immediately became an entrepreneur, supplying choice fruits and vegetables to the wealthy in their south-of-the-Loop mansions. Eventually, he became a wholesale tobacconist, prospering briefly. My mother's family came here early in the new century when its patriarch—and my grandfather—Benjamin Waldman became an economically ruined, displaced, and uprooted old-country distiller through Czar Alexander II's decision to nationalize the Russian Empire's lucrative vodka industry. So Grandpa Ben began his American career as a Halsted Street wholesale grocer—a neighbor of Jane Addams's Hull-House, where clarinetist Benny Goodman was spawned. I believe that it was in 1919—the year of my birth—that my mother's cousin Benjamin Kubelsky, destined to become Jack Benny, the suave, big-time vaudevillian and star of radio, movies, and television, left for the navy. I didn't catch up with him until years later, when I publicized one of his personal appearances. By then, my only sister, Marcella Marks, her husband, Sherman Marks, and I had exchanged our bourgeois status for Bohemian glamour. We became, respectively, a New York–Hollywood casting director; a stage, radio, and television writer and director; and a theatrical manager–press agent. My niece, ballerina Dianna Marks, danced with the American Ballet Theatre, National Ballet of Canada, Pennsylvania Ballet, San Franscico Ballet, and Chicago City Ballet, of which she became executive director.

Dina Halpern, my late, Warsaw-born actress wife, was part of an East European theatrical dynasty. Her great-aunt, the actress Esther Rachel Kaminska, founded the Warsaw playhouse that still bears her name, originally constructed with the proceeds of her pre–World War I American tours. Her son, the violinist virtuoso and composer Josef Kaminsky, was the Israel Philharmonic's concertmaster for many years. Her daughter, Ida Kaminska, headed the Polish State Yiddish Theatre and was the star of the Academy Award–winning Czech film *The Shop on Main Street.* Ida's chanteuse-daughter Ruth is the widow of the European jazz trumpet star Eddy Rosner, once known as the "Soviet Union's answer to America's Louis Armstrong." Rosner's career was cut short when Stalin (who had previously decorated him) suddenly declared jazz to be a degenerate, imperialist musical form and sent Eddy and Ruth off to ten years of Siberian exile. Erica, their toddler daughter, was raised by family friends in Moscow. She later became a graduate in English literature at Warsaw University; came to America as the ward of Dina and me; and studied film direction in New York and stage technique at Chicago's Goodman Theatre, where she collaborated with actor/playwright Jerome Kilty in drama adaptations. Now Erica has a grown daughter of her own, Amaris, who has two strapping young sons.

Alyce, my multilingual wife who speaks seven languages and uses them all backstage at Lyric Opera of Chicago, was born on the steps of a Kraków hospital where her mother had just been refused entrance by the then politically correct officials. The Holocaust era was drawing to a close, and Alyce's father, Leon Berger, a prominent physician, had recently been murdered by the Germans. Alyce's indomitable mother, Malwina, eventually brought her to Israel; then to Belgium, where Alyce became a child diamond sorter in Antwerp; then to England and France; and, finally, to Chicago, where she became the teenaged bride of physician Josef Katz, also a Holocaust survivor and a close friend of mine. Their union produced two now-grown sons, André and Leonard.

Our family's connection with the arts continues, with Alyce delighting in listening to recordings of her martyred great-uncle, the famed Bayreuth Festival bass-baritone Hermann Horner, that I found by inserting an appeal in a leading German-language opera journal. Horner had been summarily executed—along with his nine-year-old son—as he was bravely but vainly attempting to rescue him from the murder-bent Hitlerians who had gassed to death the rest of Horner's large family in a railroad car converted into a mobile gas chamber and rolled into the main railroad station of Alyce's hometown. All her remaining relatives were stuffed into it and immediately murdered.

More than sixty years have now passed since those cruel and bestial perpetrators of wholesale atrocities obliterated millions of human beings. Yet those who deny the Holocaust are everywhere, including on university faculties. I recall an evening in the 1970s, when we heard a tenured professor stating on television news that there never was a Holocaust. My late wife Dina, whose entire family was murdered at the death factory of Treblinka, screamed at our TV set, "Then, where is my father? Where are my sisters and brothers? Where are my uncles, aunts and cousins?" By then we had long known where they were done to death, because the Germans sometimes kept meticulous records of their savage depredations. We had visited those death camp sites to recite our traditional memorial prayers for each and every family member.

In mid-2002 I resigned from the Association of Theatrical Press Agents and Managers (ATPAM) after sixty-one years of membership, receiving a gold lifetime membership card and a lavish luncheon. I had previously withdrawn from the Screen Publicists Guild after ceasing to handle the midwestern premieres of major motion pictures. ATPAM is a labor union, yet—paradoxically—its manager members are, on behalf of the producers, *employers* of labor. Although ATPAM is an affiliate of the giant International Association of Theatrical Stage Employees (IATSE), it has, I believe, the smallest membership in the entire A.F.L./C.I.O., the highest minimum wage in uniondom, and only one local—in New York City. Obtaining membership when I came in was next to impossible, and there were only a few hundred ATPAM members in North America, thus keeping employment high for those on the inside. I truly felt honored to become a part of this select group of "Boswells," as our publicist members were often designated. The talent quotient of the membership was high. Some manager members had vast experience with all manner of show business, and some press agents were superb writers whose work was highly regarded by editors of newspapers and journals.

Overall, ATPAM was a fraternity of astute theatrical managers and high-level publicists, many of whom had impressive journalistic backgrounds and sometimes returned to that field. For instance, Clarence J. Bulliet, who had been on the road for Shakespearean repertory companies, was later a distinguished fine arts critic for the *Chicago Daily News,* a pioneering enthusiast for the work of Pablo Picasso, and author of a book about him, *Apples and the Madonna.* Lloyd Lewis, an alumnus of major film promotions, became the drama critic, sports, and then executive editor of the *Chicago Daily News.* He was a distinguished historian of America's pre–Civil War Abolitionist movement and, with Sinclair Lewis, co-dramatist of the Broadway production *Jayhawker.* Lloyd was my dear friend and one of my main mentors.

I was happy that ATPAM was soon so proud of me that it used a praise-laden letter about my work to convince union-shy theatrical producers to sign its basic agreement contracts during the 1940s. That particular letter from banker Abner J. Stilwell, who was then board president of the Chicago Opera Company, stated, "If Danny is an example of what your members offer, we wish that you had organized us years ago." Stilwell, a hard-drinking, florid-faced, former coal miner, had achieved education and success. In his youth he had become the main support of his impoverished siblings. I liked him at once, and he soon recognized my value to the opera company. His presidential box 16 was, at his wish, given to me for almost all performances.

Recently, in re-reading other encomia from leaders of art organizations, I noted how often they referred to the spiritual aspect of my ministrations in their behalf. The Indiana Repertory Theatre communications director wrote of Danny's "faith in us, . . . qualities ordinarily ascribed to a rabbi, priest, or minister." The Dallas Opera's Lawrence V. Kelly said, "You started a fire. We follow your procedures like a religion!" The Northern New Zealand Arts Council praised, "You really can perform miracles!" "You had a tremendous effect on popularizing opera in this country. By God, we needed you!" the Australian National Theatre added. The Louisville Ballet proclaimed me "the greatest missionary for the arts in this century," and for the *Minnesota Monthly* I was "the Messiah of the Arts." *Forbes Magazine* heralded me as "a world class evangel" and ran one of Al Hirschfeld's caricatures of me as its centerfold to illustrate critic Martin Mayer's tribute to my far-flung audience-building projects. "He's the Godfather of the performing arts in Canada" stated the Toronto International Festival. For the *Houston Post,* I was "virtually a god to literally hundreds of performing arts groups world-wide," and *Variety* declared, "He's the St. Paul of subscription sales." "Arts administrators queue up to meet him like Pilgrims to the Vatican for an audience with the Pope," noted the *Vancouver Sun.* And the Ravinia Festival of Highland Park, Illinois, affirmed, "As savior of so many arts organizations, you are Saint Danny. Boston was right to make you its Arts Angel."

Perhaps my ancestors preached in ancient Israel's "high places," and I've inherited their spirituality. And, speaking of the Holy Land, I more than doubled the subscribership of Haifa's Municipal Theatre, which thanked me for "inspiring us with the enthusiasm and faith which were so necessary for our success." "He's been likened to Moses, the prophet Mica, the Biblical Daniel, who conquered the lions, the Pope, John Cardinal Newman, Billy Graham, and the Messiah," reported the *Chicago Tribune.* "The Lord has given you a great talent and a soul which feels deeply and echoes all the joy and suffering of the artists" attested famed actress Eugenie Leontovich. "You radiate faith and wondrous creativity," glowed the Canada Council for the Arts. "Like St. Christopher, you are carrying us across the stream," waxed author Alberto Da Cruz. *Stagebill* attested, "In the church of subscribership, [you are] both high priest and theologian."

I have long been a defender of human rights, starting with my own. When I was but five years of age, in 1924, my kindergarten teacher, Miss Kindellen, at Chicago's Nathaniel Pope School denied my human right to go to the toilet. "You don't own this school," I told her, "the Board of Education does!" I stalked out, only to be given a harsh note to take home to my poor mother, who was then in the last year of her life, fast losing her struggle with breast cancer. Although I was but a child I already knew the biblical injunction "justice, shalt thou pursue," because my wonderful father was constantly and conscientiously inculcating me with our people's age-old ethical values. But how could I pursue justice for my manifestly unjustly stricken and suffering mother? As I now write, more than seventy-seven years have passed since I lost her on October 10, 1926. In 1989, my wife of more than forty years, Dina Halpern, also succumbed to cancer, as did my casting-director sister, Marcella, in the year 2000.

After my mother's death when I was six and a half, I began attending the prescribed eleven months of daily religious services to recite the age-old Aramaic memorial prayer of kaddish—in its authentic, pre-Allen Ginsberg form—for my mother. Many men who came to the minyan at the small synagogue right across the street from where I lived in Chicago's leafy Douglas Park area were elderly Eastern and Central Europeans. I would perch on their knees while they proffered sniffs of the snuff they carried in ivory-lidded little boxes and told me fascinating tales of their lives in the Old Country under Czars Alexander and Nicholas and the Austro-Hungarian Emperor Franz Josef.

For the next several years I went to public elementary schools most of the day and to Hebrew schools in various neighborhoods during the late afternoons. I also roller-skated; ice-skated; bought, recycled, and sold old bicycles; and helped my dear father care for his failing octogenarian father, whom I dearly loved. After my grandfather's death in 1929 I worked during the late afternoon and evening for a grocery store and also for a pharmacy—until the stock market crashed and previously generous tips (one nice man gave me a $10 gold piece every time I delivered his prescriptions) dwindled to thin dimes.

The Great Depression was on. I was heartbroken when a neighborhood bank closed when I was ten, obliterating my tiny savings. Federally insured bank accounts did not yet exist, and any proposals along those lines, along with ones like government-sponsored unemployment insurance, health-care insurance, and supervision of the securities markets, were branded as socialism by Republicans. I recall the vehemence with which a Lyric

Opera season wealthy contributor, usually a pleasant fellow, fulminated against such "left-wing" concepts as Social Security and Medicare.

In 1928 we lived next door to the Legler Branch Library in Garfield Park, where I devoured most books it housed in intense, highly pleasurable, and protracted sleep-starved reading splurges that, fortunately, succeeded in half educating me. As it turned out I would not be having much further higher learning. I had also plunged into amateur theatricals, for which I evidenced emerging talents and tendencies that would be important to me in the years to come.

By age fourteen I had become a precocious boy-prodigy, theatrical manager/press agent, and ever since I have worried about the economic survival and career destinies of the many artists I have encountered and also about those attempting to aid them in their aspirations—managers, publicists, and, where nonprofit organizations were involved, volunteer leaders. In contrast to many of my older professional colleagues (whose work was often good but emotionally detached), I saw myself, somehow, romantically, as fighting for the actors, singers, dancers, musicians, conductors, directors, choreographers like a medieval knight in combat for the honor of the ladies fair.

Some of those theatrical press agents were highly respected and even brilliant writers. In the commercial legitimate theater, however, press agents who toured in advance of their shows were often quite cynical, claiming that "either the public was going to come or it wasn't" and that nothing could be done to make a difference—a view I have always contested. One veteran publicist laughed at my youthful idealism. He was contemptuous of actors because, he said, "They put paint on their faces." (I later learned that he had been an actor and had certainly often used theatrical makeup.)

I proved my point many times. As one example, the 1946–47 touring *Lute Song*—a superb Broadway production starring Dolly Haas and Yul Brynner—died at the Chicago box office despite its rave reviews. Months later, however, it returned to enjoy sellout success after I took it on and "broke" newspapers with pictures for thirty-seven consecutive days, generating a head of steam that kept us happily hurtling forward for months at the 1,300-seat Studebaker Theatre.

Fifteen years later, in 1961, Elizabeth I. McAnn, who is now a noted New

York stage producer and was then general manager for New York producer Martin Tahse, said of my "handling" of the drama *Miracle Worker* at Chicago's Erlanger Theatre, "Martin is thrilled at the job you have done. No one could have worked harder to make the show a success." Tahse wrote, "I was honestly staggered by the amount of space you've been getting. The success is due to the truly remarkable job you did. I say again that you are the first press agent I have ever had who has shown me what a press agent can do for an attraction!" It must have been my seemingly inexhaustible energy and bursting good health—plus the discipline I learned as a battle-hardened World War II infantry rifleman—that enabled me to maintain a blistering, workaholic pace in the fiercely competitive show business of that era.

I worked simultaneously in the for-profit (show business) and nonprofit (performing arts) fields, but for some years now have been involved mainly with nonprofits. I was, in my early years, astonished to find that although many of their administrative practitioners—managers, publicists, and marketers—were well educated, highly cultured, and loved the arts dearly (especially the attractive lifestyle around them), they were often unwilling to undertake the necessary, unglamorous, and practical work involved. Instead, they tended to spend whole days watching rehearsals instead of being out raising funds and promoting ticket sales—life's blood to such projects. They also went to performances and sat in cafes afterward, discussing art with friends until the wee hours. Of course it was often too difficult for them to get up in the mornings and attend to business. Because I have dealt directly with a few thousand professional arts organizations over the years I've had a special opportunity to evangelize many of their employees and instill pride in doing their jobs well. *My* pride in their accomplishments has been considerable.

At age fourteen I came under the influence of a brilliant stage director, Sherman Marks, to whom I dedicated my 1977 book, *Subscribe Now!* entering its eleventh printing, and became his agent while still in my teens, providing the entering wedge for his distinguished career in national radio and television. As a dedicated "person of the theatre" I had given up my childhood obsession with the Chicago Cubs, although I still have total recall of the team's lineup in 1932: Charlie Grimm, first base; Billy Herman, second base; Billy Jurges, shortstop; Woody English, third base; Hack

Wilson, right field; Kiki Cuyler, center field; Riggs Stephenson, left field; Gabby Hartnett, catcher; and Lon Warneke, my preferred pitcher.

I also developed, in both junior high and high school, a profitable school supplies business. It was—of course—against all the board of education's rules, but I was emboldened by many kindly faculty members who admired my ambition and gumption. Encouraged by a fatherly English teacher, Abraham L. Pannitch, I became the high school newspaper's book critic and sports editor, specialties I later pursued at a junior college for which I was the National Youth Administration–hired publicist. I enrolled in a few courses there, too, but didn't go beyond the first year and never attended a university. Thus, both of my doctorate degrees are honorary ones.

During the same period I was also employed as a press associate of Bishop Bernard J. Sheil's Catholic Youth Organization (CYO), where I developed my ecumenical finesse. I also I wrote scripts for, and acted in, an extended series of radio dramas entitled *Romance and Adventure* on station WCFL, the "Voice of Labor." In two programs about Abraham Lincoln I appeared with John Huston, then a young actor, and was cast in the role of Lincoln's uncle, Tom Lincoln. In another program based on *Moby-Dick,* which Huston would years later do as a major movie after he became a celebrated film writer-director-actor, I played a boisterous old salt. During the *Romance and Adventure* series I did thirteen weeks each in the title roles of Charles Dickens's *David Copperfield* ("Please, Mr. McCawber, don't beat me! I shan't do it again!") and *Oliver Twist.*

All of this, of course, was before television. I also briefly served as personal manager for retired silent movie star Francis X. Bushman during his major radio career. I had previously convinced him to appear on the stage in the British comedy *The Bishop Misbehaves,* which I promoted. I had, during the second half of the 1940s, a profitable five-year run with the pioneering radio celebrity-interview radio show *Famous Names* for which I provided theatrical and musical arts notables who were interviewed by the golden-voiced Myron Wallace, more recently known as Mike Wallace of *60 Minutes.* From 1945 (when he came out of the navy and I came out of the army) through 1950 Mike and I had lunch together—Mondays through Fridays—with our celebrated guests at either the elegant Mayfair Room or the chic Balinese Room of the then-deluxe Blackstone Hotel. Mike was not, in those days, yet into investigative reporting. He's a good actor, however, and assumed that role beautifully for *60 Minutes,* years later. In the beginning 1950s I became national publicist for the Miss U.S. Television Contest in thirteen major cities and also publicized lectures by such prominent personalities as Eleanor Roosevelt and Cornelius Vanderbilt Jr.

Duos, trios, quartets, and larger groups offered combined star-strength for vaudeville programs. Some of the big-time variety performers I publicized included Buck and Bubbles, Block and Sully, Smith and Dale, Willie West and McGinty, the Ritz Brothers, the Mills Brothers, the Ames Brothers, the InkSpots, the Andrews Sisters, the Duncan Sisters, the Mary Macs, Borrah Minnevitch and His Harmonica Rascals, Paul Draper and Larry Adler, the Barry Sisters, the Three Stooges, Collins and Peterson, Veloz and Yolanda, *George White's Scandals,* and *Earl Caroll's Vanities.* Among the attractions I press-agented were the top-level jazz and swing bands and their charismatic leaders, like Count Basie, Duke Ellington, Ted Weems, Frankie Masters, Vaughn Monroe, Paul Whiteman, Jan Garber, Shep Fields, Charlie Barnett, Henry Busse, Stan Kenton, Griff Williams, Louis Prima, Les Brown, Woody Herman, Sammy Kaye, Lionel Hampton, Spike Jones, Tommy Dorsey, Jimmy Dorsey, Cab Calloway, Glenn Miller, Raymond Scott, Freddy Martin, Abe Lyman, Phil Spitalney, Alvino Rey, Gene Krupa, Ted Fiorito, Horace Heidt, Lawrence Welk, Clyde McCoy, Kay Kyser, Xavier Cugat, and, as they say, "many more."

Almost sixty years ago I was engaged to promote a band of fifty Blackfeet Indians—including women with babies on their backs—who arrived in dusty railroad day coaches on a cold December morning at Chicago's old Polk Street Station. They'd come as the Christmas-season attraction for children at a Loop department store. Except for the two college-educated young chiefs, the group had never been in a hotel, ridden in an elevator, or talked on telephones. They never stopped riding up and down in the elevators and soon drove the switchboard operator crazy by calling each other's rooms all night. I mined a mother-lode of print-space in the press, however. The touring *Oklahoma* was then opening at the Erlanger Theatre, and I challenged the "cowboys" of *Oklahoma* (who were only actors) to a WGN Network spelling bee, based on a question I posited: In movie serials and in dime novels, the Native Americans always bite the dust, but given a level playing field—a spelling bee—who would triumph? With my two literate chiefs and myself posing as an Indian (remember, this was before television) our side won hands down with resultant scrapbooks full of publicity!

In the mid-1940s I was handling a "personal appearance" of the Sioux Princess Whitecloud. Betty Walker, a well-known Chicago newspaper columnist and a good friend of mine (a few years later she announced my 1948 London wedding), gave Whitecloud major attention. The next day her editor received a letter denouncing Whitecloud as a fraud, not even an Indian, and a German spy (this was wartime) to boot. With my—and Whitecloud's—honor at stake, I did some hasty detective work and learned that the complainant was running a racket, demanding payoffs from theatrical Indians, and Whitecloud, a true-blue Sioux, had refused to kick in. For years afterward, journalists unjustly kidded me about having perpetrated the "Whitecloud Hoax."

Sixty-some years ago, my first Loop office was in the beautiful, Louis Sullivan–designed Auditorium Theatre Building, which faced three streets: Michigan Avenue (where you entered the Auditorium Hotel), Congress Street (where you entered the four-thousand-seat Auditorium Theatre), and Wabash Avenue (where you entered the Auditorium studios). The theater school, of which I was then the promoter, was located on the sixth floor, and my office was in Suite 1000 on the top floor of the studios section. Doing business on the Wabash side of the adjoining Fine Arts Building was my friendly competitor Norman Alexandroff, an exiled Russian who sported a turned-down black fedora and had a hundred elocution students to my three hundred drama students. His enterprise later burgeoned and eventually became Chicago's Columbia College. When Norman moved on to California, his son, Meron, became Columbia's president and retired some years ago.

My Auditorium neighbors were a colorful, *La Bohème*-like melange of arts-connected folk: voice, piano, violin, and elocution teachers, opera coaches, music arrangers, painters, writers, and booking agents—all striving for a livelihood and their places in the sun in that era of economic depression. To me, an impressionable youngster not yet out of my teens, they were all endlessly fascinating, and I was happy to enter their seductive world. Many were—to say the least—bizarre characters. I was especially intrigued by the bitter rivalries of the voice teachers. My next-door neighbor, Maestro Mario Carbone, was a volatile little retired Italian baritone who wore a pince-nez. He had—in the early 1900s—sung in Havana with Enrico Caruso, and on the strength of that important career credit he attracted many opera-singer-aspirant students, all of whom he gave screech-producing vocal exercises aimed at strengthening their diaphragms. I recall how Madame Teresa Ferrio, also a voice teacher, regularly paused when passing Carbone's door while one of his protégés was being heard in full screech. Ferrio always called out for all to hear, "He's *ruining* that child's voice!" Carbone, by the way, had a pretty, bleached-blonde wife who was insanely jealous of him, which sometimes caused complications on our floor. One of Carbone's more advanced students was a dashing Neapolitan tenor subsidized by a mysterious, darkly clad, aquiline-beaked woman whom we called "The Marquesa." She, too, was jealous of her man, and right outside my door there were some scenes reminiscent of verismo opera, replete with authentic Mediterranian passion.

Across the hall, a tiny two-room unit was occupied by an NBC music arranger—one of the few tenth-floor denizens who actually had a regular income—whose wife and daughter taught art and piano in those close quarters and also cooked there on a small gas range. Not only did all three do their respective "things" in that limited space but they also somehow turned those premises—and the hallway outside—into a charming and hospitable salon for some of the more exciting and talented arts-connected people, whom the family plied with redolent cheeses, soda crackers, and flagons of cheap wine. One regular guest was a greatly gifted young maestro, Leo Kopp, whom we all thought was certain to become the next Arturo Toscanini before he succumbed to the urgency of supporting his wife and young children and became one of the country's most sought-after musical show conductors. Another neighbor was a wild-eyed, fantasizing, mustachioed old Dutch violin teacher, who—in his cell-like studio—also penned books and manifestos and painted bad chromos with palette-knife panache so the waves of his seascapes leapt off the canvas for feet rather than inches. He insisted that he was selling his art work for hundreds of thousands of dollars. Trapping us in the agonizingly slow and old hydraulic elevator—along with our vodka-saturated, corpulent building engineer, Bill—the mad Hollander would wave those phony checks, much like Senator McCarthy twenty years later would wave his sheets of "evidence" to intimidated congressional committees.

And now a few words about two faculty members of the theater school I managed in the Auditorium Building. One was a fine middle-aged American actor who had been down on his luck and was about to commit suicide (he told me) when my call came asking him to teach for us. I staked him to extensive dentistry and a set of new clothes, and he turned out to be a marvelous teacher. Eventually, with my blessing and train fare, he returned to roles on Broadway. Another actor, an elegant Englishman who wore a monocle, kept his home bathtub filled with gin of his own manufacture. I had noted that he rarely ate anything. He claimed that he got all the nutrition he needed from alcohol. He, too, was an excellent acting teacher.

The Auditorium Theatre is hallowed territory for Chicagoans of my generation. It was there in the 1930s that I first comprehended the joys of classic dance and grand opera with the Ballet Russe's and the San Carlo Opera Company's annual visits there. There, too, I saw the youthful Laurence Olivier in *Romeo and Juliet,* Broadway musicals like *I'd Rather Be Right* with George M. Cohan, and *The Hot Mikado* with Bill "Bojangles" Robinson, whom I would handle during the 1940s in vaudeville appearances at the Oriental Theatre. And—in 1956—I was to rent the capacious Auditorium Theatre stage as the scenery-building workshop for the Studebaker Theatre Company, of which I was general manager and which shared a stage-door alley with the Auditorium. That lovely old house had long been neglected, the winter was severe, and we used electric space heaters to keep our scenic construction crew unfrozen. Fortunately, the Auditorium has since been renovated and is again handsomely appointed. I have spoken from that stage on several occasions and have marveled at that spectacular theater's wonderful acoustics, with no "sound enhancement" as present-day showpeople call their over-amplification.

We tenants deeply regretted being turned out of the Auditorium Theatre Building in 1940, as it was closed to become a USO center for the next five years. I moved my activities to the just-abandoned second-floor offices of Cohan's Grand Theatre next to the Erlanger Theatre on Clark Street, right across from City Hall. I occupied the former office of Sam P. Gerson, who had run the Brothers Shubert midwestern empire from there for some years. Gerson, who had been taken ill, left in a hurry, and I found many of his personal effects, including family photographs, which I brought to his apartment in the Ambassador West Hotel.

I've almost forgotten to mention that Philip Van Loan, my palette knife–wielding neighbor from Holland, wrote a book, *The Soul of the Violin,* which I read and which puts me in mind of famous fiddlers I've publicized. One was the virtuoso Mischa Elman, whose primacy was unquestioned in the early part of the twentieth century. Certainly he was a giant, but when music critics hailed a newcomer from Russia, Jascha Heifetz, as his successor it was a shock from which Elman never recovered. I promoted his recitals in Orchestra Hall, however, and knew him to be still capable of hearty humor. On one occasion he pointed to my broad-brimmed Borsalino and called out plaintively, "Say, Newman, who's the *violinist* here?" Such levity diminished in direct ratio to the increase in Elman's bitterness at having been declared out of fashion by the musical cognoscenti. One evening in 1952 he came home with me, presumably to listen to recordings, but—inevitably—we talked about his unhappiness despite, as I kept thinking, how much he had to be grateful for: a great and honored name; a beautiful, loving wife; fine children; wealth; a wonderful home that was an established New York salon for the cultural greats of the time; and, above all, still a full calendar of upcoming recital and orchestra soloist appearances. We never got to those recordings that night, but Mischa recounted his childhood days as a protégé of Leopold Auer, the renowned St. Petersburg teacher of great violinists. Mischa also remembered being forced to move to a different boarding house daily in order to elude the police because Jews were not legally permitted to remain overnight in a "Holy Russian City" (Auer, also Jewish, had converted to Russian Orthodoxy). Mischa glowed with pride as he told me of his subsequent worldwide successes though the first several decades of the new century, a time when violinists everywhere aspired to the ravishing "Elman Tone." Then the blow fell. Heifetz appeared on the international scene and achieved mounting success. Although Mischa lived for many more years—until 1967—I don't think he was ever really happy in all the years following the critics' discovery of Heifetz.

On one occasion after a performance with the Boston Symphony, Heifetz told me, the violin section's musicians—as if to say "if you can play like you just did, we give up"—brought a huge trash can filled with their encased instruments to his dressing room. I recounted this charming vignette to the *Chicago Tribune* columnist Lucy Key Miller, who loved it and ran it the next day. Thereupon one of her officious colleagues suggested to her editor that she had been taken in by an hyper-imaginative press agent. Lucy, understandably upset, immediately telephoned me to complain. When I reported the incident to Heifetz he was indignant and insisted that the Boston Symphony's violinists had done exactly what he reported. He dug into his briefcase and came up with the name and address of that orchestra's concert master for confirmation. Lucy and her editor were assuaged.

A few years later, when I was launching subscription drives for the Hollywood Bowl and the Los Angeles Philharmonic, a young publicist named Jay Heifetz was assigned to assist me. I asked him if he was related to *Jascha* Heifetz and he said no. Some time afterward I learned that he *was* Jascha's son. I never asked him to explain.

Violinist Josef Szigeti complained to me over breakfast at the Blackstone Hotel's charming subterranean coffee shop that many orchestra artistic directors were reluctant to program the Bartók Violin Concerto for him. As a fellow Hungarian, he undoubtedly felt a special affinity for that composer's works. That was about fifty years ago. Today, Béla Bartók's compositions are routinely heard at symphony concerts everywhere. Classical music mills do grind, but slowly. Another brilliant violinist-virtuoso, Yehudi Menuhin, who many years later became a British baron, explained why sugar was a "no-no" as he poured honey into his tea during breakfast in his Drake Hotel suite.

Ida Haendel appeared in concerts with the Chicago Symphony Orchestra at both Orchestra Hall and the Ravinia Music Festival, occasions for my reunions with her and her distinguished portrait painter father Natan Haendel, both of whom had attended my 1948 wedding in London. Ida was considered the premiere lady violinist of the British Commonwealth, much as Dame Myra Hess was its great lady pianist. Ida's dad was a lifelong buddy of the novelist Isaac Bashevis Singer, and they used to winter together in Miami Beach. Among the other violinists whose recitals and symphony soloist appearances I have publicized are Nathan Milstein, Erica Morini, Ruggiero Ricci, Zino Francescatti, David Oistrakh, and Isaac Stern.

Like most of us who are part of the musical world, I tend to idolize conductors. One of the greatest was Tullio Serafin, who was in his eighties during the seasons I worked with him in the 1950s. Before performances he appeared to be somnolent and had to be helped into the pit by two strong stagehands. Yet the moment the music began it was as if electricity suddenly coursed through his veins. He became totally alert, a *maestro extraordinaire.* When the first act was over he became inert again, as if all strength had drained from him. Yet he always came thrillingly to life again for the next act.

Georg Solti, well before his Chicago Symphony and Covent Garden eras—and years before his knighthood—came to Lyric Opera of Chicago in 1956 to conduct *Salome, Die Walküre, Don Giovanni, La Forza del Destino,* and our Gala Concert (which, recorded by London Records, has since been reissued). In 1957 he returned for Lyric's *Nozze di Figaro, Ballo in Maschera,* and *Don Carlo* productions. That *Forza,* by the way, with Renata Tebaldi, Giulietta Simionato, Ettore Bastianini, Richard Tucker, and Nicola Rossi-Lemeni (a swashbuckling, cape-twirling bass star who originated in Bulgaria and was the husband of Mirella Freni) burned up the stage. It was one of the greatest performances I have seen. Solti was born to conduct opera. He certainly deserved his reputation as one of the most brilliant maestri of the second half of the twentieth century. Later, he led the Chicago Symphony Orchestra to worldwide glory. The early career development of Georg Solti, a charming, cultivated, and tremendously talented Hungarian Jewish musician, was—of course—set back by the German blitzkrieg in Central Europe (he was stateless when we first met), although he escaped the terrible fate of so many others. We became good friends and went swimming together. He admired my work and remembered to cable me on my eightieth birthday.

Dimitri Mitropoulos, conductor of our *Girl of the Golden West,* wasn't at all upset by his tenor Mario Del Monaco's fear of the horse on which he had to make his entrance. Mitropoulos—the most good-hearted of men—was too busy planning how to give away his fees to the less fortunate.

Artur Rodziński was to conduct both our 1958 *Tristan und Isolde* and *Boris Godunov.* The announcement brought much attention because he had left the Chicago Symphony under very unhappy circumstances. Sadly, Rodziński arrived during the throes of severe heart trouble, and although he got through *Tristan* his doctor told us that he must neither rehearse nor conduct *Boris.* The doctor also instructed us not to tell him why he could not conduct, fearing that the shock would kill him immediately. When we brought in Georges Sébastian from the Paris Opera for *Boris* the outraged Rodziński complained to the press about our management's "perfidy." Talk about an opera management's painful predicaments! Several weeks later Rodziński died. I remained, through the years, good friends with his widow Halina, the aunt of my Lyric Opera colleague Magda Krance.

Lovro von Matacic, who conducted Lyric Opera's *Carmen, La Cenerentola, Jenufa,* and *The Flying Dutchman* in 1959, was a huge Croatian who towered over the orchestra. An ex-colonel of the dreaded Ustashi fascists, he had Prussian-style saber cut marks on his cheeks. He told me that when Marshal Tito's communist troops captured him, and he was about to be executed, a Jewish woman to whom he had been kind pleaded for his life. He was spared, and he married her. Once, however, as we drove to an interview, he told me, "Danny, I like you, so I tell you this about myself. Never trust me where women or money are concerned!"

Josef Krips, a major Mozart interpreter from Vienna, had been a prime mover in restoring the Vienna State Opera after World War II. During the war the Germans did not permit him to conduct, and he worked in a factory (his father was Jewish). In 1959 he did our *Così Fan Tutte* and in 1960 our *Nozze di Figaro.* I recall Krips arriving for dinner at our house, a long-necked bottle of wine under each arm. He spoke excellent English, which he had learned by incessantly listening to his hotel bedroom's radio in London. I was captivated by his exultant expression when he conducted and, from the wings, loved to watch his face during rehearsals.

John Pritchard, who later became *Sir* John, was not only a brilliant conductor but also an accomplished diplomat who could well have been the British ambassador to Washington. In 1975 régisseur Jean-Pierre Ponnelle had wanted to replace veteran Geraint Evans with a younger baritone for the title role of our *Marriage of Figaro,* even though rehearsals were well underway. So deftly and elegantly did Pritchard handle this potentially explosive matter that no blood was spilled. From 1969 through 1987 the unruffled Pritchard presided over a number of Lyric's finest productions.

Zubin Mehta's been a leading international conductor for many years. Now with the Munich Opera, he was the music director of the Los Angeles Philharmonic and New York Philharmonic and is still with the Israel Philharmonic under a lifetime contract—all orchestras I've advised. His

Ring Cycle for our Lyric Opera of Chicago (1995–96) is now happy history. This exciting Bombay-born Zoroastrian's phenomenal lingual diversity is legendary; he even speaks idiomatic East European Yiddish. He's one of my best opera friends, as is his brother, Zarin, whom I first advised when he managed the Montreal Symphony Orchestra and again when he came to the Ravinia Festival. Now, he's the New York Philharmonic's executive director. I also know Zubin and Zarin's mother, and I knew their father, the Bombay musical conductor.

Michael Lepore was choral conductor of Lyric Opera for a quarter of a century and a passionate perfectionist who drove his part-time choristers of the 1950s and 1960s to high achievements and almost rebellion, for they all also had full-time jobs, businesses, or professions. Lepore enforced perfect punctuality and to miss a rehearsal was unthinkable. He demanded the highest musical standards and complete clarity in pronouncing the words of a half-dozen different languages. World-respected music critics expressed amazement at the quality of those choristers' performances. Maestro Lepore was one of the most dedicated, idealistic musicians I have ever known.

I met Italo Tajo, bass, and the tenor Ferruccio Tagliavini when they arrived together for American debuts in 1946 with Fausto Cleva's Chicago Opera Company. Tajo seemed six and a half feet tall, and Tagliavini was five feet and a few inches at most. I recall saying to the photographers, "Well, there you have the long and short of it!" In 1948 I promoted them as Dulcamara and Nemorino, respectively, in the marvelous Italian film *L'elisir d'amore* for the *World Playhouse Theatre.* I loved Ferrucio's Angel recordings, made with his gifted wife, the soprano Pia Tassinari. Italo, after his major international career ended, sang *comprimario* roles with Lyric Opera from 1971 through 1989 and was the highly successful stage director of our *Don Quichotte,* with Nicolai Ghiaurov in the title role.

Conductor Erich Leinsdorf was doing his "restudied" version of *Carmen,* with Ramón Vinay and Gladys Swarthout, with Fausto Cleva's Chicago Opera, which I was handling in 1946. When Leinsdorf lit a cigarette during a break in rehearsals the fire guard asked him to put it out. Leinsdorf, recently arrived from Europe, where lowly staffers feared approaching maestri, became almost hysterical with rage at this "affront"—a painful episode. Prima Ballerina Alicia Markova was also displeased with her dressing room location and decided to return to Europe with no explanation to management five minutes after her 1955 arrival. Fortunately, I glimpsed her going out the stage door and followed her outside, where she was ordering a cab driver to take her to the airport. I got her to return backstage, had her dressing room changed, and she remained to open, triumphantly, the following week in the Ruth Page–Hassard Short ballet *The Merry Widow*, based on Franz Lehár's operetta, and *Revanche*, the Page–Nicholas Remisoff ballet based on Giuseppe Verdi's *Il Trovatore*.

One of the truly great dramatic sopranos of the twentieth century, Birgit Nilsson, possessed a voice of extraordinary, piercing power, all but covering up the orchestra! She sang with us over a period of eighteen years, from 1956 through 1974, and became an established star in Chicago well before she was ever heard in New York. As a press agent it was pure pleasure to have all the claims I made for her more than substantiated by her sensational performances. This unique artist was a charming woman whose terrific sense of humor was just one of her manifold gifts. One can only regret that Puccini didn't live to hear her Princess Turandot! Unfortunately, her later tiff with the I.R.S. was expensive for Lyric Opera of Chicago and effectively ended her U.S. career.

Anna Moffo was such a startlingly beautiful woman that she somehow upstaged her very beautiful voice. Although American-born, Anna's career began in Italy. Her American debut, in 1957, was in Chicago, where we savored her as Mimi in *La Bohème*, Philine in *Mignon*, Susanna in *Marriage of Figaro*, and Lucia in *Lucia di Lammermoor*. In 1958 she was our Nanetta in *Falstaff*, Liu in *Turandot*, and Lauretta in *Gianni Schicchi*. Anna was fun, and we had a lot of it when we collaborated on a newspaper picture layout of her clad in an adorable playsuit for an afternoon workout in the gym of my club. Although more than forty-nine years passed since then, this gracious lady remained in touch regularly.

In the 1960s so many leading artists of the Vienna State Opera were in Chicago during the fall season that travel agents advised clients who hoped to attend opera in Vienna to hold off their trips until at least late December, when Lyric Opera—in those years—closed its season. Among the central European stars who gravitated to the Civic Opera House were Walter Berry, Christa Ludwig, Elizabeth Schwarzkopf, Irmgard Seefried, Erich Kunz, Eberhard Waechter, Rita Streich, Hans Hotter, and Lisa Della

Casa. A similar situation held at Milan's La Scala during the early fall of each year, when virtually all of Italy's most important opera artists were to be found on Wacker Drive in Chicago.

Bulgarian bass Nicolai Ghiaurov made his 1963 American debut in Chicago, stunning the audience with his sensational performance as Mefistofele in Gounod's *Faust.* He let loose a voice of such enormous volume and surpassing beauty that he evoked salvos of extended and extraordinary applause. Through 1999 he appeared in eighteen of our seasons with continuous success. When I first met him, he had recently emerged from a communist totalitarian society. He had been head of opera's "company union" there and was suspicious of the outside world. Bit by bit we weaned him from his lifelong orientation, a task well completed by his wonderful wife, the soprano Mirella Freni. Suddenly and unexpectedly, we lost Nicolai in 2004. He is mourned by the luminous Mirella and by close friends of many years, including myself.

Joe Papp and Bernie Gersten's Central Park Shakespeare Festival was one of thirty-three various nonprofit New York performing arts projects I began assisting in the early 1960s. They wanted my advice about their plan to convert the Old Astor Street Library into a five-theater-space structure. Although Joe was viscerally opposed to having a subscription system there—he, a populist, said it was elitist to do so—Bernie prevailed on him to get my opinion (he and I had worked together in 1953 when I was press agent and he the stage manager of a legit show, *The World of Sholem Aleichem*). Joe, Bernie, and I lunched for two hours in a Fifty-seventh Street cafe while I brainwashed Joe, who—amazingly—gave in. They opened the new place with subscription, and it worked well for them for many years. Joe wrote to the Ford Foundation's satellite, the Theatre Communication's Group, that our lunch "was the most profitable two hours I've spent in a long time." Unfortunately, Joe, a human dynamo, died young, and his successors did not tend the subscription garden well. Bernie went on to run the Radio City Music Hall and then the Vivian Beaumont at Lincoln Center, where he has distinguished himself as executive producer.

At the conclusion of the 2001–2 opera season I completed my forty-eight-year, part-time assignment with Lyric Opera of Chicago, a flexible arrangement that made possible consulting activities with several thousand arts-producing entities on five continents; a twenty-year stint with the Ford Foundation and the New York–based Theatre Communications Group as its audience development guru; twenty-five years with Canadian governmental arts agencies; and many overseas assignments as well. I not only built committed (i.e., subscribed) audiences but also dealt with the other management problems and/or needs of nonprofit professional theaters; orchestras; opera companies; classical, ballet, and modern dance troupes; performing arts centers; and municipal, state, regional, and federal arts councils.

In 1961, at the urging of the visionary W. McNeil Lowry, vice president of the Ford Foundation and founder of its Division of the Humanities and the Arts, I left my remaining commercial show business activities and refocused entirely on the nonprofit professional arts. I continued assistance to the then still-infant Lyric Opera of Chicago, which would require my nurturing for many years to come. Although—primarily—I've been that company's press agent and the father of its outsized committed (sub-scribed) audience, there was hardly an aspect of its manifold and complex operations in which I was not involved, including sensitive relations with artists, participation in repertoire and casting choices, coordination of various major Lyric outreach efforts such as the Florence Flood and Italian Earthquake relief campaigns, and close communication with Lyric's various boards and auxiliaries. I also served as ombudsman for unhappy staffers, subscribers, and contributors and—overall—was the quencher of flames on all Lyric fronts whenever the fire-bell rang. Although I was not Lyric's fund-raising executive, I obtained its initial grants from both city and state and was the prime Lyric mover in obtaining the $1 million foundation contribution that literally saved Lyric's life in its 1980 economic crisis—and that was still in an era when, to quote a distinguished senator, $1 million was "real money." I even perilously frustrated an angry tenor's plan to murder a brash music critic. For more than four decades I made the clarion, unamplified, onstage announcements in our 3,600-seat Civic Opera House that so entertained both orchestra and audience. On one occasion readers of Claudia Cassidy's *Chicago Tribune* "On the Aisle" column were amused by her waggish review of a "performance" of mine: "Last night, at the Civic Opera House, the difference between Danny and the singers was that *him* you could hear!" I wrote Lyric's Ten Year Book and organized its 1979 Twenty-five-Year Anniversary Book project, prevailing upon Saul Bellow for its introduction and Claudia Cassidy to write the entire text; I then convinced the Alfred A. Knopf Publishing Company to release its chief graphic artist, R. D. Scudellari, from an exclusive contract, thus freeing him to design the deluxe Lyric Opera volume.

I established and miraculously maintained good relations with Chicago's premiere good music station, WFMT, and its founders, Bernard and Rita Jacobs, despite Lyric's founder and general manager Carol Fox's never-explained reservations about Norman Pelligrini, that station's widely respected program director and superb musical commentator, and her unwillingness to credit, as the entire field did, its brilliant operating head Ray Nordstrand's widely admired achievements in broadcasting. For a number of years the arrangements for airing Lyric Opera of Chicago's annual seasons were made at luncheon meetings involving Carol, Ray, Norman, and myself. I—who never went to a school for diplomats—had to desperately improvise at those sessions, and later explain away, somehow, Carol's unwillingness to appreciate the patently important contributions of Norman and Ray. The ship remained afloat, however, and in later years our high-powered general counsel and board officer Lee A. Freeman took over the WFMT annual negotiations—to my great relief.

I had been most concerned about the station continuing to provide us with widespread exposure and continuous complimentary subscription campaign announcements, whereas Lee aimed for maximum sponsor fees. When Ray's visionary creation, the WFMT Fine Arts Network, started to feature us continentally, Carol pressed me to find a replacement for Norman although he was clearly ideal for his job as emcee. Only when one of Carol's suggested replacements, a distinguished opera executive, told me that he could "never in a thousand years" equal Norman in that assignment did she retreat on the issue.

From 1961 through 1981 I was often on the road as the striking arm of the Ford Foundation's Division of Humanities and the Arts in behalf of our nation's nonprofit professional performing arts organizations. During the same period I traveled all over Canada for my government-sponsored tasks there or went on similar missions overseas. By 1963 I had in process some thirty different subscription campaigns for a then-great number of still-infant resident professional theaters in the United States. I couldn't keep going back that winter to all of them, so I followed up with a stream of urgent letters to their leaders. I have located, in an old file, one of my directives to Jacques Cartier, the founder–executive director of the Hartford Stage Company, which was new at the time: "Dear Jacques, I urge you not to risk the possibility of failure by box office malnutrition, and to guarantee your success via our dynamic subscription drive. You are the leader, the founder, the moving spirit—and *you* must see to it that everything we planned is carried out to the nth degree. And since your rehearsals must soon begin, better put in your sleepless nights on subscription work right now!" Some weeks later he was telling me that unless I come to Hartford and do it myself, "it can't happen." The record will show that somehow a fine subscription *was* built, and not many years later a magnificent new playhouse was as well. I always returned, however, to my Lyric home as quickly as possible. I did succeed in inculcating our series subscribers with the feeling that they were members of a superior cultural grouping in the overall society—manifested by what I called their "Esprit de Subscriber Corps."

Why do I love subscribers so much? Because, in an act of faith, they commit themselves before each season begins. They arrive at performances wanting us to succeed and are thrilled when we do. If we ever let them down (heaven forfend) they forgive us—in most cases—at renewal time. Their acceptance of repertory constantly rises, and their theatrical awareness heightens. They form and articulate opinions about performance values. They'll write to critics they think are unfair and also write to *us*—sixteen-page letters sometimes—advising on casting and repertory choices. They're hooked—finely tuned instruments on which our artists can play.

Why *don't* I love nonsubscribers? Because they never buy tickets unless they're for our biggest hit ever and/or they're observing a twenty-fifth wedding anniversary. Had it been up to them, our artists would have starved for those twenty-five years. Now they're at the box office, demanding perfect, center, fourth-row-on-the-aisle seats. Shocked when told that such locations are held only by series subscribers, they threaten to write nasty letters to the newspapers and have friends boycott our theater. I have just described—with no apologies to Gilbert and Sullivan—the "very model of the modern single-ticket buyer"!

I imbued our staff with the concept that "nothing was too good for our subscribers," which was much more than a slogan to me. Once upon a Sunday afternoon, for example, the telephone on my desk rang, as for many years it was wired to do whenever the switchboard was closed. The caller was a frantic subscriber whose wife had lost a valuable diamond from her engagement ring, perhaps the night before when she was in her main-floor seat (row S, aisle 2). I asked to speak to her. Yes, she admitted, it *could* have happened either on her way to or from the performance, although she was in no mood to be questioned. I promised to begin looking immediately for the needle in the haystack, assuring her that I would call back. Our 3,600-seat house was pitch-black, with only a small work light on the stage. There were no employes around, and I had only a small flashlight. I knew the maintenance crew would come through the next morning (Monday), and the diamond—if anywhere around—would be sucked up by their powerful vacuum cleaners and lost forever, so I went into the dark house, playing my little light around her seat but discerned nothing. The diamond, I reasoned, might have been kicked by patrons and rolled down the raked floor, so I trained the flashlight on the floor of the rows ahead. Suddenly—miraculously—the blue-white facets of the gemstone gleamed in the darkness. I reached down, retrieved it, and rushed to the telephone. The ecstatic couple immediately drove to the Civic Opera House, and I had the extreme pleasure of restoring the diamond to them. To their effusive thanks I responded, "Here at Lyric, we'll do *anything* for our subscribers!" They soon sent a handsome contribution to Lyric.

Throughout the 1960s and 1970s classical orchestra musicians everywhere were frustrated and angry at their boards' and managements' inability—not unwillingness, for they certainly were willing—to give them fuller employment, higher wages, and overall improved conditions. I'm proud that my relentless, large-scale subscription drives did solve many of the most pressing problems. Some orchestras increased subscribership by hundreds of percentage points! The influx of so many new subscribers, many of whom also soon became contributors (a major factor in the new, higher levels of fund-raising that then began) provided previously lacking credibility to inspire new and higher levels of foundation and corporate giving. The Ford Foundation gave exemplary leadership in those years with a munificent $80 million in challenge grants to orchestras. Then it sent me out to protect that investment via consistent aggressive audience developmental initiatives that the traditionally conservative musical organizations had been loath to enter into.

We finally emerged from that very unhappy period that was filled with recrimination between musicians and orchestra boards and managements. I remember a board president feeling so unfairly maligned that he literally wept on my shoulder while I comforted him with assurances that I saw a light for him at the end of the tunnel. Paradoxically, the only people in our overwhelmingly philistine society who had previously cared whether symphony orchestras existed were those same, often unfairly pilloried, board leaders and managers and their loyal subscriberships. Yet those harried good people were often being treated as public enemies. To this day I wonder why the musicians did not open an effective central lobbying office in Washington, D.C., to influence *governmental* support for the orchestras. Theoretically, the National Endowment for the Arts, which was then coming into existence, could have provided the answer had the NEA been properly funded—which it wasn't then nor has it been to the present day.

I'm proud that my own role was so significantly recognized by the American Symphony Orchestra League when—at its 1984 conference—it greatly honored me with its Gold Baton Award, given previously to such luminaries as Leopold Stokowski, Leonard Bernstein, Eugene Ormandy, and Aaron Copland. Obviously, I am neither a composer nor a conductor. I was nominated for this accolade by the New York Philharmonic, an orchestra I successfully advised for a number of years, initially through the Ford Foundation and later via a direct contract with that orchestra's management. In 2002 I was also greatly honored by the American Federation of Musicians and its Chicago Federation.

Throughout the early 1970s Peter Zeisler and Lindy Zesch—top officials of the Theatre Communications Group based in New York City (and an affiliate of the Ford Foundation)—were fearful that I, already middle-aged, couldn't indefinitely maintain the blistering pace of my constant travel and intense evangelism. Peter and Lindy kept after me to put in writing the audience-building wisdom that I had been so prolifically and assiduously dispensing to an ever-increasing constituency of arts managers and trustees, both in the United States and abroad. Although they continued to urge me to write what eventually became *Subscribe Now!* they never agreed that I should pause in my on-the-road assignments for at least several full-time months in order to do so without hindrance. It wasn't that I was shirking the task, for when pressed I will admit—with no false modesty—that I am as facile a writer-propagandist as I am a spellbinding speaker. The problem was that I usually worked at full speed, either in my Chicago office or in too many other places, from 8 A.M. to 10 P.M. six days a week, taking off only Saturday mornings. Yet I began the book in early 1975, writing from 10:30 P.M. to 12:30 A.M. and then resuming my normal regimen at 8 A.M.

The book—published by Theatre Communications Group—came out in October 1977 and had its twenty-fifth anniversary in October 2002. Its first printing, both in hard- and soft-cover editions, sold out quickly, and there have since been (as I now write) ten more printings. The reviews, ranging from very good to great, astonished me; incredibly, none were negative. The book has long been the best-seller of the arts management field. Its title was suggested by my Lyric Opera colleague Tom Blandford who had heard me a thousand times admonish would-be single-ticket applicants to Subscribe Now! Happily, I've received several thousand letters from arts producers and/or presenters I've never met, people whose organizations have prospered following implementation of my homely but sound counsel. Originally, this was a blow to my ego because I had thought it was *my* personal, ongoing consulting that made for such successes. Could one just read a book and succeed? Thinking it over, however, I comforted myself with the thought that *I* had after all written the book! I am further solaced by *Subscribe Now!* being a required textbook in university arts management courses for these many years, which has given me a patina of academic respectability I had never before enjoyed! The book, in use in thirty-one countries that I know of, was published in a Japanese translation in 2001.

Wasn't the autobiography of the great founder of the Moscow Art Theatre, Konstantin Stanislavsky, entitled *My Life in Art?* I sometimes playfully considered entitling the saga of my own long career experience as *My Life in Show Business and Its More Elegant Branches, the Performing Arts.* To delineate the vast diversity of my activities in this broad field I devised the following sort of Gilbert and Sullivanesque patter and sometimes declaimed it at arts conferences, rattling it off at a furious pace and with impeccable diction and triumphant vocal trajectory:

> In my seventy years in the lively and lovely arts, I have been intensively and often simultaneously involved on the multilevels of publicity, promotion, management, and entrepreneurship in a wide range of activities and with artists of infinite variety; in horse opera, soap opera, light opera, comic opera, and grand opera; with crooners, pop singers, liturgical singers, calypso singers, torch singers, jazz singers, choral singers, *and* opera singers (a very great number of them); with guitar and banjo strummers, mandolin pickers, and harp pluckers; tap dancers, ballet dancers, soft-shoe dancers, ballroom dancers, modern dancers, adagio dancers, exotic dancers, and folk dancers of many diverse ethnic strains.
>
> I've been an actor, barker, scriptwriter, oratorio narrator, modern dance impresario, leather-lunged change-of-cast announcer, opera lecturer, and *musicale conferencier.* I've press-agented, in my time, lion tamers, high-wire walkers, ventriloquists, pantomimics, mummers, acrobats, jugglers, ecdysiasts, mind readers, knife throwers, fire eaters, sword swallowers, magicians, card tricksters, prestidigitators, animal trainers, equestrians, bare-back riders, stand-up comics, knock-about comics, sister acts, brother acts, trampoline acts, dog acts, and pony acts.
>
> I've been associated with movie producers, radio producers, television producers, legitimate stage producers, and all of their actors, dancers, choreographers, photographers, directors, and designers. I've come up through those melodramas, musical shows, tab shows, puppet shows, tent shows, carnival shows, sports shows, wild west shows, circus shows, vaudeville shows, and minstrel shows. I've worked with little theaters, big theaters, community theaters, civic theaters, dinner theaters, repertory theaters, resident professional theaters, touring theaters, stock theaters, burlesque theaters, revue theaters, Yiddish theaters, variety theaters, cabaret theaters, Broadway theaters, off-Broadway theaters, and avante-garde theaters, too.
>
> I've labored mightily in the vineyards of symphony orchestras, jazz orchestras, balalaika orchestras, swing bands, harmonica bands, and brass bands; drama festivals, dance festivals, musical festivals, recital series, and performing arts centers, when they came into vogue. I've been a film publicist, ad writer, and owner of three movie theaters. I count 8,890 motion pictures in my promotional background.

I've handled hundreds of plays—both on tour and in residence—in the U.S.A. and overseas. I've functioned in the capacities of house manager, concert manager, company manager, stage manager, personal manager, and general manager and have functioned as guru for performing arts boards and staffs, program ad solicitor, door-to-door and telephone subscription salesman, producer, director, advance road agent, house press agent, *and* playwright's agent.

But most of this was *before 1961!*

Since then, and for the past forty-five years, aside from my heartfelt commitment to my own Lyric Opera of Chicago—an association which goes back for me more than fifty years (since its 1954 inception)—I have concentrated mainly on building those committed audiences (my euphemism for subscription audiences) for nonprofit professional performing arts organizations in the U.S.A and in such foreign countries as Canada, Australia, England, Finland, Holland, Israel, New Zealand, the Philippines, the Republic of China, and Scotland. Out of this new career, which I admit has been a fascinating adventure for me, has come the book *Subscribe Now!* published in 1977 and in use in thirty-one countries that I know of—and soon entering its eleventh printing if you count the original hard-cover edition—and recently translated into Japanese!

As I conclude this retrospective I realize how much I have left out. Many internationally famed artists with whom I have worked, some of them merely mentioned in this book, were every bit as colorful as those to whom I have devoted entire essays. If I have not given them separate, in-depth treatment, it is mainly because I'm not doing a ten-volume series, just *a* book in which I concentrate on certain individuals in various arts disciplines, about whom I have some special insights, remembrances, and information. I haven't really overlooked many I seem to have neglected. A great number are world renowned in their fields. Among them are 130 star-status vaudevillians; forty movie stars; forty-nine jazz/swing band leaders; sixty-five classical music maestri; fifty-one ballet and modern dance choreographers, ballerinas, and premier danseurs; 240 grand opera and recital divas and divos; eighty-nine opera and legit theater stage directors; forty scenic designers; seventy-seven concert pianists, violinists cellists, and other instrumentalists; and a profusion of stellar ecdysiasts, burlesque comics, movie, radio, and television producers, writers, and directors, film bookers, and so on. Some assignments from the 1930s through the 1960s that I haven't mentioned include the Kabuki Dancers of Japan, the American Ballet Theatre, the annual Kelly Bowl Games in Soldier Field, the Dancers of Bali, the Original Drive-in Theatre, the Twin Open Air Theatres, the Charlton Heston–Sophia Loren version of *El Cid*, the Chelten and Acadia movie theaters I operated (I did write about my Astor Theatre), John Houseman's *Julius Caesar* film with Marlon Brando and John Gielgud, Emlyn Williams on stage in *Charles Dickens*, the play *Night Must Fall*, the national tour of *The Fifth Season*, the national tour of Carol Channing in *Show Business*, the Dolly Haas Israeli recital tour, and the stage comedy *All Gaul Is Divided*. Other legit shows were *Josephine, American Savoyards, Bell, Book, and Candle*, and *Fig Leaf*; Martyn Green in Gilbert and Sullivan repertory; the *Paraplegic Revue*; *Season in the Sun*; Fridolin in *Ti Coq*; Dante the Magician in *Sim Sala Bim*; *Music in the Round*; Cathleen Nesbitt and Diana Barrymore in Tennessee Williams's *Garden District*; Danny Kaye's *All-Star International Show*; a four-year run at the Happy Medium Cabaret Theatre, including the two years of the revue *Medium Rare*; *A Mighty Man Is He* at the Blackstone Theatre, Chicago, and New York's Cort Theatre; a New York City Opera Tour with *Susannah, Ballad of Baby Doe*, and *Street Scene*; a national tour of *The Miracle Worker*; Jose Greco's Spanish dance company; the *Big Show Circus*; the *Celestial Circus*; and *Anastasia*. I also did a ten-year stint as executive producer for the Chicago Yiddish Theatre Association and served as advisor to the National Association of Stock Theatre Producers and the Woodstock Theatre in New York state. There must be more, but I'm sure this is more than enough.

Maybe by some miracle, even though I've passed my eighty-seventh birthday, I might (who knows?) start on the other nine volumes of the ten-volume series. It is most likely, however, that *this* book is my authorial swan song. I hope readers will enjoy and be informed by my multitudinous recollections.

1

Milton Berle, Show-Biz Whiz, Wins $20,000 and I Win $8 Betting on General Mowley in the Eighth Race at Empire! The 1930s, 1940s, and 1950s

Vaudeville meant movies; rococo, lavish "presentation houses"; five to seven shows a day (even if it meant taking a reel or two from the film); a succession of variety "acts" from acrobats to mind readers; large house orchestras in the pit; gorgeous chorus girls (both "ponies," the little, lithe, leggy, and lovely dancers, and "parade girls," who were tall, stately strutters); big-time jazz and swing bands onstage; and, in person, stars like Milton Berle, Laurel and Hardy, Jimmy Durante, Roy Rogers (and Trigger), and Sally Rand. Later in that glitzy era there was—above all—that great crowd-pleaser: AIR-CONDITIONING!

By the time I arrived on the post–World War I show business scene in the 1930s vaudeville's live entertainment was being buttressed by accompanying movies—a double-whammy that possessed enough box-office strength to extend the careers of many variety theater veterans while simultaneously providing launch pads for young, up-and-coming performers. This long-past era spawned some of the twentieth century's greatest entertainers, whose skills—polished on vaudeville stages all the way from Bellows Falls, Vermont, to New York's Palace Theatre—perfectly prepared them for future big-time employment in night clubs, big and brassy musical shows, radio, motion pictures, and, eventually, television. Milton Berle has been widely and justly credited with enticing the first huge audiences to television via his historic and celebrated *Texaco Star Theatre,* which brought the greatest show business stars of the time to early TV. It was on those programs that he also became the "Uncle Miltie" idol of America's kiddies.

A cum-laude graduate of the Catskill–Borscht Belt summer resort circuit, the young, brash, stage-mother-driven Milton Berle brilliantly and ruthlessly achieved primacy over all competitors. Milton Berlinger, born in poverty in 1908, was a child prodigy whom Charlie Chaplin engaged to appear with him in silent films. He then went on to appear in an astonishing number of "silents," all the while refining his gifts in mime. An immensely talented, versatile, and intelligent performer even in his youth, he was destined to become a nationally recognized star of the then-booming presentation houses. He was even able to command a percentage of the gross receipts! To make certain that theater managements did not falsify attendance figures (to their own advantage, of course) he employed his brother to count the customers as they entered.

Milton was fiercely suspicious of competitors purloining his jokes, yet Walter Winchell dubbed *him* the "Thief of Bad Gags"! He was also quickly combative concerning the size of his billing in advertising. Once, as I was breakfasting with a few press agent colleagues at Chicago's Henrici's Restaurant across the street from the Oriental Theatre, he burst in, waving a copy of our almost full-page ad. Most of it featured his picture and name in big, bold type. He angrily complained, however, that at the bottom of the ad I had run—in tiny, sixteen-point type—the names of the show's other acts. "Who's interested in *them?*" Milton screamed. "The public is paying to see *Berle!*"

In later years I learned that this ferocious "vodvil" leopard never changed his spots. When he became such an overwhelming success on *The Texaco Star Theatre* that producers renamed it *The Milton Berle Show,* one of his associates complained that Milton refused to give on-air mention to the show's writers. He wanted the vast audience—86 percent of everyone in the country who owned a television set, a still-unsurpassed record—to believe he wrote the show all by himself, with his own little hatchet!

This aggressive, unashamed begrudging of credit to other performers, like his anger at even the small-sized type I had given to his supporting acts on the bill at the Oriental, became Milton's normal, ego-centric, almost ego-maniacal reaction when any threat to his supremacy—even a quite minor one—was regarded as major. His son Bill's book describes the comedian speaking at a memorial for his late wife and forgetting to mention *her* name but not one line of an entire series of *his* jokes.

Was Berle, through the years, more inconsiderate of others than some of his contemporary theatrical stars? To be fair, perhaps not; even as sophisticated a smoothie as the *Today Show*'s Dave Garroway was wont, it is said, to occasionally punch his chimpanzee colleague J. Fred Muggs—of course, not on-screen. But maybe Milton went at it with special relish. Bill Berle speaks of his multitalented dad as being "the greatest comedian of history." He may well be right. Who of Miton's contemporaries could "dance with the dancers, sing with the singers, even tumble with the acrobats (sometimes to the point of upstaging the featured guest)"—not to hardly mention acting with the thespians? And what about his hilarious antic art as a female impersonator a generation ahead of Dame Edna?

Milton was an inveterate horseplayer, a big-time bettor said to be the country's champion amateur handicapper. He required a special telephone in his theater dressing rooms so he could keep in touch with bookmakers throughout the country. His bets were so big that they had to be laid off with several bookies. One morning in my presence he placed a $5,000 bet—remember, this was sixty-some years ago, and that amount would be the equivalent of $50,000 now—on a horse named General Mowley running in "the eighth race at Empire" that afternoon. At Milton's urging, I—who had never, ever, placed a bet—wagered $2 on the same race. I was astonished when the stagehand who did the deed for me came back with $8! Milton got $20,000 for his $5,000! Greatly impressed with his clairvoyance, I invested another $2 on one of his picks the next morning. This time, however, the horse ran out of the money, and I realized that playing the horses was an unreliable business. I have never again placed a bet and am—happily—still $4 ahead! In 1987 I ran into Milton at O'Hare Airport. Although more than four decades had passed since he gave me that winning horse backstage at the Oriental, when I greeted him with the words "General Mowley" he responded, not missing a beat, "Eighth race at Empire!"

Serious novitiate actors avidly hearken to the instructions of Konstantin Stanislavsky, Richard Boleslawsky, Stella Adler, Lee Strasberg, and Sanford Meisner, to name but some of the controversial Method's exponents. But the Milton Berles of the variety theater—in all its forms—never had such intellectual and academic masters to inspire them. They learned their craft/art from constantly performing with—and alongside—richly experienced and often greatly gifted veterans, making minute adjustments in their routines while appearing on stages, large and small, everywhere and relentlessly hammering out the kinks in their talents on the anvil of live performances. They developed to the point that they become finely tuned entertainment instruments who embellished the theatrical history of the twentieth century and provided momentum for the twenty-first one as well.

Milton lived a long life—expiring at age ninety-three on March 28, 2002—and was laden with honors and treasure for which the indomitable Sadie Berlinger, his adoring mother, taught him to fight so ruthlessly and ferociously.

2 Good Night, Jimmy Durante (and Clayton and Jackson, Too), Wherever You Are!

Every time yuh tuyn around, der shovin'
anuddeh drink atcha!

—Jimmy Durante

I think it was in 1942 (I hadn't yet joined the army), when I went to Chicago's La Salle Street Station to meet Jimmy ("Schnozzola," aka "the Schnoz") Durante, the vaudeville, movie, night club, and radio star (television had not yet come in) who was arriving on the New York Central's crack Twentieth Century to begin an in-person engagement at the Oriental Theatre. Usually, for such arrivals I'd be going down to the Pullman car of my quarry; I would have obtained the car number via long-distance telephone from the artist's management the day before. The 1941 Pearl Harbor sneak attack of December 7, however, had plunged us into war, and the military—wary of spies reporting troop movements—had decreed that nobody—even well-connected press agents—could go past the gates and down to the cars when trains arrived.

I had never met this gifted clown who was being called "the living embodiment of the term 'beloved entertainer'" and was chafing under the imposed restriction on my mobility—forced to stand anonymously next to a large group of people presumably waiting for friends and relatives—when I suddenly saw my man rushing up the ramp straight toward me, right to where I was standing. My first thought was that he must be far-sighted. Then I realized he didn't know me. Almost immediately, however, he was in front of me, pumping my hand. Amazed, I sputtered, "Mr. Durante, how did you know that I was the press agent sent to greet you?" Without missing a beat he responded, "Well, yuh had dat *worried* look!"

At the Oriental, our 3,200-seat, luxuriously appointed, semi-rococo venue, Durante was joined by the other two-thirds of his fabled nightclub and vaudeville act, Eddie Jackson and Lou Clayton. Together—through the late 1920s and 1930s—Clayton, Jackson, and Durante were a big-time attraction. By the 1940s, however, Durante had emerged as a star in his own right and under his own steam. Yet whenever he had a vaudeville booking he called in his old partners, strutter Eddie Jackson and comic-tap dancer Lou Clayton, while he himself literally pounded pianos to pieces, invariably gargling out his famous song "Inka Dinka Doo!" at every one of five stage shows a day.

Although we had our usual lineup of other variety acts, a pit orchestra, most often a big-name swing band onstage, *and* a line of dancing girls, *the* headline act was certainly "Jimmy Durante in Person." Eddie Jackson was a singing waiter in 1916 when he first worked with Jimmy. In 1923 they teamed with Lou Clayton and opened a speakeasy. By 1927 Clayton, Jackson, and Durante had made an auspicious vaudeville debut, their act called "Jest for a Laugh." By 1928 they were headlining at the Palace in New York, where they broke box-office records. One wit said of them, "They talk like *Variety* writes!"

Durante's box-office drawing strength was buttressed by movie successes, beginning in 1932 opposite George M. Cohan in *The Phantom President* and a half-dozen other Hollywood films, including the 1940 *Melody Ranch* opposite Gene Autry and Ann Miller. Jimmy filmed *The Man Who Came to Dinner,* in which he portrayed the Harpo Marx–like character of Banjo, in 1941; that same year he also appeared in *You're in the Army Now!* A decade later he was featured in *Music for Millions,* a Rodgers and Hart hit of three decades earlier in which he sang his famous "Umbriago" (actually, "Ubriacco"). Other films of the 1940s were *Two Sisters from Boston, It Happened in Brooklyn,* and *On an Island with You.*

For some reason Jimmy called me "Hemingway," perhaps because he knew I was a writer. We made all the publicity rounds, newspapers and radio stations, and visited the night spots that housed celebrity radio interview shows. His typical paean of pleasure at the hospitality offered us everywhere was, "Hemingway, all I can say is 'What a jernt'! Every time yuh tuyn around, der shovin' anuddeh drink atcha!"

Maybe it was the Oriental's powerful air-conditioning blowers, perhaps the theater's biggest attraction on those sizzling summer days and nights, coupled with Jimmy's copious perspiration as he assaulted the pre-smashed pianos his act required, but one day he came down with a very bad cold. I was touched by the tenderness with which Eddie Jackson and Lou Clayton, his lifetime collaborators, tucked him into his Sherman Hotel bed and plied him with nostrums of every description, including hot toddies laced with scotch, stopping short only of cupping and applying leeches. Whether it was because of—or in spite of—his pals' loving ministrations, Jimmy never missed a performance, hoarsely warbling his theme song and passionately pursuing his piano-shattering!

In 1962 Durante was featured in Broadway producer Billy Rose's *Jumbo*, which contained a devastatingly funny scene in which he is seen leading a huge elephant out of a circus enclosure. When challenged by a guard who asks, "Say, where are you going with that elephant?" Jimmy innocently responds, "*What* elephant?" In 1963 he followed with the zany movie *It's a Mad, Mad, Mad, Mad, World!* He starred, too, in radio on *The Jimmy Durante Show* and *The Camel Comedy Caravan* and won an Emmy for the *Colgate Comedy Hour* on television. His television shows included *The Four Star Revue* and the *All Star Revue*. The line with which Durante often closed his shows—"Good night, Mrs. Calabash, wherever you are!"—became as celebrated as his soft felt fedora and hilarious mangling of the language.

During the fifteen years I represented the Oriental Theatre I press-agented perhaps a thousand variety acts of astonishing diversity. Many returned to our stage again and again. Vaudeville was an invaluable—really, irreplaceable—training ground and launch pad for an army of professional entertainers *and* press agents! Our world had a familial aspect. A considerable number of artists were really talented; others were not but show business was their chosen way of life. They reveled in their U.S. bookings and those in Canada, and—for the ones in greatest demand—overseas, too.

One fine morning after we had plotted our always hectic schedule for that day's publicity rounds between shows I found myself wildly fantasizing. What if Jimmy's unlovely voice (which *did* vastly charm millions of his vaudeville, movie, musical show, and radio devotees) magically became a beautiful baritone and his gruff, growly diction somehow took on classically elegant actorial authority? Given the natural endowment of that magnificently protuberant proboscis, he could provide the American stage with the definitive Cyrano De Bergerac of our time!

James Francis Durante was born in 1893 in New York City. His barber-father bought him a piano. Although his formal schooling ended in the seventh grade, he kept up his piano lessons. At age seventeen he became a professional player at Diamond Tony's Coney Island Saloon. By the time I encountered him Jimmy was in the middle years of his rough-and-tumble but already greatly successful career—and in the upper echelon of those eternally transient, latter-day commedia dell'arte performers. A new generation came to know him when the soundtrack of the 1993 movie *Sleepless in Seattle* used his versions of "As Time Goes By" and "Make Someone Happy." He died on January 29, 1980, in Santa Monica, California, after more than sixty performing years in every entertainment field.

Undoubtedly, Hamlet, in his advice to players must have had a Jimmy of his time in mind when he cautioned them to "speak the speech I pray thee, trippingly on the tongue." Jimmy Durante didn't need *anybody's* advice—even Shakespeare's! He was not just a "natural." He was a *force* of theatrical nature!

In 1943, Danny Newman joined the U.S. Army as a private. He was sent from Chicago to Camp Wheeler, Georgia, for basic infantry training. Then he was shipped overseas to England as a rifleman replacement for casualties of the D-Day Normandy beachhead landings and spent many battle-scarred months with North Carolina's Thirtieth Division in France, Belgium, Holland, Germany, and back to Belgium for the Battle of the Bulge and all that followed. (Author's collection)

Despite a forty-year gap caused by a records fire in an army warehouse, one-time Private First Class Danny Newman was awarded a Bronze Star from Col. Stanley E. Thomas, who led a platoon into the Chicago Civic Opera House Grand Foyer to witness the 1984 presentation ceremony along with several hundred of Danny's relatives, friends, and Lyric Opera of Chicago board and staff members. (Author's collection)

Clad in a player's uniform for *Angels in the Outfield,* one of the hundreds of films Danny promoted during the 1940s and 1950s. Soon he would be off to visit the newspaper editors, columnists, and, of course, sports writers of the greater Chicago area. (Photo by David B. Lannes Photographers; author's collection)

Danny, at right, greets Eleanor Roosevelt, who was arriving at Chicago's La Salle Street Station to speak at the Covenant Club of Illinois. Between them is Danny's client Harry Zelzer, the Allied Arts manager. (Author's collection)

Ad artist Charles S. Stevens
limned Danny under the
turban of the Oriental Theatre's
Randolph Street minaret for
his 1940 holiday greeting card.
(Author's collection)

In 1972 the Houston Symphony donors presented their Gold Baton award to
Danny Newman for promoting the orchestra into box-office prosperity and to
Van Cliburn for his devotion to that organization. Conductor Lawrence Foster,
between them, was also honored. (Photo by James Benfield; author's collection)

During his whirlwind promotion of Lyric Opera of Chicago's 1971 season, Danny Newman pauses, momentarily breathless, in his "nerve center" office surrounded by files, telephones, and one of his three speedy manual typewriters. (Photograph by Howard D. Simmons; courtesy of Lyric Opera of Chicago)

In 1973 Danny provides a last-minute change of cast at the Civic Opera House. His stentorian and unamplified announcements from the stage would bounce off the second balcony's back wall. (Courtesy of Lyric Opera of Chicago)

For almost half a century the *Chicago Tribune*'s critic, Claudia Cassidy, occupied the seat in row F off the third aisle at Chicago's Civic Opera House. After her death, Lyric Opera's board of directors dedicated that seat to her friend and confidante Danny Newman and affixed his gilded nameplate to its right arm. The adjoining seat is assigned to Alyce Newman. (Courtesy of Lyric Opera of Chicago)

Schuyler Chapin, president of the American Symphony Orchestra League and the former general manager of the Metropolitan Opera, presents its highest award, the Gold Baton, to Danny Newman at the league's first North American conference, Toronto, 1987. (Photo by Norm Scudellari; used by permission of *Symphony* magazine and the American Symphony Orchestra League)

Rhumba king Xavier Cugat learned the caricaturist's art from Enrico Caruso, whom Cugat accompanied on piano at the beginning of the twentieth century. Almost fifty years later, Cugat drew this version of his press agent, Danny Newman, in lieu of his fee. (Author's collection)

HE HEARS THE BEAT OF HIS OWN DRUM!

Harry Hanson illustrated one of his *Chicago Magazine* profiles of Danny Newman during the 1970s with this drawing by William Utterback. (Courtesy of *Chicago Magazine*)

Danny and Alyce Newman at the opening night of Lyric's 1995–96 season, *Aida.* (Author's collection)

At Chicago Lyric Opera's 1999 post-premiere party celebrating William Bolcom's musical version of Arthur Miller's *A View from the Bridge. Left to right:* octogenarians Studs Terkel, Danny Newman, and Arthur Miller. Danny was general manager of the original play's world premiere at Chicago's Studebaker Theatre in 1956. (Author's collection)

In the 1930s Danny and Studs Terkel were youngsters who performed with rival Chicago theater groups, and they have been friends, and often collaborators, ever since. In the late 1970s they reminisced in Lyric Opera's Graham Room. (Courtesy of Lyric Opera of Chicago)

Stan Laurel and Oliver Hardy heeded a photographer's proposal that they pause in their in-person Chicago appearances to soothe a disconcerted duck. (Author's collection)

3 Vaudeville Headliners Laurel and Hardy Return to Their Roots; also about Roy Rogers, Trigger, Early-Days Movie Cowboy Buck Jones, and Other Show-Biz Exotica!

Laurel and Hardy, the world-celebrated premiere comedy team of motion pictures—both silent and talking—were among the major stars of the entertainment universe I publicized as house press agent of the luxurious, 3,200-seat Oriental Theatre. The Oriental offered both stage shows and movies, usually five of each, every day on Chicago's bustling Randolph Street in the 1940s. Acts were an eclectic profusion of then-contemporary vaudeville performers: mind-readers, magicians, comedians, blues singers, crooners, tumblers, tap-dancers, movie stars in person, and "tab show" musical revues of the era (*George White's Scandals, Earl Carroll's Vanities,* and the *A. B. Marcus All-Girl Revues*).

Arthur Stanley Jefferson Laurel and Oliver Norvell Hardy Jr., the respective full names of Laurel and Hardy, were both born in the nineteenth century, the former in Lancashire, England, and the latter in Harlem, Georgia. Stan—the skinny one—had in pre-film days performed with the circus and in music halls, legit theater, and variety shows. He was also once Charlie Chaplin's understudy. The rotund Ollie was a young vaudeville veteran before his 1913 beginning in silent films. Producer Hal Roach, in the mid-1920s inspired to team them, was rewarded in 1927 when they came up with a smash hit, *Putting Pants on Philip,* directed, I think, by Leo McCarey.

Timid and touchingly distressed Stan and pompous Ollie smoothly accommodated themselves to talking pictures. From 1927 through 1951 they appeared in almost ninety comedies, some full-length, some short. I have only happy memories of both "boys." They were good natured and amenable—truly gentle souls. They were fond of good food and depended on me to take them to the right restaurants. They were—in this period—at the peak of their international fame. The advent of talkies presented few language barrier problems for them because much of their comedy depended on patently hilarious situations and inimitable, polished pantomime rather than dialog. Their followers—all the way from Taipei to Timbuktu—kept increasing. For some years huge billboards in the heart of central London featured huge portraits of Laurel and Hardy, a sort of permanent exhibit. I did much work in England over the years, and every time I went the boys were still there, near Piccadilly Circus.

On one occasion in Chicago I thought it would be fun if they would accompany me to the fund-raising bazaar the Sisterhood of the Jewish Temple near my home was holding. I knew, of course, that their appearance would cause a sensation throughout the neighborhood, and you may be sure that it did! The boys ate with relish, devouring the good home cooking, including blintzes, and quaffing flagons of beet borscht with sour cream. They endlessly gave autographs and pinched the cheeks of the kiddies. I could see they were deriving pleasure from delighting the crowd.

One feature writer has charmingly and perceptively stated, "We treasure that dignified dumpling, Ollie, his trademark withering look of exasperation and 'slow burn,' all knotted up in his finger-twiddled tie. We hold in affection that bungling baby—thin-man Stan—Ollie's deceptively lamblike foil, scratching his head in perplexity one minute and poking Ollie in the eye the next—both clowns creating yet 'another fine mess' of their everyday adventures—corpulent Ollie, piloting his dirigible of pompous dignity, forever colliding with Stanley's prickly propensity for unavoidable comical disaster!"

Laurel and Hardy were among the best exemplars of those high-level nineteenth and early-twentieth-century variety artists who—with almost scientific precision—perfected, disciplined, and polished their acts through years of unremitting performing experience before live audiences of all kinds in both small-time and big-time engagements. It was an in-depth immersion-education no university could provide.

Because the Oriental was an independent venue—at a time before the courts struck down the monopoly whereby major film producers also owned chains of movie theaters—we were denied first-run rights to most important motion pictures. The Palace, for example, was owned by R.K.O. Pictures, and Paramount owned both the State-Lake and the Chicago. So we put our money into stage attractions and came off quite well competitively.

Within a few blocks of the Oriental were its Loop competitors, the Palace, State-Lake, and Chicago Theatres, all also offering vaudeville and motion pictures in tandem. There were also the United Artists, the McVickers, the Woods, the Garrick, the Apollo, and the Roosevelt, all movie houses that had been converted from legitimate stage playhouses. Then, too, there were the twin thousand-seat Harris and Selwyn and Cohan's Grand, the Erlanger, and the Great Northern, all offering live dramas, comedies, and/or musical shows. Not far away just south of the Loop were the Studebaker, Blackstone, and Auditorium Theatres, all offering plays and/or musicals. The Cort Theatre, a legit house on Dearborn just off Randolph, had recently closed, as had the Princess on South Clark Street.

There were also large-capacity, luxuriously appointed movie palaces in various outlying neighborhoods—the Uptown at Lawrence and Broadway, the Granada in Rogers Park, the Marbro on West Madison Street, the Paradise on Crawford Avenue, the North Shore on Howard Street, and a good half-dozen more like those. All, like the Oriental, employed large pit orchestras whose leaders were local celebrities and also offered weekly changes of vaudeville bills. One band leader, Paul Ash, had become so big a star at the McVickers that the Oriental was built for him; he presided there until New York's Roxy Theatre took him away.

We normally played five shows a day, seven days a week, at the Oriental, and we opened an entirely new show each Friday as staged by our resident director Charles Niggemeyer. Charlie Hogan, a feisty little showman, was our talent booker, Charlie Stevens drew our newspaper ads, and Eddie

Myer built and painted the enticing out-front displays for every change of show. Years later Myer, a serious artist of high caliber, painted marvelous portraits for me (I have them in my study at home) of Boris Christoff as King Philip in *Don Carlo,* Tito Gobbi as Rigoletto, and the legendary Yiddish stage star Maurice Schwartz as Shylock. Chester Amberg—a jolly, roundish, red-cheeked and nosed, *and* sometimes tipsy Lilliputian—was our house treasurer with whom I shared subterranean offices around the corner from the men's washroom.

We went up to *seven* shows a day for Laurel and Hardy, Jane Russell, and a few others like Roy Rogers and his Golden Palomino, Trigger, for whom we built a comfortable padded stall in the wings (stage right). Roy, if I remember, had no real Wild West credentials, having been born and raised in Duck Creek, Ohio. Some years before I worked with him I had enrolled a young acting student, Dale Evans, in a drama school I managed in the old Auditorium Theatre Building. Later she would become Roy's wife and his movie-western costar of many years.

Roy, a latter-day cowboy movie star, followed such luminaries of the silents as Tom Mix, Hoot Gibson, and Buck Jones. Whether they—the gods of my childhood—could sing as Roy Rogers did I'll never know because I stopped attending the cowboy genre by the time talkies came in. Roy and Trigger were not only my onstage stars but they also gained important media attention for me when I saw to it that they led the city's resident Black Horse Troop down La Salle, Chicago's Wall Street, all the way from the Board of Trade at Jackson Boulevard to Wacker Drive at the edge of the river. Ticker tape swirled, and thousands cheered.

I recall handling Buck Jones in a series of Chicago personal appearances in 1942, after which he was committed to a similar assignment in Boston. We had gotten along famously, and he urged me to accompany him there. I had other projects to attend to in Chicago, however, so I saw him off at the train station, having arranged for a New England press agent–colleague to take him over upon arrival in Boston. That same week, Buck, the press agent, and the press agent's wife were, unfortunately, caught in the devastating Coconut Grove night club fire that killed more than three hundred people, including Buck, who was hailed as a hero for struggling to save many victims. The publicity man was somehow unscathed, but his wife was injured. Buck Jones had been a U.S. Army cavalryman; a radio, circus, and Indian film artist; a horse wrangler; and a stuntman. He appeared in 153 motion pictures, beginning in 1918. He was—along with his contemporaries Tom Mix and Hoot Gibson—one of the true icons for wild west movie aficionados.

Increasing from five shows to seven was not easily accomplished, and doing so required taking one or two reels of film out of the movie we were showing. To my knowledge there were no complaints from afternoon patrons, a segment of whom were certainly youngsters ditching high school classes and stealthily evading Javert-like truant officers.

Our stage door alley was often the scene of volatile activity, especially when all-out bobby-soxer adoration of band-singer stars was at its height. On one occasion I had to make a perilous rescue of crooner Dick Haymes from a horde of glamour-intoxicated hysterical young girls who were literally tearing off his clothes.

Across the street from the Oriental was Dario L. Toffenetti's flagship Triangle Restaurant. (He had six others within walking distance, all featuring his celebrated and hyperbolic menus.) Next door was the dignified Henrici's, favorite brunching, lunching, and dining spot of the city's political and theatrical elite.

The five blocks of Chicago's Randolph Street between State and Wells Streets were roistering ones, jam-packed with raffish, Broadway-type folk—not unlike those Damon Runyon was celebrating. We had, for instance, the hulking King Levinsky, the punch-drunk ex-heavyweight boxer who buttonholed you to buy a loud tie, and A. B. Marcus, the wealthy international showman, on his way to a bargain lunch at the W&R Restaurant, which had free pickles and sour tomatoes on its tables.

Marcus, a charming Litvak who spoke fractured English and had run a small dry-cleaning shop near Boston, became an international theatrical impresario when a traveling musical revue's producer who had sent his troupe's costumes to be refreshed went broke and abandoned them. The canny cleaner put lovely young women into those costumes and went on to successfully tour the world with the *A. B. Marcus All-Girl Revues*, which I publicized—from time to time—in tab-show format. Although the colorful showman was not known as a fast man with a buck, he did—on one occasion—present me with a handsome cash bonus even though I was separately recompensed by the house. And he often invited me to dinners at which he regaled me with tales of sell-out triumphs in the Far East, where he received hefty percentages of the grosses and maintained savings accounts in local currencies.

The Oriental was built in the 1930s below a high-rise office building on the site of the old Iroquois Theatre, which had been destroyed in a tragic 1903 fire that resulted in an enormous loss of life and inspired Chicago to enact the nation's most stringent fire prevention laws for theaters. The Oriental remained an important venue for a full half century, finally being shuttered in 1981 and then expensively renovated and reopened as a home for touring musical shows in 1998, reduced in capacity to 2,200 seats.

The Oriental years, beginning in 1940, were happy, instructive ones for me under the tutelage of that theater's wise, kind, florid-faced manager Jack Hunt, who had been in show business since he was boy, running away from his New England home with a touring stage company. His beautiful twin daughters, Bonnie and Gloria, had been mahouts—perilously perched elephant handlers—for the Ringling Brothers Circus. Later, they opened the charming Twins Sweet Shoppe adjoining the Oriental.

It was Jack Hunt who inspired me in many ways and set me on the course of multiple employment in my profession. While still a youngster I was able to build a burgeoning press agency into a life-long career. Although he had known me only a short time, he knowingly sacrificed his own interests by seeking other theatrical clients for me, confident I'd be able to juggle a half dozen or more promotional projects at the same time, although I was then not all that confident. Truth to tell, I was sleep-deprived for the next half century. I must have thrived on that regimen, for somehow I acquitted myself honorably and successfully and have had good reason to be grateful to him ever since.

Although Jack Hunt had virtually no formal education, I came to have an almost worshipful regard for his infinite knowledge of show business and his wisdom in dealing with people. He could, with uncanny accuracy, gauge what the gross receipts would be on any given day or predict exactly the words that a disgruntled patron or a frustrated performer would use—even before the complaint was lodged. He looked out for me as if he were my father. When I came back from the war Jack had already arranged four simultaneous jobs for me. After a couple of years at a $30 per month army wage you can imagine what those four regular and generous checks meant. Now many universities have schools of arts management and teach theatrical publicity and promotion. In my youth, however, I had to learn entirely by doing—to fly by the seat of my pants. My alma maters were the Oriental Theatre and all the other many places where I served show-biz apprenticeships. I could not have had a finer professor than Jack Hunt. Although the wise and decent Jack is long gone, I remember him with admiration and appreciation and remain close to Gloria and Bonnie to this day.

Now I return to Laurel and Hardy. Their in-person engagement at the Oriental Theatre was a rare stage appearance for them and followed many years of intensive film-making. They were returning to their professional roots and the stimulation of live audiences They clearly, savored everything about the experience. Before their Oriental engagement concluded they asked me to give up all my Chicago-based activities so I could move to Hollywood, where I would presumably devote all my time entirely to them. Although I had traveled much in my work and was away for two years in the war I had never left Chicago to establish residence anywhere else. Even now, a half-century later, I haven't done so. I was born in Chicago, and my family graves are there. Certainly, I was more than touched that these two gifted artists (and wonderful fellows) wanted me to be with them permanently. I respectfully—and affectionately—begged off, however. Since then I have come to know and admire two generations of other paragons of the entertainment arts, but I now bestow my "Danny Appleseed Award" on Stan and Ollie!

4 Harry Bloomfield, Free-Spending Ticket-Scalper/ Theatrical Producer; the Young, Idealistic Frank Sinatra; and Peru's Alberto Vargas, Painter of the Ziegfeld Girls, the Varga Girls, and the Playboy Girls

Harry Bloomfield, the ambitious Broadway theater ticket broker and some-time musical show producer, introduced me to the super crooner Frank Sinatra; to Alberto Varga, creator of *Esquire Magazine*'s voluptuous Varga Girl monthly feature and its fabulously successful annual calendar; and to many other mid- and late-1940s celebs whose names were regularly to be read in Walter Winchell's nationally syndicated column that inspired his gossip columnist (calumnist?) imitators.

Bloomfield, whose touring Chopin musical *Polonaise*—starring the tempestuous Polish opera tenor Jan Kiepura and his wife, the lovely Hungarian operetta star Marta Eggerth—which I had press-agented during the 1945–46 season, had subsequently become a friend of mine. As it turned out it would become an expensive friendship for me, but more on that later. Among my many other assignments at the time I was publicist for the Oriental Theatre, around the corner from the Chicago Theatre. In the late 1940s Frank Sinatra, already widely known for singing with Tommy Dorsey's Orchestra and on the weekly radio *Hit Parade,* was making a five-show-a-day personal appearance at the Chicago Theatre. One afternoon

Harry came by and asked me to accompany him on a visit to Sinatra's dressing room. This was long before Sinatra's rat-pack shenanigans; his Academy Award movie *From Here to Eternity;* and his succession of films from 1954 through 1981, including *The Young at Heart, Guys and Dolls, High Society, Pal Joey, Suddenly, The Man with the Golden Arm, Some Came Running, The Manchurian Candidate, Von Ryan's Express, Tony Rome, The Detective,* and *The First Deadly Sin.*

At any rate, during the backstage Chicago Theatre visit Sinatra invited me to dine with him that evening at the Ambassador East Hotel's Pump Room. During the table conversation I was impressed by his knowledge of current political affairs, recent books, and films of importance. Overall, I found him to be an earnest, serious—and charming—young person. I shall judge that he was then in his late twenties. A few nights later we shared a table at Chicago's reigning night club, the Chez Paree.

On another occasion I accompanied him to the Chez Paree's private gaming room, where I had never previously been. As soon as we entered we overheard a vulgarian make offensive ethnic slurs about another patron. Sinatra angrily ran over to the offender, ferociously shut him up, and physically threw him out of the room. I loved him for doing that. Many, many years later, when he became a sort of tough guy and a rowdy, rat-pack leader who had widely publicized underworld connections, I thought back to the decent young entertainer I encountered so many years earlier and whom I admired. Certainly, he had grown into one of the twentieth century's most beloved baritone interpreters of love ballads. The *Encyclopedia Britannica* speaks of the "distinctive phrasing and pauses enhancing subtle emotional overtones that his voice expressed." He became over the years a superb motion picture actor; a big-time, sure-fire sell-out attraction for personal appearances in theaters; and a star of radio, recordings, and television.

During the same period—the late 1940s—that Harry Bloomfield introduced me to Frank Sinatra he brought me together with Alberto Varga, America's premier painter of stunning, luminous American women. He first became known for his unique creations immediately following World War I, when he became the official portraitist for the Ziegfeld Follies. Varga glorified the famed Ziegfeld Girls and then went on to Hollywood, where he designed sets and painted the portraits of Greta Garbo, Marlene Dietrich, Dorothy Lamour, Paulette Goddard, Barbara Stanwyck, and Shirley Temple.

To characterize Varga as a pin-up girl painter is to trivialize his unique oeuvre. His gorgeous watercolor technique and superb craftsmanship have been judged "perfect" and "ideal." The San Francisco Art Exchange, which represents his work, says he did more than just paint women. He *glorified* them with a passion born of respect and admiration. When asked why he painted only women, Varga responded, "Show me something more beautiful than a beautiful woman, and then I'll go and paint it!" Now, more than a half-century since I became a close friend and confidante of Alberto and his wife Anna Mae, I still recall that is exactly the way in which the gentle and idealistic Peruvian spoke. Anna Mae, his first model, posed for him when she was a Ziegfeld Girl.

I became Alberto's pro-bono publicist during his long and finally fruitless effort to free himself from what he had belatedly come to regard as an onerous, entirely one-sided magazine contract that he had naïvely signed. He had thus condemned himself to a cruel regimen of producing fifty-two paintings a year, an obvious impossibility unless quality is no consideration. Varga told me that he hadn't read the contract until years after he signed it! He had never before signed a contract. He was accustomed to just sealing deals with a handshake.

I was told by Harry Bloomfield that in 1945 alone, *Esquire*'s sales of Varga's "spinoffs" mounted to more than $1 million, while his ten-year contract, begun on January 1, 1944, called for him to receive just $12,000 per year. (These figures are given in Paul Chutkow's *The Real Vargas,* published in 1996.) Bloomfield had a stake in Varga winning freedom from this patently unfair agreement because he expected to become Varga's future manager/promoter.

When the case finally came to court I set down a heavy publicity barrage that made his exploiters very unhappy and also, I think, greatly influenced the judge, jury, and public. David Smart, *Esquire*'s publisher, threatened me in the courtroom, snarling that he'd "get me." All I had done was reveal the terms of the agreement that Varga had indeed unfortunately signed, and that was duly reported in the media. As the trial proceeded and media coverage favoring Varga mounted, the courtroom atmosphere shifted to favor the plaintiff. Our lawyer—a folksy, Clarence Darrow–like advocate who wore suspenders and, in his office, an eyeshade—scored strongly day after day, and we won!

David Smart, however, had deep pockets, and he appealed to a higher court, which—uninfluenced by the publicity-engendered sympathy for Varga—reversed the Chicago trial's findings. Alberto had, after all, signed the contract. Varga refused to accept any new assignment from Esquire for the remainder of his contract, which still had several years to run, and returned to California. When the contract finally lapsed he reverted to his original name, Vargas (*Esquire* owned the name Varga!). From 1960, and for the next eighteen years, he produced more than 152 paintings for *Playboy Magazine*. Alberto Vargas died of a stroke in 1982 at the age of eighty-six, one of the finest, most gentle human beings I have ever known.

Back to Harry Bloomfield, who at the time was proprietor of the well-known Bloomfield Ticket Service on Manhattan's West Forty-seventh Street—just across the street from the Alvin Theatre. He was also a friend and emulator of the flamboyant, risk-taking, and then creditor-dodging producer Mike Todd, husband successively to Joan Blondell and Elizabeth Taylor. Harry decided to take the plunge as a producer in his own right when the opportunity arose to take *Polonaise* on the road, Chicago being a major target.

That's where I came in. I had that fall returned from fighting during almost all of 1944 as an infantry rifleman in France, Belgium, Holland, Germany, and back to Belgium in the Battle of the Bulge. The New York office of the Association of Theatrical Press Agents and Managers, of which I had been the youngest member, had evidently recommended me to Bloomfield and, after a previous assignment that winter, to the producers of *The Second Guesser* starring the famous baseball comedian Al Schaacht (uncle of the four Marx Brothers) in Chicago's cavernous Civic Opera House.

I did the advance press agentry for the spring opening of *Polonaise* in the old Studebaker Theatre, reputedly once the site of a horse carriage factory. We opened on Monday, March 5, 1946, and the brilliant *Chicago Daily News* writer Robert J. Casey, in the role of drama critic, loved our show. He praised not only Kiepura's marvelous tenor voice but also his acting as the Polish patriot and American Revolution war hero Jan Taddeusz Kosciusko. "*Polonaise*," he wrote, "was a very good musical!"

To be honest, not all the critics were that enthusiastic, but with strong support at the box office from the eight hundred thousand–strong Polish-American community, for whom Jan was an idol, we went into a nice run. During the run I spent much time with the Kiepuras and with Bloomfield, who outside his familiar New York milieu was a fish out of water. I introduced him to many of our city's glitteratti, including celebrities in the art disciplines in which I worked, and various critics and columnists. He revelled in knowing them, but I was startled at the alacrity with which Harry went out and bought extravagant gifts for each. Evidently, that was the customary way in which Mike Todd—whom Harry so much admired—operated. Some of those same journalists have been lifetime friends of mine, and I've never given them gifts.

My decade-long association with Harry Bloomfield was costly in that I found myself constantly lending him money, and he never repaid it—not one cent. But I learned from him, too. His weaknesses, follies, and foibles, that is, underscored the worth of the solid values that my wonderful, widowed father had taught me. Harry, trying so hard and so unsuccessfully to adopt his pal Mike Todd's lavish lifestyle and imaginative career maneuvers, became enmeshed in an ever-widening web of unthought-through, misfired actions and embarrassing evasions.

I recall a perfect illustration of Harry's New York street-smart but wrong-headed attitudes. Once we were rolling through attractive Wisconsin farmland on a train. It was a late-summer afternoon, and we saw a farm family at supper on their farmhouse lawn, sitting around an outdoor table laden with food and pitchers of milk or lemonade. I remarked that it was a beautiful scene, one Norman Rockwell might well have painted. What I saw was a father, a mother, and their healthy children—and the contentment of people who worked hard and enjoyed the fruits of their labor. Harry, however, said he felt sorry for "those poor hicks," who were evidently deprived of the joys of dinners in fancy restaurants and posh hotel supper rooms. Although excellent rail connections existed and air travel saved little or no time, Harry would often fly—first class, of course—on short jumps between cities only a few hundred miles apart. When asked why he did so he said, "You meet a better class of people" on airplanes.

Eventually, he spent very little time at his ticket brokerage business in New York—paying others to run it for him—and dashed around the country in pursuit of various failing (and flailing) windmill projects. He would run up substantial bills in luxury hotels, and call me long distance, threatening to commit suicide by jumping out the window if I didn't send him money—sometimes thousands of dollars—immediately by Western Union. He seemed so distraught on those occasions—so desperate—that I feared he really would jump! So I sent the money. Bear in mind that I was then working almost around the clock at various publicity assignments, trying to pay off loans that had enabled me to lease and then buy the Astor Theatre!

After several years of being blackmailed by the awful threat of another human being's death, Harry stopped calling, and I felt it best that I let our association lapse. In later years he was, I knew, in Chicago on several occasions. I did not look him up, and I think he was ashamed to call me because he had never said that he regretted his inability to make even a token payment on his considerable debt to me. He was, I believe, in his late forties and I was in my mid-twenties at the time I met him. Eventually, I saw his obituary notice in *Variety*. I had never met his wife and son, and I sent no notes of condolence. I look back on my experience with Harry as part of my grass-roots education in the vagaries of show business.

5 Tales of Chicago's All-Day, All-Night Astor Theatre and the Peerless Menu Poet Dario Toffenetti Next Door

I came home to Chicago from overseas U.S. Army service on October 10, 1945. The next day, I arranged—at the Covenant Club—for physical therapy treatments for my wounded (and still not functioning well) left upper arm. Because club officials regarded me as a war hero they offered a special membership. Overnight, I resumed my numerous, concurrent prewar press agent assignments. Every one of my old clients had patiently waited out my long absence, and they immediately rehired me. In addition, I had new clients recommended by my friend Jack Hunt. I represented the Oriental Theatre (vaudeville and motion pictures); the World Playhouse (Italian, French, Russian, and British art films); the Original Drive-In Movie Theatre; the Twin Open-Air Theatres; Minsky's Rialto Theatre (stage shows with movies); legitimate theater venues that housed touring dramas and musical shows; impresario Harry Zelzer's classical music presentations at the Civic Opera House and Orchestra Hall; and Mayor Edward J. Kelly's annual Kelly Bowl charity football event at Soldier Field.

Almost immediately as well, I became co-producer of a pioneering, five-times-weekly celebrity radio interview show, *Famous Names,* which was broadcast at lunchtime from either the Mayfair Room or the Balinese Room of the Blackstone Hotel. The young and mellifluous-voiced Myron (now Mike) Wallace was the emcee. The program continued for the next five years, sponsored on WGN by the burgeoning Walgreen pharmacy chain.

Because I was in those years simultaneously promoting many different kinds of attractions I was able to provide a steady supply of legit theater, movie, radio, and other performing arts celebs to *Famous Names* and only occasionally had to call on other publicists for the participation of their clients. We also interviewed distinguished journalists and authors. Once, when chatting on-air with the hard-boiled entertainment feature editor of one of our city's largest newspapers, Myron asked why he so often gave big space to the shows I represented. The editor thought for a moment and then replied, "Because he's always there. He's always in our offices."

In truth, I was then visiting the city rooms, picture desks, and feature departments of all five Chicago daily newspapers every day of the week. Of course, you had to present ideas and material that made sense. One editor who respected my judgment in photographs once offered me a good job on his picture desk. I knew, however, I'd soon be in the army and demurred. Not long afterward a warm letter from him was delivered to my Dutch foxhole after the fierce Battle of Aachen on the Dutch-German border.

In my first week out of uniform I learned that the Astor Theatre—the oldest continuously operating movie house in Chicago's Loop, just off the southwest corner of Clark and Madison Streets (a high-volume location)—was available for lease. The octogenarian Roder Brothers, who had operated it for a generation, were retiring to their ancestral home in Greece. The Astor Theatre Building—a narrow, four-story structure—was owned by the fabled Dario L. Toffenetti, who ran seven successful Loop restaurants as well as a huge one in New York's Times Square at Forty-third Street. We met, talked, and, as they say, hit it off. I think he was both amused and admiring of my energy and ambition, probably because I reminded him of himself during his younger days. At any rate we shook hands on our deal.

I had to raise the $40,000 lease deposit (in 1945 that was a lot of cash), but Mr. Toffenetti proffered a long-term agreement at what seemed to be reasonable rent, and the theater's premises did not, at that time, require expensive renovation. Besides, the already air-conditioned Astor was an on-going entity. Most of its small capacity was well occupied twenty-three hours daily, seven days and nights a week, closing only between 6 and 7 A.M. for a thorough clean-up. The policy was to show double-features —westerns, family dramas, mysteries, musicals, and action stories of all kinds—that changed every day. John Wayne's movies were staples. Tickets were 15 cents in the morning, 25 cents in the afternoon, and 30 cents all night.

Putting together the money for the lease deposit, however, wasn't all that easy. I had just graduated from the army and was beginning to work again at press agent jobs, having used all my prewar savings to assist relatives while I was away. So, I invited my client Abe Teitel, who ran the World Playhouse and a foreign film exchange, to become my partner. He would, I reasoned, also provide mature show business judgment, which I greatly respected. Catherine Carpenter, one of the Astor Theatre cashiers—a fine elderly woman—volunteered to loan her $10,000 life savings. I'm happy to write that after a year I was able to repay her in full—with interest—from fees from publicity jobs. When, years later, she retired, we corresponded and spoke over the telephone until she died at a very old age. The rest of the required lease deposit I obtained by borrowing from the Equitable Life Insurance policy I took out before leaving for the army. And so I closed the deal with Mr. Toffenetti, who became my good friend for many years afterward and from whom I learned a great deal.

Now I had a movie theater to run—a decade later I also took over the leases of two neighborhood houses, the Chelten and the Accadia—and I had to do it while running back and forth to various concurrent publicity projects and the five daily Chicago newspapers and various radio stations on their behalf. I hired an experienced house manager and a part-time film booker to provide, at reasonable flat rental fees (not on percentage), fourteen motion pictures every week for my Astor's double-feature policy.

Although I already had many years of promotional experience in the film field, I was now, for the first time, an entrepreneur. I had four union projectionists on my payroll in addition to four cashiers, ushers, candy-counter help, and Charlie—a hopelessly alcoholic janitor and long-time employee whom I inherited. He couldn't handle the early-morning clean-up task, so I had to hire him an assistant. Why didn't I just fire Charlie? Well, he was a widower raising a teen-aged daughter and would never be able to hold another job. Besides, I have never, ever, been able to fire anybody!

After two modestly profitable years Abe Teitel—meaning well—convinced me to abandon our conventional double-feature programming for art films, his specialty. Our two main competitors, the La Salle around the corner on Madison Street and the Clark, kitty-corner from us, immediately took our patrons, too few of whom showed up for our new offerings. Practically from the start we were operating in the red. We tried to return to our old policy, but customers had become accustomed to the larger, more comfortable La Salle and Clark theaters, which also showed conventional double features. Wooing them back would take time and investment in renovations.

Abe Teitel lost heart and said we must sell our lease. We were losing money, however, so no buyer materialized. Eventually, Teitel asked me to take over the entire responsibility, and—using funds I saved from press agent activities—I bought him out at the price he set. I felt badly that I had invited him into what he now perceived as a failing situation. I then went heavily into debt for a new, modern, electric marquee and all-new seats. I also had the entire theater redecorated. Attendance soon improved, and the government did its part by suddenly cutting in half the federal ticket tax instituted during the war years. I felt safe in raising admission prices to 25 cents in the morning, 35 cents in the afternoon, and 50 cents all night.

A few years later, Toffenetti, needing cash to build a large restaurant in the new Greyhound bus station at Clark and Randolph streets—the station and restaurant have since been razed in favor of a high-rise office building—invited me to lunch and offered to sell me the Astor Theatre Building under generous terms. My mortgage payments, which he had arranged, were considerably less than the rent I had been paying him.

I ran the Astor, as either tenant or building owner, for a full decade before selling the property in 1955 to the board of directors of the Loop Synagogue (against my will, but that's another story). Shortly afterward, the synagogue's magnificent new structure was built on that site—*and* on an adjoining piece of land. Thinking of the Astor, I recall my tenant,

Mr. Segal, who ran a kosher restaurant there on the second floor. He had a charming little boy who helped him by setting silverware on the tables. That child, Gordon Segal, grew up to become the founder and CEO of the celebrated Crate and Barrel Corporation and a board member of Lyric Opera of Chicago.

It was through the Astor that I first came to know the astonishing Dario Toffenetti, but it was by patronizing his restaurants—particularly the flagship on Randolph Street almost across the street from my Oriental Theatre headquarters—that I came to admire the colorful showmanship of his window displays and the flamboyant wordage of his printed menus, which he created at home on Sunday afternoons after returning from church and presiding over family luncheons. Undoubtedly, the state of Idaho, which honored him greatly, had good reason to do so. As he described their tubers, "THE JEWELS OF IDAHO—HOT GENUINE IDAHO BAKED POTATOES—BIG, BULGING BEAUTIES, GROWN IN THE ASHES OF EXTINCT VOLCANOES! SCRUBBED AND WASHED, THEN BAKED IN THE WHIRLWIND OF TEMPESTUOUS FIRES UNTIL THE SHELLS CRACKLE WITH BRITTLENESS— AND WITHIN THE FARINACEOUS CONTENTS, EFFLORESCENT WITH EAGER HEAT, ABSORB THAT EVER-FRESH BLUE VALLEY BUTTER, WHICH WE SO ABUNDANTLY SERVE: WHAT A GUST OF FEELING! WHAT A DELIGHT!—JUST 20 CENTS!"

The affable Toffenetti, a Roman Catholic, was as ecumenical as they come, and his connections with—and philanthropic generosity toward— the Jewish community was well known. Nevertheless, for his *non*-Jewish clientele he glorified "DELICIOUS HOT ROASTED JUICY SUGAR-CURED HAM SANDWICHES, HICKORY SMOKED TO ENTHRALLING FRAGRANCE, LIBERAL IN SIZE, SERVED WITH PICKLE, THICKLY SLICED WITH RICH JERSEY CANDIED SWEET POTATOES—THEY MELT IN YOUR MOUTH!" Decked out in a huge white apron and chef's chapeau, and armed with the largest carving knife he could find, he personally sliced the ham daily in his big Randolph Street window, drawing large crowds of salivating onlookers, many of whom would rush inside. Overnight, Toffenetti set records for ham sandwich sales.

His exuberance in behalf of "OLD-FASHIONED STRAWBERRY SORTCAKE" knew no bounds. He called it "THE TONIC OF SPRING! A HEAPING HELPING, BE-DECKED WITH SNOW-WHITE WHIPPED CREAM. . . . DELICIOUS, MELLOW,

BEAUTIFUL, SWEET RUBY-RED GLORIOUS STRAWBERRIES—TRULY A BLOOD REJUVENATOR!" He called oysters "PRIMA DONNAS." About them he wrote, "FATHOMS DEEP IN THE CLEAR PURE WATERS OF DELAWARE BAY, THESE CHUBBY OYSTERS, RAISED UNDER UNCLE SAM'S CONSTANT SCIENTIFIC SUPERVISION, ARE SNATCHED—UNAWARE—FROM THEIR COZY BEDS, AND SHIPPED TO US FRESH EACH DAY FOR YOUR SUCCULENT SAVORING!"

Dario Louis Toffenetti was born in Italy's Dolomite Mountain (Tyrol) region near the Austrian border and not far from Milan, Padua, Modena, and Bologna. He arrived in the United States at age twenty-one, intending to work at a Cincinnati ice cream factory. When that deal didn't work out he took menial jobs until leaving for iron mines in Hurley, Michigan, for two years of back-breaking labor. Then he went on to Chicago, where he worked during the day and went to business school at night at Northwestern University. An apt student, he graduated in 1919. When I bought the Astor Theatre Building from him, my attorney told me that he had never known a nonlawyer who knew as much about American real estate law intricacies as did this immigrant young man. Even the businessman's guru Dale Carnegie wrote enthusiastically about the extraordinary Toffenetti.

The Astor Theatre's box office was at the edge of the Clark Street sidewalk, right across from the Morrison Hotel, where in the 1950s I obtained incredibly low room rental rates for my opera singers. The Morrison's owner, William Henning Rubin, was a long-time family friend of mine. Some years later when I delivered his eulogy I spoke gratefully of his largess to my artists. Next door to the hotel was the First National Bank, since moved to the site of the long-ago-razed Morrison, where I obtained the loans with which to renovate the Astor. My banker was a Mr. Snydacker, who was, I think, surprised each time I made a repayment. Financial executives did not regard show business folk as solid citizens.

Now, as I write—early in the twenty-first century—I realize how rich my Astor Theatre experiences were. I fondly recall Carol Fox and Lawrence V. Kelly, two of Lyric Opera's three founders (the third being Maestro Nicola Rescigno) coming down to my basement-level theater office in 1954 for our planning sessions concerning the new opera company's initial season that opened on November 1 of that year and featured the American debut of Maria Meneghini Callas. I also remember how six years earlier, in July 1948, from the same little underground office I placed an inspired transatlantic telephone call to London and convinced actress Dina Halpern to become my bride. A regular Astor Theatre attendee was the brilliant young lawyer and CPA Jerome (Jerry) Van Gorkom, later the CEO of the giant Trans Union Corporation, undersecretary of state in Washington, D.C., a great Chicago civic leader, and president/board chair of Lyric Opera. He was my age, and we were dear friends for more than forty years.

Mr. Toffenetti sometimes drove me home from the Astor Theatre in the evening (not very often because I worked a great deal at night), but more often he drove me downtown in the morning. I always learned something. He was amazed I didn't know how to drive. He loved the freedom and mobility that driving gave him and told me he'd rather give up his home than his car! He was by no means all business. I will never forget his spiritual sense of wonder and awe as he described the recurring miracle of seeing plants emerge each spring when he was a farm boy in Italy.

He was a good and loving family man, kind and considerate of his 1,200 employees. Having done business with him, I knew him to be scrupulously honorable and of rock-ribbed integrity. In one particular instance I saw that quality put to the test, and he passed with flying colors! Recently, I had occasion to see one of his children and one of his grandchildren. They can be justly proud of their fine father and grandfather.

6 The *Fan*tastic Sally Rand: The 1933 World's Fair Lady Godiva and Her Trusty Adding Machine

In 1933 I was beginning my work in theater by night while by day—all summer—I sold hot dogs at the Chicago World's Fair. There were a great many educational, scientific, and cultural exhibits at the ambitious, futuristic Century of Progress exposition, and there were also attractions for the demi-monde. Chief among those was the one starring the fabled fan-and-bubble-dancing, undulating Sally Rand, who was drawing huge crowds of tourists and local gawkers as well. The cultural entertainments included a small Shakespeare repertory company that presented some of the Immortal Bard's most popular plays. And one of the World's Fair Pabst Pavilion orchestra *violinists* was Jan Peerce, who *only eight* years later would make his Metropolitan Opera debut as Alfredo in *La Traviata*. Peerce, who would become one of Arturo Toscanini's favorite artists, enjoyed an illustrious international career for the next quarter century as an opera singer and recital vocalist.

Sally Rand, born Harriet Beck, said Cecil B. DeMille had provided her stage name. A young veteran of vaudeville, she had also been an acrobatic dancer in carnivals and in the Ringling Brothers and Barnum and Bailey combined circuses as well as a performer in Hollywood films. Sally met the Great Depression head-on and began improvising an effective "nude" dance routine using outsized ostrich-feather fans she fashioned herself. I put the word *nude* in quotation marks because, in fact, she so artfully maneuvered her fans that she was never revealed in the all-together.

Then came her great opportunity—the opening of the Century of Progress! Lady Godiva–like, she entered the fair grounds astride a prancing white steed, an act that led to terrific publicity and stardom at the fair's Streets of Paris concession. Her delicate fan and terpsichorean efforts were performed to the music of such great composers as Claude Debussy and Frederic Chopin. Thus, she launched a highly remunerative career that also rewarded her with international attention.

Some fifteen years later, when I was publicizing Minsky's Rialto—among a half-dozen other theatrical enterprises—Sally was booked for the starring spot at that premier Chicago burlesque theater at Van Buren and State Streets. Because she was highly sophisticated and knowledgable where publicity was concerned, it was natural for her to make an ally of the house's press agent, and we worked well together.

Sally possessed shrewd understanding of her worth at the box office and drove a hard bargain with management; her contract called for a considerable percentage of the gross. I remember being simultaneously surprised and amused when I found her in her dressing—or undressing—room between shows, avidly studying box office reports and meticulously checking them for accuracy using a full-sized, clattering adding machine that she protectively transported—along with her precious fans—from one engagement to another! Without question Sally was a strong attraction who—when added to the standard parade girls, ponies, and putty-nosed comics—made her performances profitable for the house and herself.

The "house" was Harold Minsky, scion of the celebrated New York burlesque-producing family and husband of the gorgeous ecdysiast Dardy Orlando, sister of one of the major stars of that field, glamorous Lili St. Cyr. Another sister, well married, later became an enthusiast for Lyric Opera of Chicago and subscribed to box seats, flying in from New York for each of the company's annual season's eight operas. I recall gleefully naming Dardy—a wonderful person—the "Anatomy Award Winner of 1950"—a ploy that resulted in much newspaper space, including widely distributed wire-service photographs of her (appropriately clad) playing tennis.

Sally and I touched base every once in a while in the ensuing years, and she knew I headed the press department of the young Lyric Opera of Chicago in addition to my other concurrent involvements. One day she had telephoned me there. My first reaction was one of dismay when the telephone receptionist excitedly called over to my corner of the large shared office of our tiny staff that *Sally Rand* had left a message for me. I was, after all, promoting high culture (grand opera) and—damn it—my checkered past was catching up with me!

I quickly realized, however, that I had suddenly become much more interesting to co-workers—particularly the young women—than before Sally called. Up to that moment they thought of me as a rather dull fellow. After all, they knew I didn't drink or smoke (cigars came later), had never learned to drive, lived at home with my elderly father until the day I married, and didn't at all appreciate their new, hip-gyrating idol, Elvis. The wife of a prominent gossip columnist had even been overheard characterizing me as a "square"! In a flash I had a better, more desirable reputation. The call from Sally proved I was "with it," and I quickly basked in the new way I was perceived—a now-outed closet hedonist!

I returned Sally's call from a telephone booth and suggested that she call me in the future at the office of the nearby Astor Theatre, which I owned. Sally, when I explained, understood, and—good sport that she was—laughed. We remained good friends for the years to come, and I was amused at the now more respectful attitude toward me in the opera company's office.

7

Dynamic Sam Wanamaker from Chicago's West Side: A Broadway Star, Internationally Famed Director/Producer, Theatrical Force in the West End, and Restorer of London's Old Globe Theatre

Although we were both born in 1919 and came from the same near–West Side Chicago neighborhood of Douglas Park, a largely immigrant community seething with passionate political, social, and philosophical polemic, I didn't meet Sam Wanamaker until 1936, when I, the child-prodigy theatrical manager/press agent of a civic theater company, rented the Goodman Theatre to produce Sidney Howard's *Half Gods*. I did the same thing in 1937 for the same Pulitzer Prize–winning playwright's *Yellowjack* and in 1938 for Maxwell Anderson's *The Masque of Kings*.

Part of the rental deal was that we were given, at no extra charge, a complete stagehand crew composed of the Goodman's drama students. Two teenagers on that crew were Sam Wanamaker, formerly Sam Wattenmacher ("cotton-maker" in Yiddish) and Mladen Sekulovich, who was from a steel-mill area in Gary, Indiana, and later became Karl Malden, luminary of stage, motion pictures, and television. The handsome, partially underground Goodman Theatre in the heart of Chicago's lake-front Grant Park was run by the Art Institute's board of directors. In a depression-era economy move, the board jettisoned the theater's excellent but deficit-ridden professional repertory company in 1930 but retained the drama school affiliate that broke even through tuition fees.

I was fated to encounter my stagehand friend Sam Wanamaker again in 1953, when—working in England—I sold the rights to an off-Broadway hit, *The World of Sholom Aleichem,* to the British producer Oscar Lewenstein, who engaged Sam as stage director for the show's successful London production of 1954.

In 1961 I had a hand in bringing Sam back from his eleven-year exile in England (he had been a victim of the infamous McCarthy blacklist madness) when the Goodman Theatre invited him to participate in a distinguished guest-artist program I advised the Goodman's leadership to create to bolster subscription sales. The Goodman's artistic director, John Reich, wisely cast Sam in the American premiere of Hermann Gressieker's intriguing drama about Henry VIII and his wives, *Royal Gambit.* Sam was merely magnificent as Henry, and as it turned out he also took over as the show's director.

Thus Sam relaunched his American career with a big hit, and the stage was set for the eventual resurrection of the Goodman as a professional theater. I especially reveled in acclaim from leading newspaper drama critics, whom I had invited to the Goodman after many years of their not being invited because the drama school faculty academics feared their scrutiny. The guest-artist policy made it possible for the critics to overlook the fact that we were still a school. Everybody was happy but the faculty, which adamantly resisted the participation of professionals; the professors finally seceded from the Goodman and moved to De Paul University. Soon the Goodman—after a thirty-five-year lapse—resumed being a resident *professional* theater and has become one of America's most stable and heavily subscribed companies. It enjoys the wise leadership of Executive Director Roche Scholfer and Artistic Director Robert Falls, whom I counseled years back on his outstanding work at Chicago's Wisdom Bridge Theatre.

Since our 1930s' meeting Sam had established himself in theater, motion pictures, radio, and television. Undoubtedly, it was directing and playing opposite Ingrid Bergman in the Broadway production of *Joan of Lorraine,* when he was only twenty-seven, that gave impetus to his already meteoric career. For more than a decade, however, beginning in 1949, Sam was also a force in British film and legitimate theater. He produced, directed, and costarred with Michael Redgrave in Clifford Odets's *Winter Journey* and was the Iago to Paul Robeson's Othello for the Royal Shakespeare Company. He also founded his own organization in Liverpool and for several years valiantly attempted to create a viable working-class theater there.

Then Sam's love of Shakespeare's plays, his long residence in England, and his native idealism combined to make him devote the next thirty years to the daunting project of bringing about a new and functioning Globe Theatre on the original site of the one that William Shakespeare ran. He set about raising funds throughout the English-speaking world. First, of course, he had to acquire and demolish the eighteenth-century warehouse that then occupied the land. Only then could architects be called in and the myriad problems involved be tackled. Sam neither flinched nor shirked!

Undoubtedly, many in the theater world thought he had set himself to a quixotic task that could never succeed. In England it was in some quarters considered impudent of this "outsider" (Sam was, after all, both American and Jewish) to dream he could bring about what no Englishman of the "right" origins had dared attempt. Undoubtedly, some would be delighted were he to fail. It must have been a teeth-gnashing experience for them when Prince Philip, who admired Sam, became a principal sponsor of the project. Handsome, charming, charismatic, highly intelligent, dashing as all get-out, and possessed of rare talents and skills as actor, director, and producer, Sam plunged ahead, very much like the visionaries who commenced the construction of cathedrals, knowing that completion would not come in their lifetimes. Queen Elizabeth dedicated the reconstituted Globe in 1997.

To free himself for unending fund-raising activities, Sam undertook few ambitious projects that would benefit his own career. Most were "bread and butter" assignments—in films and television—so he could carry on his higher mission—restoration of the Globe—until his demise. He still managed, though, to appear in *A Far Country* on Broadway and a dozen major television shows on U.S. networks and also undertook acting and directing assignments in films, including *The Spy Who Came in from the Cold, Those Magnificent Men in Their Flying Machines, Superman IV, Baby Boom,* and *Guilty by Suspicion* (opposite Robert Di Niro). He was also featured in such long-running TV series as *Holocaust* and *The Berengers.* The Australians brought him to open the stunning Sydney Opera House with his superb staging of Sergey Prokofiev's *War And Peace*. Always—like a virtuoso juggler—he was somehow able to keep track of simultaneous multiple endeavors.

In the early 1970s, when Lyric Opera of Chicago announced that its major American Bicentennial project for 1976 would be a monumental opera version of *Paradise Lost,* to be composed by the noted Krzysztof Penderecki, whose previous opera was *The Devils of Loudon,* and be presented in collaboration with Milan's La Scala Opera, I arranged for Sam Wanamaker to become its producer. He immediately and whole-heartedly committed himself to the complexities involved and had already accomplished the original groundwork for the production. Our composer's muse deserted him along the way, however, and we lost two entire years *and* Sam's services because he had other contracts to honor.

Sam could have made the project a success, for he was not only a gifted stage director but also an experienced and practical producer. I estimate that he would have saved us $1 million on what turned out to be an incredibly overblown physical production, much of which was abandoned without use. I have special regrets about Sam's involvement in *Paradise Lost* because I originally brought him to Lyric. In 1979, however, I asked him to stage what many have considered the most perfectly executed opera gala concert ever: our Lyric Opera Twenty-fifth Anniversary Gala, for which he also served as emcee with Tito Gobbi. Watching him do everything right for that event I saw new proof that he really did see all moves ahead on the dramatic chess board and could bring perfect order and clarity to what otherwise could easily have become (and, in fact, became) chaotic and amorphous. If only he had been able to remain the producer of our lamented *Paradise Lost.*

Sam was a good friend. When I gave my nonstop, eight-hour audience development seminars in the American Embassy's auditorium in London in 1980 he was loyally there, gamely sitting in the first row although he was certainly queasy at my brash American naiveté in daring to advise that audience, virtually the entire managerial establishment of the British performing arts, on how to build subscription audiences American-style. (Sam had paid his own dues along those lines.) A few years later when we made a number of converts and established a Subscribe Now! U.K. office across the street from the Royal Opera House, I told him, "Sam, you no longer have to blush for me. Some of your British friends have come round to my way of thinking!"

Thinking back all those years to our Chicago *Royal Gambit* premiere at the Goodman Theatre, I recall those magic moments of Sam's monologue, spoken on his knees as in the role of King Henry VIII he pleads for heaven's intercession. The effects of that speech were among the most moving I've experienced in a theater. Only such a magical actor as Jacob Ben-Ami, one of the fabled greats of the international Yiddish stage, could so instantaneously evoke such eviscerating emotion in an audience (or perhaps the brilliant British actor Wilfrid Lawson, whose searing 1953 performance in *The Wooden Dish* at London's Phoenix Theatre remains vivid in my memory a half century later). I'd had the opportunity of working with Ben-Ami over the years in several productions. The Broadway producer John Golden had starred him in the original 1920s' staging of *Samson and Delilah.* My late wife, the actress Dina Halpern, had appeared opposite Ben-Ami in *The Miracle of the Warsaw Ghetto* in New York and Chicago in the mid-1940s.

When Sam returned to the Goodman in the title role of *MacBeth* he sometimes came home with me for dinner. We talked about theater, of course. I asked him when he first thought about becoming an actor, and he replied that he would never forget the occasion. His father had taken him, a small child, to a Yiddish theater performance in which Jacob Ben-Ami was appearing. Sam told us that he was so mesmerized by what he was seeing and hearing that he knew instantly that *he,* too, must become an actor—just like Ben-Ami!

In 1993, just before he died on December 18, Sam was named Honorary Commander of the British Empire (CBE). By then he had been laden with honorary doctorates and encomia from the world over. Sam, a U.S. Army veteran of the Battle of Iwo Jima, was married and the father of three daughters, Abby, Zoe, and Jessica. His wife Charlotte, as wonderful a cook (to that I can attest!) as she was a person, is now also "of blessed memory." Zoe, held to be one of the British theater's finest actresses, corresponds with me and has introduced me to some of her most eminent London colleagues. Sam's brother, William "Bill" Wanamaker, a Beverly Hills physician, is my good friend and frequent correspondent. He was present when I spoke at the 1990 Sam Wanamaker Testimonial Dinner and again when I eulogized Sam at the 1993 memorial event. We also sat together, along with Zoe and Abby, at DePaul University's Wanamaker Tribute on May 10, 2004.

As I write, the Globe has already realized much of what Sam had hoped and prayed for ever since he first paid a pilgrimage to its original site in 1949 and found only a dusty plaque there. A fine repertory company is now ensconced in the Globe, and more than 250,000 people attended in 1999. Foreign directors are involved, and international companies appear there, too. In February of 2000 Judi Dench opened the spectacular Globe Exhibition, which dramatizes the conditions under which the Immortal Bard's plays were first written, performed, and published and drew more than 350,000 visitors in its initial year. Shakespeare Globe Centers are functioning in the United States, Canada, Australia, New Zealand, Japan, and Germany.

Theodore Herzl, another visionary not unlike Sam, once wrote, "If you will it, it is no dream!" This, of course, implies that the dreamer not only wills a dream to come true but also does something about making that happen. Sam in real life did a great deal to make his dream become a reality. He made only big plans. No discouragement deterred him. His vision has been vindicated.

8 Francis X. Bushman, King of Silent Movies Worldwide, Earned Multi-Millions before Income Tax!

In 1939 I was twirling the dial on my Atwater-Kent radio when I suddenly heard an exceedingly mellifluous baritone voice. Immediately I ceased the twirling and found myself listening to the nationally broadcast and long-running soap opera *Stepmother.* Upon inquiry, I learned that the gorgeous voice belonged to the fabulous former silent-movie star Francis X. Bushman, who in the leading role of John Fairchild won millions of new admirers across the country via the then-burgeoning wireless medium.

It happened that I was the manager/publicist of a Chicago civic theater company thinking of producing Frederick Jackson's British comedy-melodrama *The Bishop Misbehaves,* and we had been stymied for lack of the right actor for the title role. Why not, I thought, ask Bushman to take on the part? Certainly, his old-time fame as the star of some 150 silent films would provide a boost to our box office. He had begun his film career in 1911, and among his roles was a historic portrayal of the mighty Masalla, the powerful charioteer in the original, pre-talkie *Ben Hur,* with another idol of that era, Ramon Novarro, in the title role.

At any rate, I telephoned Bushman and asked him to play our bishop, pointing out that rehearsals could be fit between his radio commitments. He said that the important thing to him was that the role be "eminently suited to my personality." I assured him that it was and brought him the script to see for himself. He agreed. We came to terms, and within a few months we had a fine production of *The Bishop Misbehaves*.

Frank, as he asked me to call him, was an old-fashioned, turn-of-the-century, stock company actor, and the florid acting style of silent films had not prepared him for the developing naturalism of the legitimate stage. Fortunately, our artistic director, Sherman Marks, was a master at making an actor realize all the performing potential that voice, body, temperament, and intelligence permitted. Sometimes at rehearsals Bushman was resentful at being pushed so hard, but he was deeply grateful after the tremendous applause at the premiere and the fabulous press reviews the next day. In particular, I recall the *Chicago Times*'s erudite drama critic Robert Pollak asking, "Where has this great actor been hiding all these years, behind a microphone?"

By the time *The Bishop Misbehaves* had become a happy accomplishment we were quite good friends, and he asked me to assist him with publicity and routine managerial matters, which I did until I left for the army a few years later. When I met him, Bushman was between marriages. His most recent wife had been his costar in numerous silent films, the celebrated Beverly Bayne. They were married in 1918 and divorced in 1925.

Bushman was a strikingly handsome man, even in middle age, and had a magnificent profile not unlike that of that of his contemporary John Barrymore. He had the kind of physique that would put present-day bicep-builders and Nordic-Trackers to shame. He exercised daily—often in my presence—using dumbbells and other equipment he kept under the bed in his St. Clair Apartment Hotel residence. For many years sculptors used Bushman as a model for hundreds of heroic statues throughout the nation.

Considering the disarming charm and charisma that had made Bushman a major movie star, *and* the fact that his golden voice wasn't too high-pitched for talkies, his failure to make the transition from silent pictures was puzzling. One day at lunch, he told me what had happened. Just at the time when talking pictures were beginning to be produced he was making a highly paid personal appearance at a San Francisco movie palace as the star attraction of the accompanying stage show. MGM tycoon Louis B. Mayer, in town on business, dropped backstage to say hello. The officious stage-door man presumably went to Bushman's dressing room to report that Mayer was waiting and returned a few minutes later to say that the star was too busy to see him! Mayer, the most powerful man in the film industry and also a difficult person—to understate the case—went into a rage, stalked off, and never again forgave Bushman or spoke to him. Mayer blackballed him from the studios, all because of an offense the actor did not commit. He would not work again in the field for many years. In 1944, about fifteen years later and when he was no longer of leading-man age, he did appear as Bernard Baruch in *Wilson.* In 1951 he was King Saul in *David and Bathsheba,* and in 1957 he was Moses, a role Charlton Heston made famous, in *The Story of Mankind.* It was Heston who was Masalla in the talking *Ben Hur.*

Francis Xavier Bushman's audience had been as worldwide as it could be. Wherever motion picture projection was introduced—and that included many far-flung places—silent films, titled in an infinite number of languages, brought him a huge fandom and a multi-million-dollar annual income, much of it in the era before income tax. He traveled luxuriously, like the monarch he was, with a large retinue of retainers, including managers, publicists, masseurs, a valet, a secretary, and a hairdresser. Although he was still earning good money when I worked with him, I knew it was not anywhere like the good old days. "Frank," I once asked, "What happened to all those millions you earned?" He looked straight at me and with obvious relish said, "I *spent* them!"

9 My Romantic 1948 Transatlantic Call Results in a Fascinating Forty-Year, Five-Continent Travelog with Actress Dina Halpern

In the spring of 1948 I received an urgent call from Sam P. Gerson, the testy overlord of the Brothers Shubert interests in the Midwest. In Chicago he micro-managed eight Loop-area legitimate playhouses, including the Shubert, formerly the Majestic, where I experienced my first vaudeville show as a five-year-old. That two-thousand-seat theater was named in memory of Sam Shubert, who died young. His two siblings, Lee and J. J., bestrode a vast nationwide theatrical empire, and Gerson was their loyal and able associate.

Gerson told me that the Shuberts were backing a national tour of the American Yiddish Art Theatre production *Shylock and His Daughter,* then occupying one of their New York houses. The operetta was based on an Ari ibn Zahav Israeli novel derived from Shakespeare's *Merchant of Venice.* Maurice Schwartz, the Art Theatre's artistic director, was the Shylock; the Warsaw Yiddish Art Theatre's beloved actress Dina Halpern was cast as Portia; and American-born Charlotte Goldstein was Jessica. Schwartz, the last of the fabled Yiddish theater actor-managers, possessed a powerful, magnificent bass-baritone speaking voice and an abundance of theatrical guile. Although he was of normal height, he was so charismatic onstage that he appeared to be seven feet tall!

In 1939, when I was twenty, Gerson entrusted me with the press-agentry for the Chicago pre–New York tryouts of a musical revue—a personal project of J. J. Shubert—entitled *Cocktails at Five,* which opened at the Erlanger, not a Shubert-operated house, right across the alley from Cohan's Grand Theatre. Nine years later—in 1948—he asked me to take on the American Yiddish Art Theatre's April-May booking at the Studebaker Theatre. I was, at that time, heavily engaged on other theatrical fronts and feared I wouldn't have the time to do my best for him, so I demurred.

Gerson was obviously displeased. Although Schwartz's troupe had a top-flight agent for the Yiddish press, Gerson rightly reasoned that many immigrant Jews were already reading English-language newspapers exclusively and ought to be reached. He wanted me to do that reaching. To convince me he brought Schwartz's astute general manager, Edwin A. Relkin, from New York, and Relkin began to show me photographs taken during the show's New York run. Suddenly, like a magician triumphantly displaying the rabbit from out of his hat, he revealed several photographs of a startlingly beautiful woman. "Who is she?" I asked. He replied "Dina Halpern, our Portia." I came up for air and blurted, "I'll take the show!"

It was a decision that would affect my destiny in ways of which I had no idea at the time. The result of my decision was a more than forty-year, wonderful, perfect marriage that was tragically cut off by cancer, the plague that had cost me my mother when I was barely more than six and also killed my only sister. I have always felt that it was divine intervention that brought Dina and me together. Certainly, she was a special cultural treasure of my people—the perfect personification of the thousand-year-old, Yiddish-speaking civilization that the Germans had so cruelly and ruthlessly extirpated along with millions of innocent victims—in the twentieth century's renewed manifestation of the millennial anti-Semitic war of religious and ethnic hatred.

We were introduced by Maurice Schwartz, who for years afterward persistently insisted that I pay him *shadchones gelt* (the marriage broker's fee). Although I never paid he became a close friend and even an admirer—he kept insisting he wanted to adopt me. In fact, he and his wife, Anna, *had* adopted two child Holocaust survivors from an orphanage in Belgium,

Marvin and Frances. Originally, the middle-aged and childless couple had asked only to adopt the little boy, but he so vociferously demanded that his sister be included that the Schwartzes—deeply moved—quickly agreed to take both and lavished all manner of loving care on them. Schwartz persisted in his desire to adopt me, telling Dina, "Miss Halpern, I must adopt Danny! He understands me." I kept repeating that I would indeed be honored to become his son except for the facts that I was already grown and had a wonderful father, Jacob Newman.

If I had been transfixed by Dina's face, figure, and charm, I was totally captivated by her voice, which the Associated Press described as being "like an Amati Cello." I asked her out for coffee after the second performance, and she told me about the Germans murdering her two brothers, her two sisters, her father, and her uncles, aunts, and cousins at the Treblinka death camp in Poland in 1943. Dina, the eldest, had raised the other children after her mother's death. Overwhelmed with compassion for her, I began to cry. I was, she told me, the first American she had met who cried at her story, and when I cried, she said, she began to love me. She had lived in the United States since 1938, when she came to fulfill a contract in New York and couldn't get back to Europe because of the war's outbreak. Thus she became the only member of her immediate family to escape the German savagery.

When the show closed Dina returned to New York before leaving for London, where she was the guest star and director of the summer season at the two-thousand-seat Alexandra Theatre. I telephoned her in July and proposed. She accepted, and the wedding date was set for August 18, 1948.

Dina's Uncle Ben, her father's brother, had presciently moved from Poland to England in the 1930s and had children and grandchildren. Thus, this family arranged our beautiful wedding at the West London Synagogue. I arrived several days ahead via American Overseas Airlines, bringing both an engagement ring and a wedding ring, raisins for the wedding cake, and a box of Dial soap and other items that were hard to find in post–World War II England. Our wedding was attended by a few hundred theatrical notables and also friends I had made during my wartime convalescence in England.

Dina's London engagement was most successful. Shortly before I arrived, Sybil Thorndike, one of the British theater's great ladies, mounted the Alexandra Theatre stage after one of Dina's performances and told the audience that not since Eleonora Duse had the stage seen a tragedienne of Dina's quality. Actor Joseph Buloff arrived in time for the wedding—and to take Dina's place as stage director and guest star at the Alexandra—and we were off to a late-summer honeymoon month in France and Italy. In Paris we met with Dina's theater colleagues and with the colorful business-man–art collector Izaak Wagman, who gave us two beautiful oil paintings as wedding presents that I continue to cherish sixty years later. In Lyon we paused to dine with the widow of another of Dina's uncles who had, years before, migrated to France only to eventually be murdered by Mar-shal Petain's Nazi-compliant Vichy regime. In Milan we attended *Aida* at La Scala. After a week in Lugano, several days in Florence, and stops in London and Brussels we flew off to New York, where Dina closed her apartment, resigned from theatrical commitments there, and came with me to Chicago for a new life that would last for more than four happy decades—happy is an understatement.

In writing about Dina's many foreign tours I realize that I may be scant-ing her appearances in the United States, her home for just over a half century. Dina arrived in New York harbor on the Polish ship *Pilsudski* in 1938, a half year before World War II began and just in time for the Man-hattan premiere of the European motion picture of *The Dybbuk,* a classic in which she appeared. After the Germans bombed Warsaw in 1939, how-ever, transatlantic travel was cut off. Thus *her* life was saved, but her entire immediate family was murdered. In the 1940s she appeared with Jacob Ben-Ami's New Art Theatre, both in New York and at Chicago's Black-stone Theatre, and she also did a national tour with Maurice Schwartz, concluding with West Coast engagements at San Francisco's Geary Theatre and Los Angeles's Biltmore Theatre. In New York City she was the leading lady at the Second Avenue Theatre, and in the musical *Golden Land* she costarred with Aaron Lebedeff, Ludwig Satz, and Leo Fuchs. She was the producer/director/star of Brooklyn's Hopkinson Theatre, where she staged a series of dramas and operettas, including *Madam X, Mata Hari,* and a pre–*My Fair Lady* musical version of G. B. Shaw's *Pygmalion* entitled *The Model,* which she had done in Europe in the 1930s.

In 1951 Dina recorded an early long-playing disc, *Masterworks of Yid-dish Poetry,* which sold out overnight and became a collector's item. I have held onto three of those more than half-century-old original LPs. The recording has since been transferred to cassette, of which I have an ample supply. Throughout the 1950s she presented a succession of highly regarded recitals across the United States, "one woman shows" featuring classic poetic repertoire. In 1956–57 Dina starred in two hour-long network TV dramas on NBC's *Matinee Theatre from Hollywood* and co-starred with Ethel Waters in a third one.

Throughout the 1960s Dina, between out-of-the-country engagements, was the artistic director of the Chicago Yiddish Theatre Association, which presented classic and high-level contemporary works at the Eleventh Street Theatre and the Frances Parker Playhouse. The repertoire included works of the revered Sholom Aleichem and Jacob Gordin and also the then-contemporary poet-dramatists Itzik Manger and Kadya Molodowsky. Dina succeeded in building an audience far larger and more enthusiastic than had attended Yiddish productions in Chicago for many years. It was a golden chapter in the history of the Yiddish stage in America.

Although the great Bohemian-born German-language novelist Franz Kafka died in 1924—five years after my birth—he and I both caught the same enthusiasm in adulthood: the Yiddish stage and its larger-than-life actors. My parents, like many other European-born new Americans, spoke English and read English-language books and newspapers. We did not subscribe to the Yiddish press. Thus, I wasn't able then to communicate in Yiddish. Through Dina, however, I quickly entered the milieu of Yiddish-speaking actors, directors, designers, playwrights, journalists, lecturers, novelists, poets, and educators. I was constantly influenced by Dina's *vort concert'n* (literary recitals). Her exquisite use of the language insistingly resonated for me, and soon I began to speak Yiddish with growing confidence and started reading it as well. I had, in early childhood, learned the Hebrew alphabet. During my early years, Chicago had a number of resident Yiddish stage companies, although I was unaware of them. There were more Yiddish playhouses in the five boroughs of New York over fifty years ago than there are theaters on Broadway today.

Having been active as a novitiate theatrical manager/press agent since I was fourteen, I was not surprised when in 1939 the manager of Chicago's Douglas Park Yiddish Theatre engaged me to publicize—in the English-language media—the fabled Aaron Lebedeff, who was to open at the theater in a musical comedy, *Der Mazeldiker Bocher* (Lucky Boy!). Lebedeff was widely known as the Maurice Chevalier of the Yiddish stage. His "Rumania-Rumania" based on George Enesco's *Rumanian Rhapsody* had long been a worldwide song hit. More than a half century later it remains a centerpiece in the repertoire of Joel Grey of *Cabaret* fame. Fifty-some years ago the agronomist Ezekiel Weizmann (in whose Israeli pecan plantations I was an early investor), brother of Israel's first president Chaim Weizmann and father of its more recent president Ezer Weizmann, told me of how his young sisters waited for hours at a Pinsk stage door to catch a glimpse of their idol, the dashing Aaron Lebedeff! It was also at the Douglas Park Yiddish Theatre that—a decade later—I managed Dina Halpern's 1949 and 1950 record-breaking runs in drama critic Abraham A. Margolin's Yiddish adaptations of Philip Yordan's *Anna Lucasta* and Lillian Hellman's *The Little Foxes.*

I was already intrigued, however, with many of the Yiddish theater personalities I encountered, all of whom were consummate artists. Among them were Samuel Goldenberg and Celia Adler, eldest daughter of the star Jacob P. Adler and sister of Luther Adler, who many years later performed as Eddie Carbone in the world premiere production of the full-length *A View from the Bridge,* which I managed in 1956 and 1957. Other major Yiddish stage artists with whom I worked were Molly Picon, Joseph Buloff, Ludwig Satz, Jacob Ben-Ami, Lucy Gehrman, Menashe Skulnik, Michael Michalesko, Herman Yablokoff, Paul Burstyn, Jenny Goldstein, Menachem Rubin, and Luba Kadison. In the 1930s and 1940s touring Yiddish companies appeared in Chicago at the Studebaker, Blackstone, Civic, Eighth Street, Harris, Selwyn, Apollo, and Great Northern Theatres as well as the Civic Opera House. There were also a half-dozen neighborhood Yiddish stock companies. In addition to the classic repertoire they staged such plays as S. Ansky's *The Dybbuk* and Jacob Gordin's *Mirele Efros,* Abraham Goldfaden operettas like *Shulamit* and *Bar Kochba,* and dramas by Y. L. Peretz and Sholom Aleichem. Those years were also the heyday of Yiddish films, which were produced in both Europe and the United States. Yiddish troupes performed in many American cities.

Chicago was bursting with creative ferment during the World War II era. It boasted three daily Yiddish newspapers, three Yiddish school systems, and a network of fraternal organizations (*landsmanshaffen*). Young Muni

Weisenfreund, a native of Lemberg, Austria, who trained in his father's theater in Chicago at Twelfth and Halsted streets, became a cofounder with Maurice Schwartz of the American Yiddish Art Theatre. As Paul Muni he went on to become a Broadway and Hollywood star, triumphing in such films as *Scarface, I Am a Fugitive from a Chain Gang, The Life of Emile Zola, Juarez,* and *The Story of Louis Pasteur,* for which he received the 1936 Academy Award. His first English-speaking Broadway success was in the drama *We Americans.* (In 1937 I played the same role in a Chicago workshop staging.)

Many Yiddish artists with whom I worked during this period were superbly talented, vibrant, triple-threat performers who all acted, sang, *and* danced. They possessed large, resonant, beautiful voices that were easily heard over orchestras and bounced off the backs of balconies. Their unabashed onstage vigor was a stark contrast to so many contemporary English-speaking American actors who had begun to develop an unfortunate growing fascination with "the Method," which spawned an entire generation of morose, intellectual, and inhibited thespians who could no longer be heard in the third row. Brooks Atkinson, the *New York Times*'s drama critic, told me that when he had a night off from his usual rounds he would visit the Yiddish Art Theatre for the pleasure of finding actors *"who were not afraid to act!"* In the 1930s, 1940s, and 1950s American theater folk spoke to each other more and more, intensely and endlessly, about their art, whereas their counterparts in England, where I so often worked, usually discussed the day's cricket scores in a relaxed and pleasant manner.

Dina became a major box-office attraction in Argentina, Brazil, and Uruguay during the mid-to-late 1940s. In the spring of 1952 she returned to Buenos Aires, Rio de Janeiro, São Paolo, and Montevideo as director and guest star in a repertoire that included an adaptation of Leo Tolstoy's *Resurrection* and *Mirele Efros,* Jacob Gordin's adaptation of *King Lear* for an actress, a role Dina's great-aunt, Esther Rachel Kaminska, had played in Europe and on a U.S. tour. In that summer season of 1952 Dina also appeared in Latin American centers in the title role of Ruth and Augustus Goetz's *The Heiress,* which was based on Henry James's *Washington Square.*

I flew to join Dina in Buenos Aires in those pre-jet days, making refueling stops in Miami, Panama, Ecuador, Chile, and Peru. I was met at the

Buenos Aires Airport by Dina, her theater colleagues, and both the Yiddish and Spanish press. That night an after-performance dinner for me was hosted by the comedy team of Shimon Dzigan and Yisroel Schumacher, the funniest guys I've ever seen. Several years later I literally fell off my seat and into the aisle of a Tel Aviv theater, laughing hysterically at one of their brilliant satirical sketches. They had been imprisoned and almost starved to death in Soviet Russia for their hilarious takeoff on Josef Stalin. When the dinner party was over in the wee hours a burly friend of Dzigan and Schumacher gave us a ride to our hotel. Although the streets were deserted, he turned out to be a speed demon and perilously rounded corners on two wheels. When I asked if he had raced, he replied, "No, I used to be a tank driver in the Russian army."

While in Argentina I was receiving box-office reports by air mail from the manager of my Chicago movie theater, and because Dina was in rehearsal all day I—for the first time I could remember—had time to read. I found a bookstore on Avenida Florida that carried English paperbacks of the classics and thus compensated for my lack of formal education by devouring entire volumes of Dostoevsky, Tolstoy, and other fine novelists. I also found a theater that played triple features of Marx Brothers movies and laughed my head off for six solid hours for three consecutive days! In the previous year, 1951, I had suffered the loss of my truly wonderful father, whom Dina had so compassionately and lovingly tended in the months of his final illness. Thus, the immersion in literature and the overall relaxation I found in our visit to Buenos Aires provided much-needed balm.

Argentina was then in the mendacious grip of the Perons, who had been assiduously stealing everything out of the country that wasn't nailed down. Their spies were everywhere, even in washrooms. Friends whispered that in fifty years Argentina would still not be recovered from this monumental thievery. They were right! Where previously there had always been abundant wheat and beef there was now a breadless and a meatless day each week, the result of Juan and Eva Peron's voodoo economics. We were still in Argentina when Evita died. Thirty days of official mourning were declared, and all theaters, movie houses, night clubs, restaurants, and other public places closed, which set off a large number of bankruptcies. When President John F. Kennedy was assassinated in Dallas eleven years later no period of closing was mandated in the United States, a contrast between autocracy and democracy.

Our departure for Brazil was delayed a week, but finally we were off to Rio de Janeiro, where our impresario and a resident theater company awaited us. The ever-present and jarring juxtaposition of the most grinding, slum-ridden poverty I'd ever seen with the most luxurious residences imaginable—all against the backdrop of incomparable scenic magnificence in the world-renowned Bay City's natural splendor—was both striking and deeply disturbing. Although Dina had performed in the Rio de Janeiro Municipal Opera House, we went directly to São Paolo, where she was booked into the brand new Teatro Cultura Artistica, which had turntable stages. Her rehearsals with the local company began immediately. São Paolo was palpably pulsating with much new construction proceeding apace, fostering some of the most progressive architecture I had ever seen.

In 1965 Dina accepted the Golmulka-led Polish communist government's invitation to appear in recitals for Holocaust survivors in seven Polish cities. After the Germans' murderous depradations there, only an estimated twenty thousand Jews were left alive out of what had been a Jewish population of three million in that country. Dina had left Warsaw in 1938 and not returned. Now, with virtually all of her family there murdered, she decided to return after twenty-seven years. Although she hoped to find the grave of her mother, who died before the German murder machine arrived, she was frustratingly unable to do so in a chaotic section of the vast Warsaw Gensha Street cemetery. She did, however, find the grave of Esther Rachel Kaminska, her great-aunt, often spoken of as the mother of the Yiddish stage, in whose memory a theater in Warsaw is named and still operates with governmental subsidy.

Dina would also be reunited with her cousin and colleague, the actress Ida Kaminska, who headed the Polish State Yiddish Theatre, which the regime supported because it was eager to prove that any Polish collaboration with the German murderers was that of the previous ruling fascist government and not of the new communist rulers. Ida's husband, the urbane lawyer-turned-actor Marian Melman, accompanied us to Treblinka, where Dina's brothers, sister, and many other relatives were brutally murdered. We recited kaddish, El Mole Rachamim, and other prayers there.

This was some eight years before the Yom Kippur War in which the Israelis decisively defeated the Soviet-trained and -equipped Egyptian armies, so there was still an Israeli embassy in Warsaw, and we were invited there for Passover celebrations. We stayed at what was known as the best hotel in Warsaw, the Europejski, although the thin mattresses were stuffed with straw and an army of cleaning women, on hands and knees, scrubbed the floors every morning. There were virtually no automobiles to be seen although a car and chauffeur were at *our* disposal. Horses, buggies, and wagons abounded.

At Dina's Warsaw recital of classic Yiddish poetry the theater was packed and emotions ran high. Many of those present were from cities to which Dina had toured in various plays and operettas in the 1930s. Holocaust survivors present had not known until a few weeks before that she still lived. When she appeared onstage there was, at first, only silence and then unending applause accompanied by unashamed weeping. Years later I met a man who remembered seeing me crying in the back of the theater. When, finally, Dina raised her voice, an hour and a half of perfect communion began between audience and artist.

In Warsaw I encountered David Halberstam, the *New York Times*'s foreign correspondent who had a year or so before won a Pulitzer Prize for his powerful dispatches from Vietnam. We met in the Associated Press offices, where he greeted me warmly and spoke bitterly of communism and gloomily of its "grayness" while we looked out the window at Piekna (Beautiful) Street below. He had just married a gorgeous Polish actress but was being thrown out of the country, he told me, because of his negative articles about the Gomulka regime. Dina was being interviewed by Warsaw journalists who were rapt in their admiration of her impeccable, classic Polish speech. She told me that the Polish then spoken had evidently deteriorated under the communist regime. When Dina attended Warsaw University during the era of Jósef Pilsudski she was required to sit on separate "Jewish benches" apart from the students of presumably pure Polish ethnicity, who would thus remain uncontaminated.

We attended seven productions at the Polish State Yiddish Theatre, including classic works as well as a then-recent Arthur Miller play, *All My Sons*. Although many brilliant Yiddish actors and actresses of the 1920s and 1930s had been murdered by the Germans, the management presented some fairly acceptable casts that included non-Jewish performers who worked from transliterated scripts.

Dina and I often had dinner at Ida Kaminska's spacious apartment on fashionable Jerosolimska Street, where she lived with her husband; her daughter Ruth, wife of the famed European jazz trumpeter Eddy Rosner; and her granddaughter Erica, a bright and beautiful twenty-two-year-old just graduating from Warsaw University. (Dina and I soon brought Erica to Chicago, where she spent two years with us.) I was surprised and bemused at Ida having three household servants and a chauffeur in this "egalitarian" communist society.

It *shayn opgeret* (goes without saying) that Dina was a widely admired actress, yet she was so much more than that. A life-long, impassioned student of rare intelligence and sensitivity, she constantly sought and absorbed a wide range of knowledge with the zeal of a Talmudist sitting at the feet of East European sages. She mastered English at Columbia University and studied Russian there, too, and then she studied Hebrew at Chicago's College of Jewish Studies, where she was her graduating class's valedictorian and declaimed the works of Israel's national poet, Hayyim Nahman Bialik. Her feats of memory were phenomenal—for example, two-hour recitals of Yiddish literature with no text in hand. She was also a skilled writer whose articles appeared in journals in the United States and abroad. Our home was a warm, hospitable salon where Dina entertained countless creative people of the arts and sciences who savored her mouth-watering cooking. Her devotion to both secular and religious individuals and their myriad causes was intense, compassionate, and unflagging. On the day following press reports that Hadassah had named her the "Ideal Jewish Woman" nationally she was seen—on hands and knees—thoroughly scrubbing our neighborhood synagogue's kitchen floor. I took pride in having such an absolutely wonderful wife who spoke of me as her *oytzer* (treasure). I felt that heaven had placed her in my keeping, and I strove to be worthy of the responsibility that accompanied that joy.

After an intense month in Poland we departed for home. As we left the hotel early in the morning, the middle-aged woman desk-clerk, who had never spoken to us, suddenly sang out the lyrics of a ballad that Dina had made popular in Poland many years before. We paused for a moment and then went through the door.

Just as we arrived in Warsaw, Ida Kaminska returned from Czechoslovakia, where she had been featured in director Jan Kadar's marvelous film *The Shop on Main Street*. Two years later Ida telephoned me in Chicago with the news that Hollywood's Academy Award Committee was naming it the year's best foreign film and wanted her to come there to accept the honor. They didn't, however, send her an airplane ticket, and although she had plenty of Polish zlotys they had no value in the foreign currency context. Acting on Ida's behalf, I telephoned the Hollywood people, and they immediately agreed to provide round-trip transportation and all other expenses. Shortly afterward, Ida and her husband Marian Melman arrived for the first time in the United States and spent a week in our Chicago home. I arranged for my lifetime friend Studs Terkel to interview her on WFMT, Dina serving as translator, and several receptions were given by the art film theater that would shortly be opening *The Shop on Main Street*.

The couple went on to Hollywood, where Ida was "lionessized" before returning to Poland just in time to be exiled for refusing to sign a Soviet statement asserting that the Israelis had attacked the Arabs in the Six Day War, something the world knew to be untrue. Although Golda Meier offered her a subsidized theater in Israel, Ida and her husband moved to the United States, where her fair-weather Hollywood admirers, to her deep disappointment, did nothing to assist them. She appeared in several American stage productions and a movie opposite Harry Belafonte; eventually moved to Israel; and they returned to America, where she died in 1980. She lies in the cemetery of the Hebrew Actors Union in Long Island. My Dina was the eulogist at her funeral.

Dina often presented Yiddish-language literary recitals in larger Canadian cities and was affectionately and enthusiastically received. Canada's liberal immigration laws brought many European Jews there between the two world wars, and Holocaust survivors began to arrive in the mid- and late 1940s. Many of those refugees had been Dina's devotees overseas and were ready-made audiences for her appearances in Canada. Some refugees had been poets, novelists, and essayists in Eastern Europe who found their ways to various Canadian communities, including Toronto, Calgary, Winnipeg, and especially Montreal, where the Bronfman Center, the Yiddish Library, Yiddish schools and press, and a Yiddish drama ensemble were already established. There was also a growing religious life, with Talmudic academies and fine synagogues that boasted some of the generation's most gifted resident cantors.

Dina also began to appear in Australia. On our first trip there we flew from Chicago to San Francisco to Honolulu to the Fijis and finally reached Down Under—so many thousands of miles away—that you fell asleep in the plane on Monday night and when you awakened it wasn't Tuesday morning but Wednesday morning (which was somewhat unsettling). We stayed for a few days in the Fijis, astonished that all Fijians seemed to look alike. We arrived in Adelaide—heart of Australia's wine-growing country—one beautiful morning and were met by newspaper photographers and reporters. By late afternoon Dina's pictures were prominently appearing in the press, and she began to receive many telephone calls at the hotel from people who remembered her from Europe. A number came to see us, and some later visited us in Chicago.

In 1972 and 1977 Dina performed in both Sydney and Melbourne, which had a good-sized Yiddish-speaking community and a well-rooted Yiddish stage ensemble at the Kadimah Theatre, where Dina performed poetry recitals and musical dramas. In Sydney she had the great joy of reuniting with the Brodaty family, her cousins from Warsaw who had miraculously survived the German death camps. Henry, their brilliant young son, was born in a displaced persons refuge. Dina sent his father an industrial sewing machine—from Chicago to Sydney—and with that beginning he had created a thriving business by the time we arrived there: an automated textile factory that eventually made the family financially secure. Over the years we remained in regular touch with the Brodatys and saw Henry become a distinguished professor of medical research, specializing in gerontology. He was eventually married to the lovely daughter of another family of Holocaust survivors, and they adopted two beautiful Peruvian children whom they brought to visit us in Chicago on several occasions.

Although Dina is no longer alive I still hear from the Brodaty children and keep au courant concerning their progress. In connection with Henry Brodaty, I often think of the two million children murdered in the camps and the good possibility that some of them might also have become professors and medical researchers. Perhaps like Jonas Salk and Albert B. Sabin, both of whom solved the dread polio puzzle, they might have found cures for cancer and AIDS. Then I think of the reality. The madness of the "Herrenvolk" continues, a half-century later, to afflict the world and there are endless consequences for their unspeakable crimes of so long ago. As Shakespeare wisely wrote, "The evil that men do lives after them."

In the early 1950s Dina began to receive letters from European Yiddish actor friends who had somehow survived the Holocaust and arrived in Israel, only to learn that despite the large potential audience for Yiddish theater there the government—committed to the not-easy task of establishing Hebrew as the national language—suppressed the opening of Yiddish theaters by denying them licenses to perform. In effect, you could act and sing in French, English, or Arabic but not in the language that had been the *momme-loshen* (mother tongue) of European Jewry for the past thousand years. I called this absurdity to the attention of my friend Max Bressler, a great admirer of Dina and then-president of the Zionist Organization of America. Max verified what I told him and protested personally to Israel's president David Ben Gurion, himself a native Yiddish-speaker from the Polish town of Plonsk. Overnight our actor friends were informed that the ban was lifted.

When Dina and I arrived in Israel in the spring of 1955 impresario Josef Lichtenberg had already engaged actors, actresses, scenic and costume designers, and an orchestra plus a stage manager and crew for us. At a Tel Aviv press conference we announced that Dina would direct and star in three plays, all with musical elements: two dramas with music (*With Open Eyes* and *The Governess*) and a modern version of the old Abraham Goldfaden operetta *The Enchantress* with a modernized text by the major poet-dramatist Itzik Manger. The latter offering was strongly opposed—before its premier—in the Hebrew-language press because it limned Jewish poverty and persecution in Eastern Europe. Doctrinaire Hebraists had skipped that era of Jewish history and had taught their Israel-born children (sabras) that all their forebears were biblical heroes. Over time, however, Manger was greatly honored by the county's literary establishment. Many years later I had the satisfaction of passing a street sign in Tel Aviv: Avenue Itzik Manger.

At any rate, all three of our 1955 productions were smash hits, and at the box office our Yiddish company outdrew all three top Hebrew theaters—the Habimah, Ohel, and Cameri—combined. We toured to thirty-three towns and cities, and there were no empty seats, even when the summer heat began and we moved into huge outdoor venues. In some sense we were embroiled in a culture war, striking good blows for our side. Dina, however, who also loved Hebrew poetry, which she recited from memory, wisely said about that bitter struggle for supremacy between Hebrew and Yiddish, "You don't have to hate your father in order to love your mother."

Dina was beloved throughout the country by the time we finished our five-month tour of Israel. Even non-Yiddish-speaking Sephardic Yemenite immigrants came to our performances. In the audiences, as expected, were many who had attended Dina's appearances in East European cities before the war, but she won thousands of new enthusiasts. She also accomplished what had been deemed impossible, winning over the militantly anti-Yiddish Hebrew press of that era. Ofra Alyagon, the important critic and commentator, wrote in her Hebrew-language journal *Dvar Hashavuah* (Word of the Week): "I say to Israel's theatre producers, a great actress is here with us. Don't let her go! Her place is here!" But Dina did go. She had a husband who had his own irons in the fire back home. She did return for several other wonderful tours in later years, however, which I joyfully managed.

Just as we were about to begin our next theatrical tour in the Holy Land in 1957 we found ourselves stranded on New Year's Eve—in Paris. We had flown very pleasantly via Air France from Chicago to New York to Paris, expecting on arrival at Orly Airport to fly on to Tel Aviv, where a company of actors and musicians was awaiting our arrival to begin rehearsals for an operetta that Dina would both stage and perform in. To our consternation, however, a moment after we landed an official informed us that an international strike of airline pilots had begun that morning. There would be no planes that day. For how many other days they didn't know! I rushed to the Air France reservation desk, where the bad news was confirmed. "You mean," I asked the official incredulously, "that we are *stranded* here?" A look of disbelief and incomprehension came over his face, and he responded, "But monsieur, YOU MAY BE STRANDED, BUT YOU ARE STRANDED IN *PARIS!*" It didn't take long for me to understand his bewilderment. Air France, at its expense, put us up in a fine hotel on the Boulevard Haussmann, where the chef turned out incredibly delicious gourmet meals for the excellent dining room. By the time we finally were able to fly on to Israel several days later, my understanding of the implications of being stranded had broadened considerably!

In 1955 I wrote a series of magazine articles about the many Christian religious denominations in Israel and their relations with the government there. I also wrote articles for the *Chicago Sun-Times* about the exciting and burgeoning Israeli entertainment arts life. Later, in the 1980s and accompanied by Dina, I held consulting sessions with almost all of the professional performing organizations there, including the Habimah Theatre, the Israel Philharmonic Orchestra, and the Haifa Municipal Theatre (for which I inspired and directed a campaign that netted more than thirty thousand season ticket subscribers). In the mid-1990s, at the direction of the United States Information Agency, I gave a seminar for all the professional performing arts managements in Israel at the Habimah Theatre and assisted the New Israel Opera for the opening of its new opera house.

In 1988, although plagued with cancer, Dina again toured Israel, not in staged productions but in recitals of classic poetry. The city of Haifa presented her with its silver medallion celebrating the forty years of Israel's statehood. Bar-Ilan University, which houses the Dina Halpern Institute for the Yiddish Performing Arts, awarded her an honorary doctorate. Mayor Teddy Kollek awarded her the Medal of Jerusalem. Two days later she was in Paris and giving a brilliant recital performance at the Salle Bernard Lazare with Yiddishists from all over France in attendance. Many in the audience had been present in the 1940s when she was at the Theatre Antripo and the Sarah Bernhardt Theatre in Paris with her repertoire of classic dramas. Two days after that she was in a Chicago hospital. She never performed again. The final curtain had rung down on her distinguished career, embracing appearances in more than a hundred cities on five continents.

During the summer of 1988 a conclave of poets, playwrights, novelists, and journalists of international stature met in the Helena Rubenstein Art Museum in Israel and presented Dina—in absentia—with the highest award in world Yiddish literature, the Manger Prize. The honor was quite remarkable because she was an actress not a professional writer, although she did write a series of excellent and charming essays about theater colleagues for New York and Paris newspapers. Present at the Manger Prize event was the venerable poet-laureate Abraham Sutzkever, who stated that although there were many things he *didn't* remember about life in Europe in the 1930s he *did* recall the large number of writers who had been in love with Dina Halpern.

Dina died on February 19, 1989. I received a tremendous number of condolences, many from people I didn't know but who had seen Dina perform in an astonishing number of places since the 1930s. The great novelist Saul Bellow, who knew and admired her, wrote, startlingly, "Reflecting on Dina, I reach the conclusion that I would rather have had her read of *my* death. There are people like that, more deserving of life. You are offended when they die. They *shouldn't* be taken away. Dina was a source of life for others—that's how I classed her."

More than seventeen years have passed since my great loss. Each year I place a memorial statement in various publications: "A great actress, an irreplaceable treasure of Yiddish cultural life, for whose honor she fought all of her life. She was the personification of goodness and kindness. And she was my beloved partner-in-life for more than forty beautiful, creative years."

10

Russia's Tempestuous Madame
Eugenie Leontovich: Actress,
Director, Playwright, Producer,
Teacher, and Great Artist

In my many years in the theater world, beginning in the mid-1930s, I have encountered charismatic actresses. One I especially adored was the Russian-born, internationally admired Eugenie Leontovich, whose extraordinary, even magical interpretive qualities were universally lauded and applauded throughout her seventy-year career. Twice she won Broadway's coveted Antoinette Perry Award for best actress, as the empress in Guy Bolton's *Anastasia* in 1954 and as the queen in William Saroyan's *Cave Dwellers* in 1957. Although I am a press agent—a professional praiser—believe me that Eugenie Leontovich, who died at the age of ninety-three in 1993, was a truly *great* actress who was also amazingly versatile. She was an accomplished playwright and stage director and a brilliant educator in the theater arts.

Genie (her students called her Madame Leontovich, but she insisted I address her as Genie shortly after we first worked together in 1947) was the original Grusinskaya of Herman Shumlin's celebrated New York production of *Grand Hotel* although Greta Garbo's enormous box-office strength won her that role in the film of the same title that followed. In 1932 Eugenie scored another Broadway success as Lily Garland opposite Henry Hull and Sam Jaffe in the Ben Hecht–Charles MacArthur comedy *Twentieth Century,* with Carole Lombard and John Barrymore doing the movie. She was Natasha in the Jed Harris production of *Dark Eyes,* which was co-written by her and Elena Miramova, for 230 Broadway performances in 1943. Producer Gilbert Miller, for whom Genie had been the Maria of his *Candlelight* production, presented her 1935 London debut as Tatiana in the Jacques Deval–Robert Sherwood play *Tovarich,* with Cedric Hardwicke as costar (some years later, when I was working with Cedric in a production of George Bernard Shaw's *Androcles and the Lion,* he complained to me that Eugenie's passion for perfection had been "exasperating"). When on an American tour in 1937 she came with *Tovarich* to Chicago's Harris Theatre, the fine actor McKay Morris in her support, I was in attendance and entirely captivated.

In Los Angeles she appeared with Charles Laughton in *The Cherry Orchard* and codirected it with that distinguished British theater artist. Some of her other theatrical roles included Cleopatra in Shakespeare's *Anthony and Cleopatra* in London and on a tour of the United Kingdom and Nadya in *Obsession,* which she performed opposite Basil Rathbone in Chicago and New York. She also coauthored, with George S. George, the play *Caviar to the General* for London's West End and a U.S. tour.

From the beginning of April until late August in 1955 I had been managing my actress-wife Dina Halpern on a thirty-three theater tour of Israel. Just as we were leaving for home a cable arrived from Elaine Perry, the New York stage producer, asking me to undertake the promotion of the Chicago run of *Anastasia,* which was scheduled to open that fall at the venerable Blackstone Theatre. Madame Leontovich would be the grand duchess, and Dolly Haas would appear in the title role. I had press-agented Dolly along with Yul Brynner a decade earlier at Chicago's Studebaker Theatre in the exquisite Raymond Scott–composed musical drama *Lute Song.* By return cable I informed Miss Perry of my agreement. During the run of *Anastasia* in that 1955–56 season Genie, Dina, and I developed what turned out to be a close and enduring friendship. Both women had been in the theater all their lives and shared many cultural values. They became like sisters.

Eugenie had appeared in a half-dozen Hollywood films with colleagues like Jose Ferrer, Loretta Young, Gregory Peck, Anthony Quinn, Richard

Burton, Lana Turner, and Fred MacMurray. Because she had a pronounced Slavic speech pattern she was, of course, limited to roles that permitted foreign accents. She had a fairly jaundiced view of the bad taste and materialistic motives of some motion picture producers, especially when they tackled the Russian classics. As she wrote to me, "I do not believe that MGM botch has anything to do with Tolstoy! Somebody there decided to shoot *Anna Karenina,* and they certainly did it!"

A year later, in 1956, I asked Genie to arrange a leave of absence from her playhouse and drama workshop in Los Angeles and leave her comfortable Santa Monica home to come to Chicago and stage a production of Ivan Turgenev's classic *A Month in the Country* at the new Studebaker Theatre Company, of which I was the co-general manager and subscription promoter. Genie knew I would never let her down, and undoubtedly difficult as it was for her to join me at that time she didn't disappoint. She came, however, into an excruciating situation for a director. The brilliant young American actress Geraldine Page, whom we had just expensively bought out of a contract in London, was going through an artistic crisis and for the moment had lost her performing self-confidence to the extent that she couldn't (or wouldn't) project her voice across the footlights (chapter 12). Eugenie, even with her extraordinary sensitivity, was unable to solve our problem. But our project brought her back to Chicago, where she remained for subsequent successes as both actress and director.

In 1957 I undertook to build a subscription audience—virtually from scratch—for Chicago's Goodman Theatre, which had, years before at the onset of the depression era, jettisoned its professional company (it had been losing money) and kept its drama school (which had been "making it" on tuition revenue). In 1984 the Art Institute of Chicago, which ran the theater, called on me to assay what could be done to improve things within that academic framework and without greatly increasing the budget. I recommended that guest artists of distinction from the professional theater be brought in to inspire the students and improve the quality of performances by their participation.

The Art Institute agreed to my insistence that a top-level artistic director be brought in, and John Reich, who had been associated with Max Reinhardt at the Salzburg Festival, was engaged. I introduced John to Eugenie, and she agreed to be one of the new program's distinguished guest artists, beginning with Saroyan's *The Cave Dwellers*. She would appear as the queen and also direct. For the role of the king, I suggested Studs Terkel, my friend since the 1930s, who proved to be ideally cast. He loved Genie's direction, she loved his performance, and the public loved them both. The show was a big success. Drama critics, who had been purposefully uninvited at the Goodman for the past several decades and whom I asked to come when the guest artist program began (a program that seemed to enrage the drama school's professors), loved the show, too, as they did other Goodman productions in the seasons to come.

Genie found a tenant for her Los Angeles Playhouse and moved to Chicago to begin seven years of resident artistry at the Goodman, bringing along her darling sister Mary Koutkowsky, happily a marvelous cook. Genie staged a number of plays for the Goodman Theatre School, including *Anna Karenina* (her own adaptation, which she had done off Broadway) with the splendid Catherine Ellis in the title role. Catherine, who came under Genie's artistic influence and inspiration when she was very young, had become her close associate and devoted friend of many years. Whenever the Madame was grappling with a difficult project, wherever it was, you could count on Catherine Ellis quickly arriving on the scene. Even though Eugenie is gone I remain in touch with Catherine, a theater person whom I regard highly.

Genie also directed and taught at Smith College, at Amherst College in Massachusetts, at Chicago's Columbia College, and at London's Studio 68. Her theater studies began in Moscow under the tutelage of Konstantin Stanislavsky, the original Method advocate. She took advanced training with such giants of the Russian stage as V. E. Meyerhold, Yevgeny Vachtangov, and Victor Komissarjevzky but was the most dedicated, honest, serious, and unpretentious drama teacher I have known. She was an idealist and entirely unaffected by the cynicism of conventional show biz culture.

Eugenie's husband of many years had been the colorful Russian-born actor and film director Gregory Ratoff, a poker-playing pal of some of Hollywood's top movie producers. I came to know him in 1948, when we were seat partners on my honeymoon Swiss-Air flight from London to Zurich. When he asked how long Dina and I had been married. I replied "Since yesterday." He responded in a thick Russian accent, "Okscyus me for osking!" Although they were already divorced when I met Genie in

1947, it was clear that she remained deeply in love with Ratoff for the rest of her life. She spoke of him often to me and with apparent tenderness. She rarely mentioned his follies and foibles, and his photograph was always with her.

Eugenie, usually vigorous, fell ill—a victim of some very wintry Chicago days and nights—just a week before the premiere of *The Cave Dwellers*. Her voice disappeared, and she was so weak that she couldn't stand. I telephoned a top throat specialist and rushed her to his office. He gave her the time and attention, now a rarity, and worked a miracle—perhaps aided by Eugenie's prayers (she was deeply religious). Thankfully, she regained her strength, her voice returned, and we opened the play on schedule and to critical raves.

I cherish the message she sent me at that time: "The human part of you is so strong and shining. It is a privilege and joy to know you. My words fail to put in writing my gratitude for your inspiration. Stay Glorious! Genie." More than forty years have passed since she wrote those words, and I remain deeply grateful to her for her kindness and noblesse oblige. Hers was a truly noble soul. May her memory be a blessing for us all.

Postscript: In 1993 I telephoned to inform the *New York Times* of Genie's passing. The fact that the young woman who answered at the obituary desk had never heard of Eugenie Leontovich was undoubtedly due to the generation gap. When I assured her of Genie's eminence, however, she grudgingly agreed to look her up in the newspaper's library, asking that I wait a few minutes. She soon came back on the line and apologetically reported that she had indeed found a huge amount of material. I then faxed her my information, and a fine, full obituary notice appeared in the next day's edition.

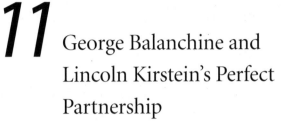

11 George Balanchine and Lincoln Kirstein's Perfect Partnership

George Balanchine and I became good friends in the early 1950s when I was promoting his New York City Ballet's annual visits to the Chicago Civic Opera House and its enchanting production of *The Nutcracker*. On one visit, and using attendant razzmatazz publicity, I arranged a *Nutcracker* "handicap" at a local racetrack, with Balanchine and dancers including Taniquil Le Clerc, Jacques d'Amboise, Edward Villela, Francisco Moncion, Maria Tallchief, Diana Adams, Melissa Hayden, Andre Eglevsky, Nora Kaye, Violette Verdy, and Patricia Wilde in attendance. Balanchine had a wonderful time, and through the years whenever we were together the celebrated choreographer happily recalled the event. It was the first and only time I have been to a racetrack.

Later, the Ford Foundation assigned me to assist all the New York City Center's constituent arts companies housed on West Fifty-sixth Street (the old Mecca Temple). I advised the New York City Ballet and the New York City Opera and, later, the Joffrey Ballet to plunge into the subscription format. Unfortunately, Morton Baum, the City Center's feisty board chair, didn't understand the enormous potential of subscription for those companies. I chose, however, not to argue the issue with him because he was then very important to what I knew were delicate, difficult, and even Byzantine negotiations whereby the handsome New York State Theatre was being conceived and constructed in the heart of Lincoln Center, the new home for both the City Center's Ballet and its Opera, although the facility had been primarily designed according to Balanchine's dance-oriented specifications. More than a decade before the move to the new building I succeeded in establishing—for the New York City Opera—a subscription base that later came to full flower in Lincoln Center, to the point that the company eventually achieved a subscribership of almost forty thousand committed, annually renewing series-ticket-holders!

For at least fifteen previous years I was unable to budge the determination of the New York City Ballet management to continue presenting a too-small number of performances to often very poor attendance, subjecting its wonderful dancers to frequent periods of unemployment. The company's management staff thought it had to be that way, much as our grandparents believed that polio was heaven's will and nothing could be done about it.

The Ballet's managing director, Betty Cage, was adamant about not only pleasing Baum but also protecting Balanchine from my influence. She insisted that he would never, ever, agree to having subscription. Besides, the new New York State Theatre was now in the offing, and its management would, it thought, soon be hearing from many single-ticket-buying dance enthusiasts, who it was assumed were salivating at the prospect of luxuriating in the new theater's lavish surroundings, including its contemporary sculptures in well-appointed lobbies.

When the new theater opened that fall, attendance, in box-office parlance, "died." During all those years, I had always assumed Betty was discussing my advice with Balanchine and that he was turning it down for his own reasons. I didn't want to go over Betty's head and did not directly approach Balanchine in the matter. His wishes were sacred to all who revered him as the most gifted leader in American performing arts. Predictably, from my experience, single-ticket buyers will cherry-pick the most popular works but ignore other elements of a repertoire that subscribers accept along with the favorites.

W. McNeil Lowry and Marcia Thompson at the Ford Foundation, which continued to be the major backer of the company, told me I must get there immediately and once more advocate the beginning of a subscription campaign, to begin in time for the crucial spring season to follow. After such a defeat the theater's management would surely give in. When I came to my meeting with Betty and her staff at the New York State Theatre, however, they again said no.

Fortunately—and fatefully—at that moment Balanchine, whose office was next door, was passing the open door of our meeting room. Seeing me, he waved hello. "Mr. Balanchine," I called out, "could you give us a minute or two?" Stepping into our little conference, he asked, "Ah, Nyooman, what is it?" I replied, "They say that you will never permit subscription here." He paused for a moment and then asked, "*Who* says?" Pointing to the culprits—Betty and her yes men and women—I replied, "*They* say." He paused again and asked in a reasonable tone, "Tell me, Nyooman, will it be *good* for business?" "Yes, Mr. Balanchine," I responded, "it will be *very, very good* for business!" Without pausing, and looking straight at Betty and her cohorts, he said, "Then vee *do!*"

At that moment I realized that butlers in the houses of the rich are more snobbish than their employers. Betty, I understood, undoubtedly had been speaking for a small number of old-line balletomanes who were always deliriously happy about there being lots of unsold seats because they could then have their pick at the last moment. They could continue to feel superior to those subscribers not from the right side of the tracks, who, the single-ticket-buyer snobs patronizingly insisted, might bring sandwiches in brown paper bags to performances. They wouldn't even know when to applaud! That was the tenor of the letters received by New York newspapers when our initial campaign sold more than twenty thousand series subscriptions overnight! Stubborn aesthetes who refused to subscribe were furious that they could obtain only our left-over seat locations. One complainant wrote to the *New York Times* that every parvenu subscriber would become an "albatross round the company's neck!"

The day after that letter's publication I was strolling through the New York State Theater's backstage corridors when Lincoln Kirstein, Balanchine's elegant associate, spotted me and ran over to gleefully shake my hand. I am almost too modest to recount that he exclaimed, "Mr. Newman, you *are* a genius! And, by the way, can you find me another twenty thousand albatrosses? I'll take as many as I can get!" Kirstein was the co-creator with Balanchine of both the School of American Ballet and the New York City Ballet. He also wrote six important books on ballet and edited the authoritative seven-volume *Dance Index.* Prolific and eclectic, he published plays, novels, memoirs, and critical studies on the visual arts, motion pictures, music, and literature. Born in 1907 and deceased in 1996, he was one of the twentieth century's most respected American cultural figures. He had devoted his life and personal fortune to the support and promotion of the arts.

The success of that 1966 subscription campaign was to have far-reaching effects not only for the New York City Ballet but also for dance in North America, which has since—under the impetus of wide-spread subscription campaigning—undergone incredible growth. I mourn for those lost years during which the subscriptionless New York City Ballet so unnecessarily suffered the lack of audience support. Its financial problems could have been eased. Fuller employment could have been provided for its dancers. What many dilettantish arts administrators in the nonprofit field often fail to understand is that those who create art want to perform it for *audiences*—the more the better! I recall an artistic director, rejected at renewal time by subscribers (and for good reasons they thought), told me, "We're well rid of them. Those boors don't share my artistic vision."

Philanthropy Magazine, in its January-February 2001 issue, stated that the "subscription revolution's impact is seen today in nearly every city in America, as well as around the world." In the spring of 1966, however, when we launched the New York City Ballet subscription series with such overnight success, Clive Barnes, the dance critic editor of the *New York Times* was deluged with mail from protesting single-ticket buyer aesthetes who weren't at all embarrassed to ask—as one did—"what is bad about being a snob in the arts?" Their horror at what they considered, from their self-serving viewpoint, an unwelcome invasion of barbarians into their temple of art was monumental.

By the fall season of 1966, however, subscription soared still higher, and Barnes was attacked for embracing it as "desirable, democratic, and providing a practical and pragmatic solution to the survival needs of ballet and modern dance." He also wrote that subscription provides the artistic direction with "an almost unheard of freedom" in programming. Suddenly, subscription nay-sayer Morton Baum, who had done yeoman's work in getting Lincoln Center's New York State Theatre built, telephoned. Would I, he asked, drop by his office? I did. He looked me straight in the eye and said, "Mr. Newman, *you* were right. *I* was wrong" (the exact words that had come to me in a letter from Baum's admirer John S. White, the New York City Opera stage director-turned-manager). White had—in loyalty to Baum—refused to attend staff meetings I held at City Center to establish a subscribership for *his* company. I probably would not have been able to proceed with my plan for that company in 1964 had it not been for a close relationship with Julius Rudel, who had finally succeeded to the general directorship. He was one of the conductors during the New York City Opera's seven years of providing fall opera seasons in Chicago (1947–53), which I promoted. Although both Baum and White had said nay to subscription, Julius said yea. Happily for the destiny of the company, and for my promotional leadership, he prevailed.

Expansion of New York City Ballet seasons went on apace, and within a very short time I was establishing "charter" subscription audiences for Barbara Weissberger's Pennsylvania Ballet in Philadelphia, E. Virginia Williams's Boston Ballet, and William Christensen's Utah Civic Ballet (Ballet West) in Salt Lake City. All were "Balanchine-advised." I also was able to restore the lapsed subscription of Lew Christensen's San Francisco Ballet, which had gone back to being basically a school but with subscription could resume professional seasons. North of the border—and still in the mid-1960s—I inaugurated the charter subscription concept at Arnold Spohr's Royal Winnipeg Ballet, Celia Franca's Toronto-based National Ballet of Canada, and the Alberta Ballet of Edmonton and Calgary. (Eventually, I completed twenty-six years of audience-building throughout Canada for all the performing arts—and some museums—with, I am proud to say, fabulous results.) I then assisted dance impressari in England, Australia, Holland, Belgium, and Finland. I doubled back to New York City to advise the Alvin Ailey Dance Company and the Dance Theatre of Harlem. The momentum of the Balanchine-Kirstein subscription success confirmed Clive Barnes's prediction that "ballet would never be the same." Certainly, its audiences greatly increased along with its income.

Certain myths persist in performing arts circles. One is that somewhere out there are hordes of single-ticket buyers who will turn out for events if only we knew how to attract them. Admittedly, *some* cultured folk (hardly hordes) do show up for a performance here or there, but they are not to be found at *most* of the attractions we present. Their absence has been the main cause of the opening and quick closing of ballet and other art companies in our society throughout most of the twentieth century. Fortunately, the subscription revolution—of which I have been the striking arm—reached ballet by the mid-1960s, first with the Balanchine-Kirstein New York City Ballet and then with so many others, including a greater number of new companies generated by the burgeoning movements. Of course, the huge increase of regular attendees brought higher levels of financial support from subscribers and, as in other art disciples, increased business and foundation funding, even from government sources.

My day-to-day assistant for that 1965–66 New York City Ballet's turn-around was Harvey Lichtenstein, a Ford Foundation intern who I had known twenty-three years earlier, in 1953, as a young modern dancer in Sophie Maslow's New York–based troupe, for which I was tour manager and backer. Upon my intervention with Morton Baum, Harvey was asked to establish a central subscription promotion office for City Center affiliates: the New York City Ballet, the New York City Opera, and the Joffrey Ballet. Later, in one of my roles—that of consultant to the New York State Council for the Arts—I was able to recommend Harvey to head the Brooklyn Academy of Music, one of the country's pioneer complexes for the performing arts. I had also recommended his predecessor in the position. Harvey, from the beginning, did a great job at BAM, and I continued to advise him there throughout my Ford Foundation years. His accomplishments there are now among the major success stories of the arts in our time. He became one of the titans of the international arts management field. I have known Harvey for more than a half century and am proud to have influenced him so greatly.

Balanchine's company never advertised its dancers as stars, but Maria Tallchief was unquestionably and widely held to be one. Maria, a resident in Chicago following her retirement from the New York City Ballet, was the principal ballerina–guest artist of Lyric Opera of Chicago for our 1957 and 1959 productions of *La Gioconda,* and she returned for *Orfeo ed Euridice* in 1962. Ruth Page's Chicago Opera Ballet, which toured widely for years as an independent entity financed by her husband, Thomas Hart Fisher, provided Lyric with its dance sequence requirements from its 1954 inception through its 1968 season. From 1969 through 1973 I arranged for E. Virginia Williams's Boston Ballet, with which I had long worked (under my Ford Foundation mandate) to provide the dance requirements for Lyric's annual seasons.

In 1974, inspired at a dinner meeting with Tallchief and Balanchine, I proposed to Carol Fox, Lyric's general manager, a newly constituted Lyric Opera of Chicago Ballet that would become another Balanchine-advised company. Maria would be its director. Balanchine pledged to supply scenery, costumes, and his own participation if necessary. He choreographed our 1975 *Orfeo ed Euridice* and our internationally televised *Faust* in 1979. In the late 1970s, Lyric Opera of Chicago was undergoing an economic crisis and asked Maria to create a ballet entity, to be separately financed. She did so by founding the Chicago City Ballet, which performed in the city and on tour throughout the 1980s.

Maria, who had previously been married to Balanchine, was universally famed as one of the great exponents of his choreography and widely acclaimed as the top ballerina in the United States. I was electrified by her performance in Igor Stravinsky's *Firebird,* which Balanchine had choreographed for her—Marc Chagall provided the stunning stage settings—when she returned to the New York City Ballet after a three-year stint in the early 1960s with the American Ballet Theatre. I was the press agent for one national tour she did with that company. At that time I also urged Lucia Chase, founder and backer of the American Ballet Theatre, to lose no time in initiating the development of a subscription audience in what I saw as a wide-open market for New York City's as yet uncommitted dance lovers. She demurred, and it was left to Balanchine, Kirstein, and company to pluck that prize a few years later at my initiative and because of my Ford Foundation–sponsored promotional initiatives.

Maria, born on an Osage Indian reservation in Oklahoma on January 24, 1925, and her sister Marjorie, also a celebrated ballerina, were of Osage and Scots-Irish descent. From 1942 to 1947 Maria was an important artist in Ballet Russe de Monte Carlo, and in 1954–55 she was the New York City Ballet's prima ballerina. For eighteen years she was a stalwart of that company, retiring from it in 1965. Among her most acclaimed performances were those in the *Firebird, Orpheus, The Nutcracker, Sylvia pas de deux, Scotch Symphony, Pas de dix,* and *The Ground Symphony.* In 1996 she received Kennedy Center honors and was inducted into the National Women's Hall of Fame. Her autobiography, *Maria Tallchief: America's Prima Ballerina,* was published in 1997. I recall that when consulting with the board chair of the Royal Opera House at Covent Garden I lingered in its ornate lobby to savor a lovely portrait of Maria, pictured onstage in full splendor. When Maria had just had her daughter Elissa, I immediately came crib-side with a *Chicago Daily News* rotogravure section photographer. The resulting sepia-toned photo layout was proudly exhibited on the wall of Maria's North Lake Shore Drive studio for many years. Little Elissa, now a beautiful and elegant woman, is an established poet and has a daughter of her own, Alexandra, whose color portrait Maria sent to me, introducing her darling granddaughter as "The newest Sugar Plum Fairy!"

George Balanchine was born Georgy Melitonovich Balanchivadze on January 22, 1904, in the then-czarist St. Petersburg to a Georgian family. He studied dance at the Marinsky Theatre's Imperial School of Ballet and music at the Petrograd Conservatory. By 1920 he had begun choreographing experimental works such as Jean Cocteau and Darius Milhaud's *Le boeuf sur le toit.* Later he partnered with Alexandra Danilova in key European cities and joined Sergei Diaghilev's Paris-based Ballets Russes, for which he choreographed ten works, including *Apollo* (1928) and *The Prodigal Son* (1929). Throughout the 1930s he worked with the Royal Danish Ballet and the Ballet Russe de Monte Carlo. In 1933 Kirstein, impressed with Balanchine's avant-garde company Les Ballets, invited him to the United States to organize the School of American Ballet and the American Ballet Company. Thus a unique and lasting partnership was launched that was to greatly influence the destiny of dance in the United States and throughout the world.

In the United States, Balanchine's magic was seen at the Metropolitan Opera, and he was an early choreographer for both Broadway and Hollywood, including the 1936 "Slaughter on Tenth Avenue" in *On Your Toes.* In 1941 he created *Concerto barocco* and *Ballet Imperial* for the American Ballet's tour of Latin America. By 1948 Balanchine and Kirstein's New York City Ballet, which presented Balanchine's repertoire of 150 works, including the full-length *Nutcracker* and *Don Quixote,* began at the New

York City Center. After consistent artistic successes there it moved in 1965 to the New York State Theatre in Lincoln Center.

Dance patronage history was made in 1966 when the W. McNeil Lowry–led Ford Foundation Program for the Humanities and the Arts made an unprecedented, almost $8 million grant to the company, its affiliated School of American Ballet, and the country's half a dozen Balanchine-advised dance entities. During the second half of the 1960s, all of the 1970s, and into the early 1980s Balanchine and his forces were at the vital center of ballet in the United States, where, as Lowry's audience development associate in this unprecedentedly ambitious program on behalf of dance and dancers, choreographers, scenic and costume creators, and lighting designers, I entered into a new and exciting phase of my vastly variegated, arts-oriented career.

Ill-health finally forced Balanchine to retire in 1982. He died on April 30, 1983, at seventy-nine. One of the most influential and most success-ful classical ballet choreographers of the twentieth century, he inspired and trained an extraordinary number of superior dancers. Ballet com-panies everywhere continue to program his creations; some of his best-known works overseas are set to Johannes Brahms's *Liebeslieder Walzer* (1960), Hershey Kay's *Western Symphony* (1954), and Robert Schumann's *Davidsbundlertanze* (1980). Balanchine's long and special relationship with Stravinsky began in 1925 with *Le chant du rossignol* (The Song of the Nightingale). He also collaborated with Arnold Schoenberg and Charles Ives. Balanchine was a serious musician and his studies of the scores he choreographed were intensive. His decades-long partnership with the brilliant Kirstein, an American "Renaissance man" has been described as "the most productive collaboration between a great artist and a great patron in the modern history of the performing arts." I was privileged to have known and worked with both of them.

12 Geraldine Page, a Brilliant Young Actress and Casualty of the Method

During my many years in the performing arts (show business), I have either witnessed or been victim of every possible catastrophe that can afflict managers, producers, or publicists. I've seen scenery collapse on performers during crucial scenes. I've had a world-renowned opera basso sustain a four-week attack of hiccups, which even a great neurologist was hard-pressed to cure. I've somehow lived through a famed prima donna decamping under cover of darkness between performances, returning to Europe without saying a word to management. I've witnessed so devastating a snowstorm that neither the audience nor Luciano Pavarotti could get to the concert hall. I've seen an opera tenor so enraged by a critic's merciless attack that I had to stop him from murdering the offending journalist! I've worked through many, many weeks of preparations for a show only to have its backers, heartbreakingly, pull out at the last minute. I've been driven out of performances by storm, flood, and—in one especially memorable case—by the death of a South American dictator's wife!

In 1956, however, I went through an experience so bizarre that I'm sure it is unprecedented in the annals of the performing arts. When I was general manager of Chicago's Studebaker Theatre Company a brilliant actress refused to speak her lines. We had bought the greatly gifted, thirty-two-year-old Geraldine Page out of her long-run London engagement in *The Rainmaker* to star in three successive plays. We opened our initial season with G. B. Shaw's *Androcles and the Lion* starring Ernest Truex and staged by Cedric Hardwicke. Then came Geraldine's plays: Eugene O'Neill's *Desire under the Elms,* Ivan Turgenev's *A Month in the Country,* and Andre Gide's *The Immoralist.*

Page, the darling of the then very fashionable Konstantin Stanislavsky–inspired Method school of acting, was abundantly talented and would have been a terrific actress, I'm sure, even without aid of the highly introspective indoctrination central to that system. How much more introspective can you get than entering into the then-fashionable arena of psychoanalysis? Whether Geraldine's regimen was Freudian, Jungian, or Adlerian I never learned. Suffice it to say that it seemed to render her erratic. Her stage directors for the O'Neill and Turgenev works—Boris Tumarin and Eugenie Leontovich, respectively—were totally mystified when at performance after performance *her lips moved but no sound issued forth!* Our new subscription audience, then the largest of any theater of good plays in North America, was driven to despair and revolt. Holders of second-row seats asked to be moved to the first row. Because her lips moved, they thought the problem was that they just couldn't hear her!

For Geraldine's third show, Gide's *The Immoralist,* we brought in David Pressman from off Broadway. Pressman, a steeped-in-the-intricacies-of-the-Method director, amazed us by getting Geraldine to talk throughout the run of that drama, thus placating at least some of the abused subscribers. As he explained her blockage to me, she had somehow become convinced that she was an inept (he said "lousy") actress, and the only way she could prevent the public from finding that out was to *make sure they didn't hear her!*

What Pressman said to Geraldine I don't know, but evidently he somehow restored her belief in herself. Her miasmic indulgence in psychological fantasy had been ruinously costly to our project, and not even with our vastly successful follow-up production, the world premiere of Arthur

Miller's full-length version of *A View from the Bridge,* a fourteen-karat hit directed by George Keathley and starring Luther Adler, could we regain momentum.

The Studebaker Theatre Company was organized and backed by a group of young, culturally oriented but theatrically inexperienced business executives unaware of the demands and complexities of the project they envisioned. When they asked me to become the general manager I decided I must share the job with another showman, Danny Goldberg, a former *Variety* mug, playwright, stage producer, and former partner of the controversial producer Mike Todd, husband to movie stars Joan Blondell and Elizabeth Taylor and producer of *Around the World in Eighty Days.* Mike, who had produced three of Danny's plays on Broadway, was the son of a rabbi, and Danny's dad was a kosher butcher. Danny and I, good friends, had long been fellow Randolph Street denizens. When I was the press agent of the Woods Theatre—now, along with the Harris and Selwyn Theatres replaced by the Goodman Theatre Center—Danny's office was on one of the floors upstairs. At the Studebaker we proved to be excellent partners—complementing each other well—and became closer than ever before.

Missouri-born Geraldine Sue Page, a magical artist of the professional legitimate theater for well over four decades, also won eight Academy Award nominations and finally an Oscar for best actress for her performance in the 1986 film *Trip to Bountiful.* Her quintessentially neurotic characterizations saw her starred opposite such luminaries as John Wayne and Paul Newman. In all, she appeared in thirty-eight motion pictures and was featured in a dozen important television dramas. Geraldine and the actor Rip Torn were married for many years, and she had a daughter and twin sons. Born in 1924, she died in 1987 while starring on Broadway in a revival of Noel Coward's *Blithe Spirit.*

Certainly, Geraldine was one of the most important American actresses of the second half of the twentieth century, and as I write, fifty years have passed since she drove me to such distraction. Yet painful memories of that experience haunt me still. I long relived them in nightmares in which time and again I would be on my knees in her dressing room, pleading that she speak out. "Danny, please, I'll try. I'll try" she would mouth as she cried piteously. Some years later we both spoke at a fund-raising event for the Milwaukee Repertory Theatre, and she approached me and asked that I forgive her for what had happened in Chicago. I did so but can never forget the agonies through which she put me. When in 1962 she starred on Broadway in Tennessee Williams's *Sweet Bird of Youth* while I was working at Lincoln Center, I wanted to see the play but couldn't bear to see *her* onstage. I learned that her understudy was stepping in for the matinees, so *that's* when I saw the show!

Undoubtedly, many of the fine actors with whom I've worked all over North America and abroad have employed their own ways to achieve high-level performances. Most often, they are not handicapped by the psychological hang-ups that often plague practitioners of the various versions of the Method, whether Stanislavskian, Strasbergian, or whomever. Many British actors and their colleagues throughout the Commonwealth favor rock-solid technique and exquisite clarity of speech. They rarely talk about it. American artists, however, tend to talk volubly and endlessly about their performance-priming approaches. Many French Canadian actors are inspired by the classic theaters of France although they also share in avant-garde activities. Overall, I have seen the Method as a retarding factor in the American theater's development. I am convinced that our most truly talented theater artists would succeed with or without the encumbrance of the Method. I deeply regret the ongoing and painful frustrations of so many clearly untalented persons who say, "We'll just keep at it until we master this marvelous Method, and then we'll surely become stars!"

13

Samuel Goldwyn (Shmuel
Gelbfisz) Walks from Warsaw
to Hamburg, Is a Blacksmith in
England, a World-Champion
Glove Salesman, and Wealthy
Hollywood Producer in America

In 1960 I received a call from the famed Hollywood movie producer Samuel Goldwyn, who had recently completed the filming of George Gershwin's musical show (no one then dared call it an *opera*) *Porgy and Bess.* He wanted me to promote its planned midwestern premiere at Chicago's McVickers Theatre. Its success there, Goldwyn reasoned, would influence the number of bookings in the surrounding region throughout Illinois, Indiana, Wisconsin, Michigan, Iowa, and Minnesota. He was willing to come in and work with me, which he did several times.

Although Goldwyn's strong cast included such luminaries as Sidney Poitier, Dorothy Dandridge, Sammy Davis Jr., Pearl Bailey, Diahann Carroll, and Brock Peters, he also wanted a strong advance promotional campaign. He'd been told that I'd publicized the brilliant 1952 stage production of *Porgy and Bess* starring Leontyne Price, William Warfield, and Cab Calloway that Blevins Davis, a novitiate producer, had wanted to close during the unsuccessful Dallas tryout performances. I convinced him, however, to keep it running and nursed it through to eventual triumph. Goldwyn—a fighter himself—was impressed with my seminal role in the survival of that historic stage production, which went on to become a success in both the United States and Europe.

Shmuel Gelbfisz, born in Poland in 1879, later became Samuel Goldfish and even later Samuel Goldwyn. At age sixteen, perilously stealing across international borders, the hungry youngster walked all five hundred miles from Warsaw to Hamburg, Germany, where he paused long enough to learn the rudiments of glovemaking. With the kindly help of co-workers he bought a one-way, cross-channel ticket to England. Then he walked 120 miles from London to Birmingham, where he was apprenticed to a blacksmith. Finally, he arrived in Gloversville, New York, and became a glove factory worker. Soon he graduated to the front office, becoming the world's most successful glove salesman. Thus he raised the capital with which to enter the movie business with his brother-in-law, Jesse Lasky.

The two men produced one of Hollywood's first full-length feature films in 1913, Cecil B. DeMille's *The Squaw Man.* They next merged with Adolf Zukor's Famous Players Film Company, with Goldwyn becoming board chair of the Famous Players–Lasky Company in 1917. In that same year the ex-glover founded the Goldwyn Picture Corporation, and in 1924 he joined the formidable Louis B. Mayer (with whom he never got along) in founding Metro-Goldwyn-Mayer. As an independent producer, Goldwyn later distributed his films through the United Artists Corporation founded by "America's sweetheart" Mary Pickford, the dashing Douglas Fairbanks, the great Charlie Chaplin, and the pioneering D. W. Griffith and then through RKO (the Radio Keith Orpheum Circuit).

Goldwyn recruited superior writers, directors, actors, and cinematographers, and his high-quality products were notable for their literary level, including *Dodsworth* (1936), *Wuthering Heights* (1939), and *The Little Foxes* (1941). Other Goldwyn successes were *The Best Years of Our Lives* (1946) and, later, the Technicolor musical *Guys and Dolls.* He introduced to movies such stars as Bebe Daniels, Pola Negri, Will Rogers, Vilma Banky, and Ronald Colman. Goldwyn's consistent success was not only due to his relentless drive and business acumen but also his good judgment in assaying the quality of stories he could turn into films.

He had participated fully in the silent film era and was also was on hand for the chaotic early days of talking pictures. The stage play *Once in a Lifetime,* George S. Kaufman's satire of that hysterical period, has a Philistine movie producer named Glogauer yelling at his yes-men, "From now on, I make a new ruling! Before we produce a script, somebody here has first got to read it!"

Goldwyn, who died in 1974 at age ninety-five, was celebrated for his "Goldwynisms," among them "Include me out!" and "He should have stood in bed!" On one occasion when he had ordered an aide to obtain movie rights to a recent Broadway smash, he was told, "I don't think you'll like it Mr. Goldwyn. It's a very caustic piece." "I don't care how much it costs!" Goldwyn responded. "Get it!"

His wife Frances Howard, who was handsome, dignified, and strong-minded, accompanied him on one of his working trips to Chicago. Howard, a talented legitimate stage actress, had defied her anti-Semitic mother to marry Goldwyn. A woman of valor, she fought valiantly for her man for some four decades, and he was—to understate it—greatly influenced by her. Goldwyn was a health-food faddist, and when we lunched together in his hotel suite he was clearly disappointed in my lack of enthusiasm for the bland viands he ordered for me. He was invariably kind, however, even when I once took him to the wrong airport. O'Hare had just opened, and by force of habit I instructed our limousine driver to go to Midway Airport, which was older. Goldwyn didn't reprove me but quickly hired a helicopter to get him to O'Hare in time for his flight. Perhaps he felt warmly toward me because my wife Dina was also a native of Warsaw.

His commitment to *Porgy and Bess,* he told me, was of long standing. He had bought the film rights many years before but couldn't proceed because militant black organizations opposed the dress and dialect of the Catfish Row residents being shown and heard on screen. After making many artistic concessions whereby their grammar and clothing were "sanitized," which may well have had a negative affect on the film's overall impact, Goldwyn made the movie. It was not an immediate box-office smash in the United States, but, fortunately, it was much more successful overseas and did much better in subsequent U.S. showings.

Sam Goldwyn, an East European Horatio Alger, could very well have long ago preceded Norman Podhoretz's autobiographical *Making It* with colorful recollections of his own upwardly mobile and ultimately success-ful struggles. Having known Goldwyn, and considering his youthful years of continuous striving and his long life of consistent accomplishment against tremendous odds, I can only wonder at the breadth of his vision, his infectious optimism, and his never-flagging determination.

14 Carol Channing Parlays "Diamonds Are a Girl's Best Friend" into a Half-Century Career Climaxed by Her *Hello, Dolly!* Mega-Triumph!

In early 1960 I handled a bright new musical revue, *Show Business,* starring the unique, statuesque, and immensely talented Carol Channing, already a major star in the musical comedy genre and a big attraction at the nation's poshest supper clubs. We enjoyed a four-month engagement at Chicago's venerable Erlanger Theatre, right across the alley from Cohan's Grand Opera House on Clark Street. The Erlanger faced City Hall and was next door to Gust C. Terzakes's restaurant, Drake's, where politicians lunched. Just around the corner on Randolph Street was Henrici's, where actors and their managers and press agents gathered.

Although our show was solidly entertaining—custom-made for Carol's special comedic and terpsichorean gifts—and did respectable business throughout its run, it was not a smash hit in that it wasn't in the ticket-scalper "demand" category. The actors, musicians, and stagehands were all happy with their on-going employment, however, and the producer and theater owner seemed satisfied with their respective percentages of the gross. The only one who was unhappy was the box-office chief, a dour, sour fellow who wasn't getting enough "ice"—illicit bribe money—from scalpers. Working for just his salary, which was quite good, was unthinkable!

He constantly tried to convince us to leave for the road as soon as possible, figuring that a new, greater-demand show might come in and put him back on the gold standard. We finally did leave—when *we* were ready—for a twenty-two-city national tour. Touring was far from ideal for me because I had many other Chicago-area irons in the fire and didn't need the road. Nevertheless, I did go out in advance of the company, publicizing the show in city after city, making shared-advertising deals with house managers, reserving hotel rooms, and, of course, visiting newspaper critics, editors, and columnists to seek publicity.

At the Erlanger, George Wilmot, the genial house manager as well as my ATPAM union brother and good friend of many years, provided figures on our gross receipts each week to *Variety*. To George's embarrassment, however, he found that Carol's husband and personal manager, Charles Lowe, was calling ahead of him and providing inflated figures to *Variety*. I suppose Charles was overly anxious to prove his value to Carol's career. An efficiency wonk, he kept voluminous records of every review and feature story about Carol from earlier appearances in every city. In Chicago, for instance, where she appeared in *Gentlemen Prefer Blondes* at the R.K.O. Palace and at the Palmer House's Empire Room, journalists who had written about her then were invited to her "Show Business" performance and arrangements were made for new interviews. Charles, now deceased, was indeed indefatigable about his work.

Carol was a charming, pleasant, and delightful colleague. She was born in Seattle in 1921, and her father, an important newspaper editor, was prominent in the national leadership of the Christian Science movement. An alumna of Vermont's Bennington College, where she majored in drama and dance, Carol became an instant star on Broadway and toured as Lorelei Lee in *Gentlemen Prefer Blondes,* in which she memorably sang "Diamonds Are a Girl's Best Friend!" Tossing a number of fake diamond bracelets into the audience each night—and at matinees—was a regular feature of her *Show Business* performances. Carol is very disciplined and careful of her diet. I arranged for the restaurant next door to the Erlanger to deliver a choice cut of steak to her dressing room, well before the start of each performance, for her nightly main course. Carol's son, Channing Lowe, has become a Pulitzer Prize–winning cartoonist.

Fourteen years after *Show Business* Carol won the coveted Antoinette Perry Award for best actress in a comedy for her role in *Hello, Dolly!* on Broadway, and she's still going strong! For four decades she has never let a holiday go by without sending me a message, and I appreciate it.

I have rarely observed the degree of rapport between performer and audience that Carol enjoys with her adoring fans. I can liken it only to the love affair I used to see between grand opera star Renata Tebaldi and her devoted aficionados. Probably neither Carol nor Renata's overwhelming star quality would please devotees of the Method, but she's a living doll!

Sally Rand almost bared her all in her second sell-out year, 1934, at the Chicago World's Fair. (Library of Congress)

Sam Wanamaker and Danny Newman met at Chicago's Goodman Theatre School in the mid-1930s and remained close friends and professional associates for the next fifty years. (Courtesy of Lyric Opera of Chicago)

Dina Halpern in the title role of
Philip Yordan's *Anna Lucasta,*
Chicago's longest-running-ever
Yiddish stage hit, 1949. (Author's
collection)

Dina Halpern, star of
stage, screen, radio,
recital platform, and
television, as Portia in
Maurice Schwartz's
adaptation of *The
Merchant of Venice,*
presented by the
American Yiddish Art
Theater in 1947–48
as an operetta with
music by Joseph
Rumshinsky. The
production was
performed in New
York, Chicago, and
throughout North
America. (Author's
collection)

Dina Halpern, 1961.
(Photo by David H.
Fishman; author's
collection)

Dina Halpern at home in Chicago, 1987, next
to a Natan Haendel portrait of her done in
London in 1946 that is now in Chicago's Harold
Washington Library Department of Special
Collections, along with her library of books in
Yiddish. (Photo by Al Podgorski; as published in
the *Chicago Sun-Times.* Copyright 2005 Chicago
Sun-Times, Inc. Reprinted with permission)

Maria Tallchief and Danny Newman have worked together since the early 1950s when she starred in an American Ballet Theatre national tour. Years later, they are pictured with Lyric Opera artistic administrator Ardis Krainik and Henry "Buzz" Paschen, Maria Tallchief's husband. (Courtesy of Lyric Opera of Chicago)

Carol Channing starred in the musical revue *Show Business* at Chicago's Erlanger Theatre and on national tour in 1955, with Danny Newman providing advance press agentry and micromanagement. (Author's collection)

Danny Newman commissioned a
Lucile Leighton portrait of Dolly
Haas, who costarred with Yul Brynner
in *Lute Song* at Chicago's Studebaker
Theatre during the 1946–47 season.
Left to right: Dolly Haas, Louis
Hector, Lucile Leighton, and Marian
Leeds. (Author's collection)

Tenor Richard Tucker, a pillar of the
Metropolitan Opera and idol of Lyric
Opera of Chicago audiences as well as
a renowned cantor. (Photo by Nancy
Sorensen; courtesy of Lyric Opera of
Chicago)

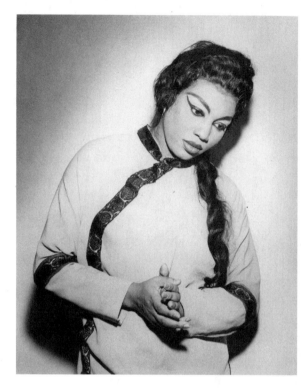

Leontyne Price, the supersoprano who soared to international stardom in the second half of the twentieth century, appeared as the tragic Liu in the Chicago production of *Turandot* in 1959. (Photo by Nancy Sorensen; courtesy of Lyric Opera of Chicago)

Baritone William Warfield, known for appearances in opera, vocal recital, and musical theater and also as a music educator, was Porgy in Lyric Opera of Chicago's historic 1952 production of *Porgy and Bess.* (Courtesy of Lyric Opera of Chicago)

David Poleri, whom Danny Newman has called "one of the three best American lyric tenors," along with Richard Tucker and Jan Peerce. (Courtesy of Lyric Opera of Chicago)

By day, Ardis Krainik typed Danny Newman's publicity releases, but at night she sang mezzo-soprano supporting roles. Here, cast as Myrtale in Lyric Opera of Chicago's *Thais* (1959), she greets baritone Michel Roux and conductor Georges Pretre. (Courtesy of Lyric Opera of Chicago)

Ardis Krainik just before her *comprimaria* appearance as Rossweisse in Lyric Opera's *Die Walküre* (1956). She was excited that one of her cast colleagues was the formidable dramatic soprano Birgit Nilsson. (Courtesy of Lyric Opera of Chicago)

Renée Fleming and Danny Newman backstage at Lyric Opera in the late 1990s. Fleming's exquisite voice and impeccable singing technique invite comparison with the sopranos of opera's early decades. (Courtesy of Lyric Opera of Chicago)

15
Danny Kaye, the All-Time Great Who Felt That He Must, Wherever He Was, Wow Everyone within Range!

In 1963 one of my big-time New York City legitimate-theater press agent colleagues subcontracted me to handle one of his mainstay clients, the comedian Danny Kaye, who had already become a major movie star and was big on the radio and in early television. Danny was set to come into the 3,600-seat Chicago Civic Opera House in the quickly put together *Danny Kaye Revue,* which would feature the hilarious material for which he was known and that had stood him in such good stead over the years. Much of it was custom-created by his greatly gifted wife, the writer Sylvia Fine. He had not, in my memory, appeared in much legitimate theater for some time although he enjoyed sensational success in the post–World War II George and Ira Gershwin musical show *Lady in the Dark* with Gertrude Lawrence.

One of the major multitalented people in mid-twentieth-century American performing arts, Danny could sing, dance, and act up a storm. His acceptance was universal. He was beloved of the British Royal family, and UNICEF children were in his thrall the world over (he was UNICEF's goodwill ambassador from 1954 until his death in 1987) as was nearly every entertainment lover everywhere, including me!

David Daniel Kaminsky had come up through years of experience in Borscht Belt and Catskill resorts, long a unique finishing school for comedians. He was a highly skilled, quick-on-the-trigger variety artist, sensitive at every moment to how he was going over. He proved overwhelmingly successful in every branch of show business. I cannot think of any other performer who could so completely compel audiences on so many levels and with such seeming ease and authority—even in that era of theatrical greatness!

Because our show—which Danny would headline—was being organized overnight and there had been little advance notice before we put tickets on sale, we didn't assume that it would be an automatic sell-out. It was decided that we would stimulate the local market quickly by doing newspaper, radio, and television interviews, to which Danny obligingly agreed, some days before opening and for the early days of the engagement. Wherever we were, whether on a sidewalk, crossing the street, or in a hotel elevator, a restaurant, or a radio studio, there wasn't a moment that Danny was not in entertaining action. He was always on, always testing his powers and trying to wow 'em or murder 'em. At first I delighted in it and joined in the fun. After a while, however, I began to feel like the manager of a prizefighter who never stops indiscriminately punching, left-hooking and right-crossing all passers-by and interviewers. Even with all the fun and excitement involved it somehow became too much—sometimes even embarrassing.

As soon as it was announced that Danny Kaye was coming to Chicago for in-person appearances I began to receive imploring calls from an interviewer on the Chicago ABC (now CBS) radio station WBBM who desperately wanted Danny to appear on his program. We had more requests of that kind than we could honor, and I couldn't give the man an immediate yes. He pleaded that his career was at stake and having Danny Kaye on his show was crucial to him. So even though it didn't fit the plans I'd made, I told Danny about the situation. "Oh, what the hell," he said, "let's do it!"

Danny not only did it but also took over the man's show, giving it his all. I doubt that any radio program in America that day, that week, that month, or that year was as great. The host was beside himself with pleasure. He had provided listeners with a program they would long remember, and he no doubt gained credit from his bosses. I should mention, however, that the same radio guy turned me down not many weeks later when I asked him to interview a lesser-known actor from another legit show I was press-agenting. "Sic semper" something or other!

I have been fortunate over the years in having happy relationships with newspaper folk. Studs Terkel, my friend of more than sixty-some years, wrote about my unique status with the working press in a chapter devoted to me in his *Coming of Age: The Story of Our Century by Those Who've Lived It* (1996). An unfortunate press relations incident took place during my work with the *Danny Kaye Revue,* however, that was the only truly unhappy one in the more than seventy years since I began to visit newspaper city rooms. It was certainly no fault of Danny's, who greatly charmed a journalist who interviewed him the day after our opening. Unfortunately, her husband was unable to accompany her to that performance, and she asked if I could provide a ticket so he could see the show later that week. Ordinarily, her request would have been no problem. A press agent generally has a few pairs of top-location tickets for each performance in order to take care of VIP press requests. I immediately agreed to have a ticket in his name at the box office, I think for a Thursday night (we had opened on Monday). The fact that we became a hot-ticket show immediately after reviews came out would normally have made no difference. When I came into the box office the next morning, however, I learned that Danny's New York management people had been there ahead of me. Invoking their authority as his personal representatives (I represented the *show*), they stripped me of my press seats for the entire engagement. They needed them, they said, for VIPs they were bringing in from out of town to catch the show. As it was, I had to scramble to get *any* main-floor seat for the journalist's husband, and it was not a prime location. She didn't talk to me for a long time. That was more than forty years ago, and I think she has long ago forgotten the incident. I, however, have not.

I have heard rough language in my time—in the army, in various echelons of show business, and in other environments as well—but the most utterly foul-mouthed person I have known, I regret to write, was Danny Kaye. I could hardly believe that such a wonderful person would and could talk like that. I always thought of him talking endearingly and properly to UNICEF youngsters. I had supposed that because he had a radarlike sensitivity to how he was going over, at all times and under all circumstances, he sensed my shock at his obscenities and was having fun with me. I soon realized, however, that he really did talk that way, as did other show-biz veterans. My reaction was not a factor.

Whenever we met in later years Danny was as charming and gracious as I could have wanted. Shortly after my book *Subscribe Now!* was published he saw me coming down the aisle of a theater. He was standing next to the front-row aisle seat a few minutes before the curtain went up and yelled out to me, "Ah, subscribe now!" Perhaps he had read the marvelous *Daily Variety* review of that book and its title stuck in his incredibly retentive mind. Years later, backstage at the Metropolitan Opera, I was coming out of Plácido Domingo's dressing room, headed for the stage door through which Danny and his estranged wife Sylvia were entering. Again he called out, "Danny! Subscribe now!"

16 They Loved Me in Scotland (but I Didn't Love the Deathly Damp and Dreary Underheated Winters)

In 1973 I began to receive letters from Thomson Smillie, chief publicitor of the Scottish Opera, which was headquartered in Glasgow and also performed in Edinburgh, Aberdeen, Dundee, and other Scottish cities. Could I, he asked, arrange to meet with that company's general director, Peter Hemmings? Because I was then at the peak of my subscription audience–building activities throughout the United States and Canada I wasn't able to go abroad at just that time. After much correspondence back and forth, however, Hemmings decided to come to Chicago and arrived in the fall of 1974.

We met backstage in the Civic Opera House after a Lyric Opera performance. He told me that his company was in the process of restoring and eventually reopening Glasgow's long-abandoned, 1,600-seat opera house, the Theatre Royal. He said he'd been receiving my publicity releases and brochures for some time and that he—a staid Cambridge graduate—had become fascinated with my flamboyant prose and uninhibited selling stance. He was envious of Lyric Opera's vastly successful subscription series system whereby sold-out houses in our 3,600-seat theater were the norm for seasons that increased in length from year to year. Hemmings had also heard that I was not only the promoter of subscription sales at Lyric but also had been successfully introducing the concept to numerous professional performing arts organizations in North America and overseas. Perhaps, he suggested, I would come to Scotland, where I might convince his board of subscription's efficacy.

It must be remembered that—at that time—there had never been an opera subscription series in the United Kingdom, although I had built committed audiences in a few other Commonwealth nations—Canada and Australia—and would soon begin work in New Zealand. By 1976 I would be working in the Mother Country with the Birmingham Repertory Theatre, the Royal Opera House, and the English National Opera. Into the 1980s I would be conducting seminars for the managerial establishment of the British performing arts, even opening a London office (Subscribe Now! U.K.) in partnership with my friends Keith Diggle, an experienced British arts publicist and promoter, and Tony Gamble, publisher of London's *Classical Music* journal. Together, they have since founded England's important Rheingold Publications.

At any rate, in the winter of 1975 I arrived at Glasgow's Prestwick Airport and immediately evangelized the Scottish Opera's board of trustees—the majority of whom seemed to be flinty-eyed bankers, other skeptics such as shipping and mining magnates, and various other forbidding, CEO types. I was much younger then and even more passionate than now, and somehow I managed to convince them that subscription was a good idea. Within twenty-four hours after they agreed to launch a charter subscription drive I had designed and written a lively brochure. It certainly would have won no prizes in a graphics design contest, but it would, my whip-cracking, American-showman instincts assured me, sell the needed subscriptions.

The brochure proclaimed simple, straightforward, not arty statements of our bargain offers, which I devised on the spot: 10 OPERAS FOR THE PRICE OF 7 (3 OPERAS *free*), OR 5 OPERAS FOR THE PRICE OF 4 (1 OPERA *free*). Seductive descriptions of each opera accompanied each offer. I used the following enticement for Benjamin Britten's *A Midsummer Night's Dream* based on William Shakespeare's play: "Love's erratic progress under the full moon weaves mythically, magically, and musically through the Freudian forest of our sub-conscious, whilst men and maids disport themselves, faeries flit like fireflies, and this completely captivating extravaganza flashes 'twixt the peaks of high and low comedy, casting an evening-long spell of enchantment." To plug *Così fan Tutte,* I wrote, "Jubilant music bubbles and then bursts into magnificence, as two dashing officers, egged on by a cynical bachelor, assume disguise to woo each other's fiancees—who seemingly succumb—or is it that they're onto their lovers' little ruse? Thus, the master composer and his inspired librettist pose but do not answer their ultimate question on the reflexes of the sexes!" Complementing the exuberant text was an order form of such exquisite clarity that a child could use it.

In the event that we might need additional campaign components I indoctrinated Thomson Smillie in a dozen of my other favorite sales strategies. As it turned out, we required only a few. Smillie, a sophisticated publicist and valuable factotum of the Scottish Opera, was then elegantly moonlighting as artistic director of the annual summer Wexford Festival in Ireland. For me, he was an ideal collaborator and became a valued friend.

For part of three winters (1975–77) I worked in Glasgow with Scottish Opera in its administrative center in a very old and crumbling mansion. My "office" was a huge, unheated (and unheatable), high-ceilinged room where I typed, somehow, with gloved hands and wearing a muffler and overcoat. After my first day of this frigid duty I looked forward to checking into the hotel, thinking that surely my room would be heated. No such luck! The howling wintry winds came in as if there were no walls. To be fair, the management did attempt to provide heating, but it was insufficient—similar to most places I visited in Glasgow. Tuck-pointing must have been a lost art in Scotland. Macho Glaswegians, by the way, don't wear gloves and think it unmanly to do so. Many buildings there are ancient, and the dampness and dankness of centuries permeated the rooms.

Glasgow—Scotland's largest city—was founded in 550 A.D. Every day on my way to the office I passed its impressive, twelfth-century cathedral, which was still in daily use. I recall lunch and libations in a charming nearby pub that had—happily—a huge, roaring fire. I remember, too, a lovely dinner party at the manorial baronial home of Peter and Jane Hemmings when Dina was present along with the Gavin Boyds (he was the opera company's board chair). During my second visit—the following winter—to Scottish Opera, I also began to work with the Royal Scottish National Orchestra, which shared the services of Sir Alexander Gibson as music director and principal conductor with the opera.

Over the several years of my assignment I had the pleasure of immediately and enormously increasing the subscription audiences of the Scottish National Orchestra's various series in Glasgow, Edinburgh, and Dundee, all locations where the opera also performed. When my ministrations were first selling out both Scottish Opera and the orchestra, London's *Music News* asked, "Did these amazing statistics indicate some kind of classical music renaissance in Scotland?" The real reason for those increases, the *News* reported, was that *I* was guru for both organizations. Sir Alex wrote to me in high good humor that I had so inspired the populace that "the single ticket buyer was rapidly becoming a member of a fast dying race!" I hope it's not too immodest to admit that I loved his words. Moreover, I will always happily recall Thomson's letter to me of May 22, 1975:

> Our campaign, now only in its fifth week, is outrageously successful. Everyone in Scotland is astonished and people in the profession simply cannot conceive of an opera company in the United Kingdom having sold out grossly unpopular operas right through the end of next February. It is not an overstatement to say that you have effected a revolution in the theatre going habits of one section of the British public, and I promise you that all your funny expressions like "charter subscriber" are now used here as if they had been part of standard English since Chaucer.

Then he went way overboard, and I almost (but not quite) blushed when he told the *Birmingham Post* that I was "a genius" who had "attracted more people to live performances than any man in the world!"

Not everyone, however, was joyful about the subscription landslide. Stubborn single-ticket buyers, who had—in past years—obtained good seat locations because so many tickets were unsold, were chagrined by the sudden shortage the new series system generated. The Scottish Arts Council, long the provider of the opera's major subsidy, also protested on behalf of self-disenfranchised nonsubscribers. I proposed we hold back 10 percent of tickets for the unhappy taxpayers, and that was agreed upon. We ended the campaign with almost 90 percent of the capacity subscribed for a much longer season than had ever been attempted.

Thomson eventually came to the United States as manager for Sarah Caldwell's Opera Company of Boston and later for the Kentucky Opera in Louisville. Peter Hemmings and I remained close. Even before he arrived at his next assignment—the general directorship of the Australian Opera, where I worked three times in the 1970s—he cabled to ask me to meet him in Sydney when he arrived there. I did so, and my powerful promotion campaign resulted in a big box office success for his inaugural season there. The following year I returned to promote his first joint season with the Victorian State Opera in Melbourne—a wonderful sell-out experience! Then we collaborated on the London Symphony's premiere season at the new Barbican Centre (which, I admit, was not such a great success). Finally, Peter became the general director of the Los Angeles Opera, and I met him there to launch its initial subscription season in the 1980s. I'm happy to say that he enjoyed a fine decade there. I regret, however, to write that after too brief a retirement at his home in England he died of an on-going illness. Peter Hemmings was one of the finest arts managers I have known, and I am proud to have worked with him in perfect harmony on four continents.

My three-year Scottish Opera involvement began in the 1970s, but I first went to Scotland in the wartime 1940s, when, just released from a U.S. Army convalescent center in England, I was given a ten-day furlough, which I spent in Glasgow. There, I stayed in Geneen's Family Hotel in the long-since redeveloped Gorbals slum area and relaxed from the rigors of the war and the military discipline that had extended to the hospital and nursing facility from which I'd just emerged.

When, after a thirty-year hiatus I returned to Glasgow on Peter's invitation, newspapers ran my photograph. That night I found a telephone message from the Geneens' daughter, who remembered me although she'd been only a child when I was a guest at her parents' hotel. She had married a fine man and had children and a host of friends, many of them among the community's cultural elite. A few evenings later I met them in her beautiful home. Later in the week I accompanied my hosts to a splendid Scottish National Orchestra concert, and we continued to correspond for some years. I also squeezed in some sightseeing—including in Edinburgh, which was only a thirty-minute train ride away—and learned a lot more about Glasgow and its citizenry than I had come to know on my wartime visit three decades earlier. I returned to Scotland once more in 1980 to conduct performing arts promotional seminars for the Scottish Arts Council's constituents.

Just a few days after I'd checked into Geneen's Hotel in 1945, it was suddenly V.E. Day, the end of the War in Europe; V.J. Day, the end of the War in the Pacific, was still some months ahead. I didn't know it then, but I was soon to be back in France and then again Scotland, where I flew from Prestwick Airport back to the United States. Although I certainly cannot recommend Scotland as a place to visit in the winter I can enthusiastically recommend the Scots (in any season), so many of whom I have found to be warm, friendly, and helpful to visitors. I've also been to Scotland in summer when it's most beautiful.

17

Jan Kiepura, Grand Opera's High-D Specialist, and His Wife, the Adorable Operetta Star Marta Eggerth, Enchant Sentimental Audiences Everywhere!

In the 1945–46 season I handled—following its Broadway run—*Polonaise,* a touring show of Frédéric Chopin's music and starring Jan Kiepura and Marta Eggerth. The Polish-born Kiepura, then winding down his grand opera and film careers, was recklessly willing to risk his still potent voice by submitting it to the cruel rigors of an eight-performance week legitimate theater regimen. In an era of great tenors he possessed one of his generation's truly thrilling voices, powerful, ringing, and exciting. He was fearless in the upper range. Eggerth, his leading lady in *Polonaise* and wife in real life, was a lovely Hungarian blonde who starred in operettas and—like Kiepura—was the *liebling* (darling) of central European audiences. Before World War II they also costarred in such movies as the international hit *Be Mine Tonight* from the UFA Studios in Germany. During the war the couple lived in the United States, where he appeared at the Metropolitan Opera and in Erich Wolfgang Korngold's Hollywood musical *Give Us This Night.*

In the 1950s the Kiepuras made a succession of farewell appearances in major European centers, where they played to packed houses of adoring, sentimental audiences. In the United States they presented annual sold-out recitals and operetta performances in Chicago, Buffalo, and Hammtramack (a virtually all-Polish suburban enclave near Detroit), those three great centers of Polish American population. The couple lived in a New York City apartment building they owned on East Ninety-sixth Street off Madison Avenue. Artist though he was, Jan was in certain respects a practical man and possessed considerable business acumen. He was always able to recognize a good real estate investment when he saw one.

They also had a farm in upstate New York where Jan's brother, the tenor Ladis Kiepura, resided. Jan discouraged Ladis's singing career. "If he performs badly," he told me, "the public might think it's me!" In that post–World War II era the brothers sometimes followed one another in successive stage revivals of the popular Stanislaw Moniuszko opera *Halka*, appearing before primarily Polish American audiences. In Chicago the presenter was always impresario Harry Zelzer, which ultimately caused the *Tribune*'s Claudia Cassidy, doyenne of the city's music critics, to write, "If Harry brings *Halka* here once more, I'm going to start calling him Halka-Zelzer!"

Marta Eggerth, laden with talent and charm, was adored by audiences everywhere and was a gracious and tremendous asset to Jan in their many joint appearances. She was also a doting mother. I recall accompanying her as she strolled down Chicago's Michigan Avenue with her first child, Scarbecek, in his baby carriage.

Jan would end his principal *Polonaise* aria, "Now I Know Your Face by Heart," to tumultuous applause on a beautiful A and then give a rousing encore, upping the ante with a concluding high C. The audience would go wild, inspiring him to still another encore that finished on a thrilling high D! Pandemonium would break loose—and he did that *at all eight performances,* every week!

Jan, who had a keen sense of the importance of public occasions, was often called upon to appear and make statements on matters concerning the Polish American community. Sometimes his words tended toward grandiloquence. On one occasion we returned from a publicity appointment to learn the sad news of the death of a prominent Polish American journalist. Jan asked me to connect him with Western Union and then intoned in accented English to the widow, "Dear Lady: From the depths of my pure Polish heart, I send you my deepest sympathy." Our publicity rounds brought us to all manner of social gatherings in Polonia, Chicago's Polish neighborhood, and often to dances where Jan threw himself with unfeigned fervor into the polka and *krakowiak*, partnered by ethnically costumed young women who were giddily gleeful and ecstatic at the momentous occasion. They had danced with the great Jan Kiepura! Once we made a courtesy call at Wieczorek's Pharmacy on Milwaukee Avenue, which was our extension box office for his Orchestra Hall concerts. A crowd gathered on the sidewalk and around the block, everyone thrilled to catch a glimpse of their national cultural hero.

Jan greatly admired the elegant Polish spoken by my Warsaw University–educated actress-wife Dina Halpern; Marta, too, fell victim to her charm. Over the years, they entertained us on various occasions in Chicago, New York, and London.

A special laryngological instrument enabled Jan to study the color of his vocal chords before performances. If you were a good friend he permitted a quick peek into the reflecting mirror, and I was accorded that privilege. Although I didn't think of him as a hypochondriac, Jan did travel with a considerable arsenal of medications, both prescribed and patent, which were crowded haphazardly onto his dressing table.

I publicized what turned out to be Jan's final Orchestra Hall appearance in Chicago as I had the previous ones. We not only had to sweat out the problem of his increasing need to often sing at less than full voice but were also concerned about a complete box-office boycott by Chicago's Poles. That previously faithful group was angry at a statement Jan made that they considered conciliatory to the Polish communist regime. At issue was a vain and misguided effort to retrieve a luxurious mountain resort hotel—the Patria—in Krynica, which Jan built before the war and was used by German army officers during the war and then later confiscated by the Soviets. (Jan, in an obviously conciliatory statement, had in effect said that, after all, both the present occupants of the Patria Hotel and my family are good and loyal Poles.) When hostilities ended, the new Polish communist regime seized the Patria, declaring it national property.

American Poles—overwhelmingly bitter anticommunists—considered Jan's well-intended statement an act of unforgivable betrayal. With the Chicago recital only days away and our ticket sales paralyzed, concert manager Harry Zelzer and I sought the advice of our friend Sig Sakiewicz, the *Polish Zgoda* (Polish Daily News) English-language columnist. With his guidance we arranged for Jan to sing mass on the following Sunday at St. Stanislaus Kostka Church, thus demonstrating that he was not in sympathy with the atheistic communists but still a practicing Catholic.

The Chicago-area Polish press and radio immediately trumpeted Jan's return to the righteous path. When we arrived at the church that Sunday morning it was filled to overflowing and the surrounding sidewalks and streets were jammed with those who couldn't get in. We climbed to the choir loft, and soon the religious service began. I don't know what was running through Jan's mind, but *I* was *very* worried because I had been with him the day before when he rehearsed for the recital with piano accompanist Alexander Aster. He was, I noted, certainly not in his usual good voice.

How would he be able to render the mass? I wondered. As it turned out I need not have worried. Incredibly, his voice was suddenly as firm and strong and beautiful as when I first heard it years before. As Jan sang on, and with deep feeling, I was standing opposite him, so moved that I began to cry. Seeing the tears roll down my cheeks seemed to inspire him all the more. I heard him on many later occasions tell people how I had sobbed that day in the choir loft. Although we had been warm friends before, I now felt that he had come to love me. When the service was over a platoon of priests accompanied our walk to the nearby rectory for lunch while hundreds of parishioners gaped and cheered. The boycott was immediately over. A few nights later Jan and Marta performed to a sold-out Orchestra Hall.

Earlier that week Jan had learned that the tenor Moshe Kusevitzky—a renowned cantor in Warsaw during the 1930s who survived the Holocaust by taking refuge in Russia—was to give a Chicago recital. Would I, he asked, take him? Jan told me that as aspiring young singers he and Moshe studied with the same voice teacher in Poland. Kusevitzky had escaped German death camps by taking refuge in Soviet Russia, where he became a successful opera and concert singer through the early 1940s. For the Chicago concert that Jan and I attended he programmed some of the most difficult opera arias of the tenor repertoire and executed them with ease. Kusevitzky also sang several major Hebrew liturgical selections, making his mastery of that highly specialized field evident. At the intermission Jan and I paid a polite visit to Kusevitzky in his dressing room, and I noted that Jan became distracted during the second half of the evening. When we met the next morning he was still pensive and said, "I was greatly affected by the music I heard last night. My heavens, how much the Jewish people must have suffered in order to create music like that."

Then Jan told me a story I had not heard about his origins. He said that his father, the young son of a Polish baker in Sosnowiecz, and a teen-aged Jewish girl had fallen in love, eloped, and were secretly married by a priest. Her deeply religious Chassidic parents mourned her for dead, and she never saw them again. When Jan was born (according to age-old Jewish law, a child born of a Jewish mother is automatically considered Jewish), a group of Jewish elders came to insist on a religious upbringing for him, but a large force of angry Poles set upon them and beat them off. "So," Jan concluded, "if the Jews had attacked in greater force, I would probably be a Jewish cantor like Kusevitzky today!"

I first came to know Jan well more than a half century ago. He was essentially a European who never quite adjusted to American ways. He hated the salted butter served in many restaurants, for example, preferring the more familiar sweet European version. One day when we were at breakfast in the Congress Hotel dining room, he called over our waiter and, pointing to the butter on the table, asked, "What is that?" "That is butter, sir," the waiter replied. Whereupon Jan responded in a powerful voice heard all over the room, "In Poland, we give such butter to *pigs!*" He also complained that the way the Congress's windows opened didn't admit enough fresh air.

Jan couldn't understand American critics' often negative reaction to his florid acting style while European critics wrote mainly about his thrilling voice. Neither did he appreciate the bantering, kidding style of some journalists, one of whom wrote that "the passionate love affair 'twixt Jan and Kiepura is positively scandalous!" To his credit, however, Jan was a good sport. When the Hearst drama critic Ashton Stevens called him a "Polish Ham," we went to a Polish neighborhood butcher shop, where he posed for newspaper photographs while contemplating a real ham in the display window! He was enthralled when I told him, "Jan you're not just the best tenor in the world, you're the best tenor in the world *and* suburbs!"

He thought that U.S. audience responses were tepid compared to those abroad. It was not unusual, he told me, for aficionados to scoop him up when he emerged from a stage door after performing in Germany, Austria, France, or Italy and sweep him onto the roof of a nearby car. They would then demand that he sing on and on for them from his perch—and he would happily comply. "You Americans," he stated, "are cold fish!"

Jan was not inclined to express admiration for other tenors. Once I took him to Chicago's celebrated Chez Paree night club, where Kenny Baker, the light lyric tenor star of Jack Benny's early radio show, was appearing. After Baker's first set Jan applauded politely then turned to me and—not exactly in a whisper—uttered the ultimate put-down for a tenor: "He eez *barrritone*, no?"

All opera tenors I know carefully husband their vocal resources, limiting performing to two or three—at the most—times a week. Jan, however, told me that he could easily sing *every* day, just as enjoying sex daily was his norm (he said). Was he as serious about the sex as the singing? Perhaps, in America, he had learned about kidding!

One morning before we left the hotel for a publicity appointment he stopped at the desk to cash a check and identified himself as "Jan Kiepura." When the cashier asked for official identification he couldn't believe that she didn't know who Jan Kiepura was. Perhaps he assumed she *did* know but thought that *he* was an impostor. "I'll show you that I *am* Jan Kiepura" he insisted and emitted a piercing high note that electrified everyone in the lobby—including the manager who rushed over and cashed the check immediately.

When in 1966 Jan Kiepura died at the age of sixty-four, the Associated Press reported that a million Poles lined Warsaw streets to view his funeral cortege. Although he had not been in his native land since before World War II, his people still idolized him along with Chopin and Ignacy Paderewski as one of their nation's musical giants.

18

Yul Brynner, Macho Celebrity, and Dolly Haas, "Wisp of a Porcelain Actress," Star in Touring *Lute Song:* Thirty-seven Days of Passionate Press-Agentry

On Monday, September 16, 1946, *Lute Song,* that exquisite music-drama costarring Dolly Haas and Yul Brynner, began its national tour at Chicago's Studebaker Theatre. Its Broadway run was respectable, but the show wasn't a commercial hit in New York. In Chicago it played several weeks sponsored by the Theatre Guild's American Subscription Society. Although the show received great reviews, including an all-out rave from the *Tribune*'s brilliant critic of all the performing arts Claudia Cassidy, no immediate individual ticket-sales momentum was generated that could have resulted in an extended run. *Lute Song* left for its West Coast subscription bookings, where single-ticket sales proved insufficient to encourage extending those engagements.

The management, contractually obligated to bringing the company back to New York, decided to "break the jump" by returning to Chicago for a few weeks. There had, after all, been some positive action at the box office just before the show left that city in the fall. On the show's return engagement to Chicago, I became its press agent. How that came about went back to the night of September 16, when the production had its

Chicago premiere and I was in the house as guest of *Lute Song* company manager John Charles "Charlie" Gilbert.

I emerged from the theater that evening in a state of exaltation, swept away by what I thought to be my most enchanting theater experience. The lovely Dolly Haas was entirely believable as the pious and devoted wife and daughter-in-law; her performances could well have served as an effective antidote for the cynicism of the postwar era. As Claudia Cassidy described Dolly, "A wisp of a porcelain actress who turns out to your delight to be a creature of flesh and blood and full theatrical dimensions." About Yul Brynner she wrote, "He is precisely right in appearance, in voice the texture of rough silk, in swift, supple movement, in that look of integrity that makes sense."

In the theater lobby that night a radio interviewer asked audience members about their impressions of the entertainment they had just witnessed, thus beating the print journalists whose reviews would not appear until the next day. When the broadcaster, who was my friend, spied me, he ran over, put his mike in my face, and asked my opinion. "If I were the producer of *Lute Song*," I replied, "I'd be very proud tonight" and went on with much enthusiasm. I didn't know that the show's producer, Michael Myerberg was standing close by. Several months later Gilbert told me that Myerberg had whispered to him, "Who is this guy?" Gilbert told him that I was a press agent pal of his. "Why in the hell didn't we get him for the *Lute Song* tour?" Myerberg asked.

Gilbert didn't forget Myerberg's question, and before the show returned to Chicago he sent me a contract. I was in promotional charge when *Lute Song* reopened at the Studebaker to a new welcome of press praise. The production deserved such hosannahs. In addition to Dolly Haas, who had replaced Mary Martin while the show was still running on Broadway, and Yul Brynner, Meyerberg assembled a brilliant ensemble and top-level creative people. Among them were the dramatists Sidney Howard and Will Irwin, who had done the adaption of the popular Chinese classic *Pu-Pa-Ki*; composer Raymond Scott; lyricist Bernard Hanighen; the fabled scenic, costume, and lighting designer Robert Edmond Jones; stage director John Houseman; and choreographer Yeichi Nimura. Some of the actors who appeared in the New York and/or Chicago casts were Clarence Derwent, Augustin Duncan, McKay Morris, Rex O'Malley, Ralph Clanton, Mildred

Dunnock, Nancy Davis (later to become Nancy Reagan), and Virginia Gilmore (Mrs. Yul Brynner). Myerberg, whom I came to know well, told me that in his eagerness to obtain box-office insurance he had mistakenly cast the young star Mary Martin, primarily a singer, in the lead when what he needed was a dramatic actress who could also sing well. Dolly, a luminary of the pre-Hitler-era German stage and screen, was exactly that.

The renewed Chicago run of *Lute Song* in early January 1947 gathered steam at the ticket wicket. Instead of a few weeks it went on for months as I stoked the promotional fires, beginning with thirty-seven consecutive days of picture breaks that included a high-speed diapering contest between Dolly and Yul, each of whom had an infant on tour with them. We also hogged virtually all of the many radio interviews (television had not yet become a factor). We were able to earn back some of Myerberg's earlier tour losses, and the show went on to new bookings in Detroit and Washington before finally closing as the summer came on.

Dolly had many friends who came to see her in her upstairs dressing room at the Studebaker. I particularly recall novelist Thomas Mann's daughter Erika; the golden-voiced actor Jose Ferrer, then appearing at the Blackstone Theatre in *Cyrano de Bergerac;* and orchestra conductor Otto Klemperer, whose painful back injuries forced him to conduct sitting down. In later years his son, the actor Werner Klemperer, gained fame as the bumbling Colonel Klink on TV's *Hogan's Heroes.*

Dolly's darling infant daughter, Nina, stayed with her throughout the season while Dolly's celebrated husband, the caricaturist Al Hirschfeld, was away on a round-the-world assignment with his buddy S. J. Perelman, the sophisticated humorist. Via Al's relentless and ingenious placement of her name in his drawings for the *New York Times* since her birth in 1945, Nina long ago surpassed the fifteen minutes of fame predicted for us all by Andy Warhol. Until his death in 2003 at the age of ninety-nine, Al worked imperturbably from his time-battered barber chair in his lofty Ninety-fifth Street (Manhattan) aerie, flaunting his jaunty, Jovian beard—like Cyrano's plume—as he continued to chronicle in inimitable fashion *everybody* who was *anybody* in our wonderful world of the entertainment arts—the whole spectrum!

More than fifty-seven years have passed since I came to know the Hirschfelds, including Dolly's mother and Al's parents. Like them, Dolly is long gone. Yet I salute her daily as I pass through our dining room and see the exquisite Lucile Leighton oil painting of her, caparisoned, coiffed, and made up as the lovely Tchao-Ou-Niaong in *Lute Song*. Undoubtedly, as Myerberg predicted, the presence of Dolly Haas infused the production with dramatic validity that made all the difference in its audience impact.

Nina, long a Texan, stops off between trains in Chicago to visit with us. Louise Kerz Hirschfeld, Al's luminous wife of recent years and a highly valued person of the theater arts, also remains a dear friend of my wife Alyce and me. We treasure the drawings that Al gave us over the years, including two caricatures of me, one commissioned by Theatre Communication Group in 1981 and the other by *Forbes Magazine* for a centerfold in 1984 that illustrated Martin Mayer's essay about my unremitting pursuit of arts audiences.

Our producer, the shrewd Michael Myerberg, who owned New York's Mansfield Theatre (long ago renamed the Brooks Atkinson Theatre), discovered Yul playing his guitar in a New York City nightclub and signed him for the leading role of the young student Tsai Yong, a wonderful opportunity to make an important Broadway debut. Undoubtedly, Myerberg thought Yul to be a charismatic performer, and he was right although Yul was still five years away from his big career breakthrough in the 1951 production of *The King and I*, for which he shaved his head and won a Tony Award. Yul, who was balding when I met him in 1946, wore a lacquered, Chinese-style wig for *Lute Song*.

He was certainly one of the most fascinating young performers I have encountered. Although still far from true stardom, he comported himself as if he had long been an established major celebrity. His special blend of impudence, arrogance, and charisma somehow made him irresistibly charming, especially to young women. Certainly, he was a dapper, dashing bon vivant and heartbreaker if there ever was one! Yul loved to be seen with important people. I recall how pleased he was when the renowned couturier Mainbocher would come in from New York to visit him. Yul spun for me, with much pleasure, a multitude of outrageous tales about the exciting, dangerous, and glamorous life he led. Because he was only thirty-one at the time, I realized that he could not have possibly done—or experienced—more than a tiny percentage of what I came to think of as fantasies. He did, I think, come to *really* believe them, however!

Once I thought I'd have some fun with him. Sitting at the old Underwood typewriter in the counting room next to the theater box office, I quickly fabricated a wildly imaginative version of his life story. Led on by his high-powered, exciting, and fanciful tales, I imagined him to be a formidable, Jackie Chan–like martial arts martinet who had been mentored under the severe regimen of ascetic Buddhist monks in the snow-clad mountain fastness of Tibet. There, I posited, he was tutored in all manner of kung fu, karate, and jiujitsu. Knowing Yul, I was sure he'd love it all—and he did. I convinced a columnist friend to go along with my jape.

When my piece appeared in the newspaper several days later I tacked it to the backstage call-board and awaited Yul's entrance through the stage door. When he appeared I pointed to the call-board. He went to it and read the column thoroughly, his face becoming wreathed in smiles. He then rushed over to me, jubilantly pumped my right hand, and exclaimed, "Danny dear, how did you know that it was all *exactly* that way? Thank you! Thank you!" Talk about savoir faire, sangfroid, composure, cool, or what have you. Yul had them *all*—and in spades! For years afterward, especially after his major success in *The King and I,* when I read about Yul and heard him interviewed I couldn't help but suspect that he was claiming some of my 1946–47 untruths about him as authentic experiences. We'll never know! According to his curriculum vitae, Yul was a native of Sakhalin Island off the Siberian coast. Also, we're told that his father was a Mongolian mining engineer and his mother a Rumanian gypsy and that he was once a trapeze performer in France, a student at the Sorbonne, and so on—ad colorful!

Yul had been a director early in television before the original stage presentation of *The King and I,* and through that production he came to the stardom to which he felt entitled. In later years Yul and Richard Rodgers and Oscar Hammerstein had a veritable cash cow in touring revivals of the exotic musical show that followed the 1956 film version's success. Yul also starred in many movies. Among the forty-some with which he is credited are *Anastasia, The Ten Commandments, The Magnificent Seven,*

Westworld, The Brothers Karamazov, The Buccaneer, The Journey, The Sound and the Fury, Solomon and Sheba, Taras Bulba, Cast a Giant Shadow, and *The Madwoman of Chaillot.*

Before he died in 1985 at the age of seventy after suffering from lung cancer, Yul taped antismoking commercials that were posthumously aired. His wife was the actress Virginia Gilmore. Although I've been involved with hundreds of stage productions, two of them—both musical shows—remain on high pedestals in my memory: the 1946–47 *Lute Song* starring Dolly Haas and Yul Brynner and the 1952 *Porgy and Bess* starring William Warfield, Leontyne Price, and Cab Calloway.

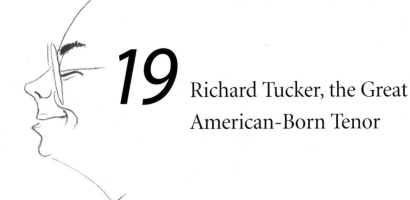

19 Richard Tucker, the Great American-Born Tenor

I first heard Richard Tucker's gorgeous, passionately produced voice more than sixty years ago on the nationally heard WGN/Mutual Broadcasting Company radio program *Chicago Theatre of the Air,* which featured beloved operas and operettas sung in English. After I came to know Richard well I found it hard to reconcile his super-perfect, polished renditions of English-language lyrics with his off-microphone, off-stage, classic Brooklynese patois. I recall listening to a radio baseball broadcast in 1947 with Richard and his little—now middle-aged—son, Barry, in the Tuckers' Brooklyn apartment. When an umpire's close decision went against their beloved Dodgers, Richard, in no way favoring his valuable vocal chords, screamed "Moider da bum!" (the umpire). (Richard sent me a photograph more than forty years ago of himself, Barry, and his younger sons David and Henry playing touch football on their front lawn.) After the broadcast, Sara, Richard's wonderful wife who is now also of blessed memory, served a delicious dinner. Her widowed father Levi Perelmuth, who was also the father of tenor Jan Peerce, lived with them, and Richard's affection and respect for him was obvious. How odd of God, I thought, to have made this sweet old gentleman the father and father-in-law of America's two greatest lyric tenors. Richard's original name was Reuben Ticker, and family and old friends addressed him as Ruby; Richard Tucker was his professional name.

In Chicago I publicized a number of Richard's Orchestra Hall recitals; his work with the old Chicago Opera Company, the Metropolitan Opera, and Lyric Opera of Chicago; and also his affiliation with the Austro-Galician congregation, where he was the High Holy Days cantor, and his thirteen years with Chicago's Park Synagogue. I prize the wristwatch, its numerals in Hebrew, that he gave me in the mid-1960s; its reverse is inscribed "Sincere Thanks, Everlasting Friendship, Richard Tucker."

Richard followed up his 1945 Metropolitan Opera debut in New York with a Chicago Opera Company debut in 1946. He was Edgardo in *Lucia di Lammermoor* opposite the sixteen-year-old Patrice Munsel in the title role, with Fausto Cleva conducting Gaetano Donizetti's florid feast of thrusting tenor brilliance and coloratura fireworks. Most operagoers are unaware that Richard was then an established cantor who attracted large crowds of worshippers to the Brooklyn Center Synagogue for ten years before his debut at the Metropolitan. When Edward Johnson, the Met's general manager, heard Richard's ideal lyric tenor voice and savored his impeccable musicianship he did something without precedent by signing him for the leading tenor role of Enzio in *La Gioconda*. A tenor who had not sung a supporting role started out at the top! Richard had studied opera for years, paying for the lessons by selling fur coat linings in the Manhattan garment district.

Pietro Moranzoni—who had been Chicago Civic Opera's conductor during the 1920s and 1930s but was now retired—showed up backstage with no advance notice and asked for a seat for the premiere of *Lucia di Lammermoor*. We were entirely sold out, all 3,600 seats, so I invited him to sit with me in the wings. Although it was a fine performance and the young but as yet not internationally famous tenor sang gloriously, the aged maestro made no comment until the final act and completion of Edgardo's passionate and melting double aria "Fra poco a me ricovero. . . . Tu che a Dio spiegasti l'ali." While the audience was going wild with seemingly never-ending applause for Tucker, the veteran conductor at my side uttered his first words of the evening: "Theesa tenorr, he ees Eetalian, no?"

"No, Maestro," I replied. "He's American." The applause continued, and Moranzoni shot another question at me, "Eesa poppa and momma, they Eetalian, ah?" I answered in the negative, adding that they were Rumanian Jews. As the ovation went on he tried again, and this time he thought he had me when he asked, "Eesa stody in Eetaly, ah?" I deprived him of all hope when I said that Tucker had made all his career preparations in New York City. As the applause was near its end Moranzoni turned to me and stated defiantly, "Ah donta care, eesa the best Eetalian tenor ah ever hear!"

Richard's Chicago opera debut was an all-out triumph with both public and press. Claudia Cassidy, who admired him for the rest of his life, compared his *Lucia* tomb scene with that of the fabled Beniamino Gigli, and Chicago operagoers loved him forever after. He made annual visits with the Met tour and also appeared in fourteen Lyric opera productions from 1956 through 1970, including *La Forza del Destino, La Gioconda, Simon Boccanegra, La Bohème, Lucia di Lammermoor, Rigoletto, Un Ballo in Maschera, Tosca,* and *Don Carlo.*

A rift between Richard and Carol Fox, Lyric's founder and general manager, interrupted his appearances there for a few seasons. He had missed an important rehearsal because he flew via tiny commuter airplane through a perilous blizzard to upstate New York to chant the funeral liturgy for his old friend Arthur Winarick, owner of a Catskill Mountains summer resort, the Concord. On another occasion when he felt Fox slighted him Richard notified us that he wouldn't sing as contracted. I was assigned the task of getting him to relent. At first I failed, but then I reached Sara, who was always wonderful to me, and she got him onto the next airplane for Chicago.

In the early fall of 1948 Richard was the guest cantor for one of Milwaukee's largest synagogues. While rehearsing there with the choristers, he called to ask that Dina and I join him for dinner. We did so the next day, riding the electric train ninety miles to Milwaukee and arriving in the late afternoon. Richard was awaiting us on the train platform. When Dina made her American debut in New York in 1938 Richard had been in the audience. At dinner that evening he told us that the year before, 1947, he had sung with a fabulous young soprano in Verona. Her name was Maria Callas. Six years later—in 1954—she would make her historic American debut with Lyric Opera of Chicago. Richard prophetically predicted a great career for Maria, although he told us that she would have to lose some weight. She did—about a hundred pounds!

When Richard was High Holy Days cantor of Chicago's Austro-Galician congregation during the early 1950s I brought press photographers to choral rehearsals. His choir leader—a Mr. Tappo—was so carried away with Richard's deeply moving and highly emotional incantation of the penitential Slichos service that he fainted at exactly the same high point of those sacred prayers—*two years in a row!* I greatly admired on both occasions how Richard continued to sing, not missing a beat, while the stricken Mr. Tappo was carried off the platform.

Richard, who fought an eternal battle with his weight, loved late-night, post-performance orgies involving lox, bagels, cream cheese, and scrambled eggs at Fritzel's Restaurant with boon local companions that included his press agent. His backstage dressing room–salon was always packed with colleagues and pals. While his makeup was applied and his wig was being adjusted he somehow managed to scrutinize the score of an opera he was to perform in a few days, check baseball scores and stock market quotations, and make inquiries concerning the health of friends' wives, children, and grandchildren. It was lively in that tiny dressing room!

Alfred C. Stepan, a chemical tycoon and Lyric Opera of Chicago board president, regarded Richard as the generation's greatest tenor. As a major donor to Notre Dame University, Al prevailed upon its president, Father Theodore M. Hesburgh, to present Richard with an honorary doctorate from that very Catholic institution, a fact widely noted in the press. When Richard sang at the Ravinia Music Festival, Al threw a lavish "mother of all postperformance parties" on the grounds of his Winnetka estate. We once sat together at a Lyric-sponsored, off-season recital by Luciano Pavarotti. At its conclusion Luciano "murdered 'em" with his celebrated rendition of "Nessun Dorma" from Giacomo Puccini's *Turandot*. As the monumental applause finally was ending, Al turned to me, grabbed my arm, and loyally and fiercely whispered, "Danny, it *ain't* Richard!"

Both Richard and Luciano—unlike most opera tenors—raved about other artists of their genre. In Luciano's foreword to James A. Drake's *Richard Tucker: A Biography* (1984) he writes three remarkable pages of praise, including the observation that Richard's and Jussi Björling's careers proved that non-Italians could become "great *Italian* tenors!" He also recalls Richard's La Scala debut in *Luisa Miller,* when "the audience didn't merely applaud, they *erupted,* screamed, stamped their feet, tore up their programs, and showered him with the confetti." "When I was studying voice," Luciano remembers, "Richard was one of my idols. His technique was as close to perfect as one can get!" The gracious Sara Tucker sent me that newly minted biography and inscribed it "Danny, you will love reading about Richard's life and career, and you were part of it."

Lyric's artistic director Bruno Bartoletti also headed the opera in Florence, Italy, and was a frequent conductor at Teatro Colón in Buenos Aires. An ardent admirer of Richard's Chicago performances, Bartoletti exported him to Italy and Argentina. The maestro told me of arriving at Richard's Buenos Aires hotel one morning for a prerehearsal scan of an opera score and finding his tenor wrapped in a large prayer shawl and wearing phylacteries. Although Richard's career precluded full religious observances, he managed to adhere to a traditional Jewish way of life in many ways and wherever he was. Indeed, he possessed a fierce pride in being Jewish. If he really was one of the great tenors, he wanted it known that he was a tenor who was Jewish. That belief was undoubtedly rooted in Richard's knowledge of the anti-Semitism that once barred European Jews from careers in Western music. Although Richard had great belief in his abilities and capacities as a singer, he always credited his gift to God. He felt that the Ribono Shel Olam (master of the universe) had given him that voice for a higher purpose than his own benefit. It seemed to me that the higher purpose was not only that Richard serve the cause of the musical arts but also bring honor to the Jewish people.

If Richard possessed a considerable sense of his worth as an artist, he—like Luciano Pavarotti—was capable of humility in the presence of other greats. He was full-hearted in his admiration for Leonard Warren, his baritone colleague, and for the cantor Moshe Kusevitzky, the fabled master of the high tessitura. Richard was the finest cantor America had produced, but Kusevitzky, the cantor of Warsaw, was his mentor. "Danny," Richard told me, "all of us cantors can learn from him." The men were neighbors in Great Neck, New York, and Richard regularly visited and comforted the older man during his final illness in the late 1960s.

As Richard entered his sixties—an age at which most opera singers are long past their prime—there was no diminution of his vocal prowess. I heard him for the last time in late 1974, and he had it all, the ringing, luminous, silvery trumpet sound of his youth matured into a new, rich and lustrous baritonal quality. He was still in total control from top to bottom with a diamond-hard musical focus and surpassing sweetness and warmth that was, as one critic wrote, "more to be expected in tenors from Naples than tenors from Brooklyn!"

On January 8, 1975, I was working in New York and staying at the Biltmore Hotel with Dina. At 6 P.M. I turned on the radio for the evening newscast only to hear the shocking announcement of Richard's death. I could only utter the traditional words Jews repeat upon hearing such news, "Boruch dayan emes" (blessed be the true judge).

We stayed on for the chapel visitation the next evening. On the following sad, wintry day, and in the presence of four thousand mourners, deeply moving funeral ceremonies were held onstage at the Metropolitan Opera House. Richard's voice had rung out and been heard and treasured by opera lovers there for a full thirty years and in thirty roles. Then the Met's great golden curtain closed for the last time on Richard Tucker. "May his memory be for a blessing."

Richard's willingness to assist aspiring singers was legendary. Thus, the Tucker family and Richard's friends and admirers established a perfect living memorial for him in the Richard Tucker Foundation, which materially and successfully backs the careers of young opera artists.

20

Truman, Stalin, and a Daring Ticket Sales Strategy for *Porgy and Bess*

More than half a century has passed since I came to know and cherish those fine artists and gentle persons who remained my lifelong friends: baritone William Warfield and soprano Leontyne Price. In December 2000 I was given the honor of being the sole speaker at Bill's eightieth birthday celebration, a magnificent and moving musical tribute in the jam-packed Pick-Staiger Hall at Northwestern University. On that occasion I reprised the unusual circumstances of our meeting in 1952.

Leontyne was the tragic protagonist of the *Porgy and Bess* stage production that brought us all together. In later years I publicized her in the title roles of such memorable Lyric Opera of Chicago presentations as *Turandot, Thaïs, Aida,* and *Madama Butterfly* as well as for various concert and recital events. She and Bill plighted their troth in 1952 while we were busy with the historic legitimate-stage production of *Porgy and Bess,* the George Gershwin musical show that was nine years in the making and that experts have only recently begun to admit is a full-scale opera.

In mid-1952 the producer Blevins Davis asked me to publicize his major stage revival of *Porgy and Bess.* I was over my head, however, with other show business assignments. I was house manager of Chicago's Selwyn Theatre, where Joan Bennett starred in the hit play *Bell, Book and Candle;* press agent for Russian, Italian, French, and British art films at the World Playhouse; handling vaudeville and pictures at the 3,200-seat Oriental Theatre; and managing my own Astor movie house at Clark and Madison Streets. I was also preparing for my annual promotion of the Kelly Bowl football extravaganza in Soldier Field and the upcoming annual visits of the New York City and Metropolitan Operas. *And* I hoped, somehow, to get away for a few weeks of vacation in Buenos Aires, where my wife Dina Halpern was performing in a Ruth and Augustus Goetz drama, *The Heiress,* based on the Henry James novel *Washington Square.* In addition, I was publicizing a series of almost weekly Sunday afternoon recitals and concerts at Orchestra Hall that concert manager Harry Zelzer, my colorful friend and the Chicago retailer for the equally colorful New York wholesaler and impresario Sol Hurok, was presenting. And then there were Columbia Artists and the few other major concert managements who represented visiting orchestras, dance troupes, choruses, vocal soloists, pianists, and violinists. There was every reason then why I should *not* undertake the responsibilities involved in promoting a new *Porgy and Bess* production.

But the joy and excitement of it all lured me in! Too, I was more than touched by Davis's "I won't take no for an answer" insistence that I take on the project. *Porgy and Bess* was to come to the Civic Opera House for a crucial four-week run after a few weeks of tryout performances at the Dallas State Fair Grounds Auditorium. It would then go on to the Big Apple.

Blevins Davis lived in Independence, Missouri, and had never produced a show. He was, however, a close friend of President Harry Truman, who rescued him from the sheltered life of a teacher by introducing him to Democratic politics and to a fine and very wealthy woman, Margaret Sawyer Hill. They married and shortly thereafter Blevins became her widower and heir. He had always wanted to enter show business so he backed Robert Breen, a brilliant New York theater director wanting to stage a new production of *Porgy and Bess.* Breen then assigned Wolfgang Roth, a refugee artist, who created the show's marvelous scenic designs. For the role of Porgy, he signed the already-celebrated young singing actor William Warfield, who was handsome, exciting, noble of mien, and possessed of a beautiful baritone voice of considerable amplitude. For Bess, Breen chose the supremely talented and rising young soprano Leontyne Price, and for the role of Sportin' Life, the incomparable Cab Calloway of "Hi-Dee-Hi-Dee-Ho" fame. I was amused when Breen later told me that the great Calloway "had no rhythm." He wasn't criticizing that famed maestro's musical beat but his acting, which, Breen said, was wooden and required the kind of painstaking instruction usually provided for theater novices. As musical director and conductor, the noted Alexander Smallens, who had conducted the work's world premiere in 1935, was engaged.

Our *Porgy and Bess* opened in Dallas to a marvelous press reception but terribly disappointing attendance. One of the reasons may have been that Cheryl Crawford's revival production just a few years before had taken the edge off. Another reason concerned the on-going sociological metamorphosis of the African American community as long-simmering resentment began to fester and then foster higher levels of militancy. Such emotions boiled over at representations of African Americans as the illiterate, shabbily dressed, and superstitious folk of Catfish Row and above all at the fact that DuBose Heyward and George and Ira Gershwin, the creators of *Porgy and Bess* whether in book, play, or musical show form, were white.

By the time Davis and Breen were readying their revival those resentments had turned into a serious boycott, and there was continuous pressure against the work. Some eight years later, when Samuel Goldwyn engaged me to publicize his movie version of *Porgy and Bess,* he told me he'd owned film rights to the project for many years but was blocked time and again by black activists. They finally prevailed. He was forced to make many changes, which eventually compromised the production's artistic and financial success.

Now that we had opened in Dallas I was busy with the advance campaign for the four-week run at the Chicago Civic Opera House, but it appeared that—as in Dallas—advance ticket sales were disastersville! The box office ticket racks remained full despite strong publicity and heavy advertising. Blevins, who was with the show in Dallas, and I were talking back and forth daily. Deeply disappointed, he wanted to post the closing notice immediately on the call-board there. That, of course, would be the end of the project, blasting the hopes of all the artists involved and causing him immediate and extensive financial loss.

I couldn't get the superlatives of the Dallas reviews out of my mind, however, and those thoughts triggered an idea. If the show was really as great as reported, and if I could, somehow, fill the house for the entire opening week in Chicago, then word of mouth—so important to our business—might well perform the miracle we needed. I was young in those days and even more passionate and eloquent than I now am, so I convinced Blevins to hold the closing notice until he had seen me in the Chicago Civic Opera House the next morning. He must have gotten a 7 A.M. flight out of Dallas, for he met me before noon. I showed him four weeks' worth of racked-up tickets, hardly touched, and although we were due to open in Chicago only a week later I proposed to personally *give away* the entire capacity for the first week—twenty-eight thousand seats for eight performances! Thus I would create an overwhelming word-of-mouth pressure.

Blevins was intrigued by the idea although he must have had reservations concerning its chances for success. At any rate, with his go-ahead I began one of the hardest jobs I've ever tackled, distributing my largesse on every floor of every office building in the Loop area. I also went to myriad shops, outlying factories, and universities. By the day before the Chicago opening I had given away more than twenty-eight thousand complimentary reserved seats, all passes, and every one of them had to be punched by hand in those precomputer days.

The opening night was jammed to overflowing, and I saw the production for the first time. It was stunning! It was staged so brilliantly, and the performing talents were so great, that the audience was ecstatic. There had never been enough people in the Dallas house to go out and tell others how marvelous the show was. In the Civic Opera House, however, a bank of about eight telephones was located just opposite the elevators that went up to the boxes and balconies. During both intermissions our enthusiastic freeloaders lined up ten deep at each telephone to call friends and relatives and rave about what they were enjoying so much. I had never seen anything like it, and it continued at every other performance that week. The Chicago critics' reviews were terrific! They had experienced the show on opening night in a full house unlike the Dallas house that had many empty seats. By the time we reached the end of our first Chicago week, long lines were at the box office all day, buying—for real money—*all* the tickets for the final three weeks of the run. What resulted were the biggest grosses the cavernous venue had ever enjoyed.

Need I underscore what that sudden 1952 success meant to Blevins Davis, Bill Warfield, Leontyne Price, and all the marvelous artists involved? They were all in seventh heaven now that victory had been snatched from the jaws of defeat and the future of the show was suddenly bright! A few nights before the end of the Chicago run, our company manager, Zelda Dorfman, asked me to come backstage immediately after the final curtain. The company remained onstage, and Davis, Breen, Leontyne, Bill, and Cab made little speeches thanking me for saving their show. They also presented me with a beautiful leather wallet that more than a half century later is still in pristine condition. The following day I flew off on a long, many-legged (five stops for refueling) flight to meet my Dina at the Teatro Mitre on Buenos Aires's Avenida Corrientes.

Mentioning dear, eccentric Zelda Dorfman reminds me of an unfortunate occurrence during the *Porgy and Bess* Chicago engagement. She accepted, on behalf of the entire company, an invitation to a post–Saturday night–performance supper at the home of a noted Russian-born Chicago painter, Alexander Zlatoff-Mirsky. He prepared a magnificent late-night repast for our large company, but Zelda *forgot to tell* our performers and staffers, including myself, about the event. She suddenly remembered during the Saturday matinee and told me the sad story. By that time, however, it was too late because everybody had made their own plans for after the performance. With understandable trepidation *I* accompanied Zelda to the Zlatoff-Mirskys' Near North Side home late that night. There were just the two of us. I think it was the most embarrassing experience I've ever suffered. The aggrieved painter, who was very kind to us under the circumstances, was the father of the violinist Everett Zlatoff-Mirsky, then a small child and now the middle-aged and retired concertmaster of the Lyric Opera Orchestra.

The *Porgy and Bess* triumph in Chicago changed the show's previous touring plans overnight. Instead of going to New York it headed for Europe, with Hamburg, Germany, the first stop and then Soviet Russia. Blevins wanted me to pick up the show in Hamburg and take on the fateful and wonderful tour of the Soviet Union, then still under the heel of that heel

Josef Stalin. My negative feelings about Germany ran deep, however. I suffered greatly during the war; moreover, by 1952 I was aware that the Germans had tortured and murdered six million of my co-religionists *and* that Stalin's long-simmering anti-Semitism was becoming increasingly rabid. I felt that I should forego the tour and tend to my fast-growing number of assignments on American soil.

Porgy and Bess's Russian tour was sensational on both artistic and political levels. Upon arrival the company met the press, which—like the Soviet citizenry—had long been brainwashed to believe that African Americans were *all* uneducated victims of an exploitative imperialist system and that the artists were very much like the characters they portrayed—illiterate and simple-minded. In fact, numerous members of the company had university degrees and could more than hold their own in interviews. When that word got out (the controlled Soviet press being unlikely to point it out), a vast word-of-mouth campaign ensued. The U.S. State Department was overjoyed. The musically knowledgable Russian audiences adored Gershwin's heartfelt melodic feast. Undoubtedly, American art and American artists were successfully striking blows for our side.

At long last the Davis-Breen production of *Porgy and Bess* had its New York premiere at the Ziegfeld Theatre and the acclaim it deserved. By the next year it was again off on its long-delayed American tour, and I again handled publicity in Chicago. Over the many years there have continued to be new mountings of the work, but I judge ours, which I loved so much, to be the best.

One of the main reasons for the show's success was Leontyne Price, who scored a major success as Bess. I was further smitten by her luminous personality and vocal opulence when she appeared as Floria in Maestro Peter Herman Adler's pioneering televised version of *Tosca* in 1955. In 1959 she was the title-role artist in our Lyric Opera of Chicago's *Thaïs* and Liu in *Turandot,* and in 1960 she was our Aida and Cio-Cio-San. She didn't make her Metropolitan Opera debut until 1961, as Leonora in *Il Trovatore.*

Leontyne Mary Violet Price was born in Laurel, Mississippi, on February 10, 1927, to James A. Price, a sawmill worker, and Kate Baker Prince, a midwife. Leontyne studied at Central State College in Wilberforce, Ohio, and at the Juilliard School. Leontyne was inspired to become a singer by hearing the great Marian Anderson, famously barred from the stage of Washington, D.C.'s Constitution Hall by the Daughters of the American Revolution. Until 1985, when she retired from public appearance, her lovely, ravishing, and resonant *lyrico spinto* voice was heard in a wide-ranging soprano repertoire in London, Vienna, Verona, Paris, Milan, Berlin, San Francisco, Salzburg, and all the other ports of call for important opera stars. She was also, of course, presented by virtually all of the world's major symphony orchestras under the musical direction of the generation's most distinguished musical maestroes. Critics loved Leontyne; Harold Schonberg of the *New York Times,* for example, declared her the "Stradivarius of singers." She delighted in the presence of early friends and backers at her performances. Mrs. Alexander Chisholm, whom I met on several occasions, was from Leontyne's hometown and had befriended her greatly from the beginning. As a prescient voice teacher once told the aspiring soprano, "Your voice is like a brook that some day might be Niagara Falls!"

William Warfield's early 1950s success as Joe in the MGM movie version of the great Edna Ferber–Jerome Kern musical *Showboat* made him an international star. His magnificent bass rendition of "Ol' Man River" is unforgettable. He became a major attraction in every field open to a singer's art and was admired and respected wherever refined vocal artistry is cherished, whether in recitals, operas, symphonic appearances, films, oratorio narration, musical shows, radio, television, or legitimate theater. Although born in West Helena, Arkansas, Bill's early home was Rochester, New York, and he earned a bachelor of arts and a master's degree at that city's renowned Eastman School of Music. He then served in the U.S. Army and later appeared importantly in the national touring company of the Broadway hit *Call Me Mister* along with his vastly talented colleagues Buddy Hackett, Carl Reiner, and Robert Fosse.

Through the years Bill accumulated a formidable number of awards and honorary doctorates, made more USIA-sponsored foreign tours than any other American artist, and became known as one of the world's most accomplished singing actors, accounting for his extraordinary success as a recitalist. His starring role as "De Lawd" in the NBC-TV Hallmark Hall of Fame production of Marc Connelly's *Green Pastures* was a triumphant demonstration of actorial authority. He won three Grammy Awards in the "spoken word" category for his brilliant narration for Aaron Copland's *Lincoln Portrait* recording on the Mercury Phillips label.

Until his passing in late 2002 Bill continued to appear widely in concerts and conduct master classes at many institutions of higher learning. For more than a quarter century he was professor of music at the University of Illinois, where he became a beloved father figure and taught and inspired a generation of aspiring artists. Although I was his senior by one year, Bill Warfield also inspired me for the half century we knew each other. Happily, I saw him regularly because he was long an active board member of our Lyric Opera of Chicago's Center for American Artists.

In January 1981 Lyric Opera of Chicago presented Leontyne in a vocal recital at the Civic Opera House, and we had a pleasant reunion. We also sometimes met in airports. Not many years ago, although retired from opera, she was presented in recital by one of my clients, the Connecticut Opera Company in Stamford, and I was happy to tell her how well she was performing. The magic was still there.

Blevins Davis—Truman-indoctrinated—remained an enthusiast for the Democratic Party, and he invited me to various political and social events of importance. He never forgot that I had used what he believed to be prophetic knowledge to stop him from making the biggest mistake of his life. He had greatly enjoyed his new eminence as a successful theatrical producer. A novice, he tasted and savored the sweetness of show business success and was grateful to me for having steered him to it.

Gershwin's fascination with the African American musical idiom began when he was very young and was heightened by his discovery in 1926 of Heyward's novel, which was the literary progenitor of his opera-to-be. So intense was Gershwin's fascination with African American culture that he gave his own short shrift. In 1929, for example, he accepted a commission from the Metropolitan Opera to compose a work based on an S. Ansky drama *The Dybbuk,* but he seemed never to have proceeded with the project. This proved especially interesting to me when I was engaged by the Illinois Humanities Commission to create and present a lecture entitled "The Jewish Roots of George Gershwin's Music." The assignment was not only pleasurable but also highly informative because my research led me to answer a question, Did George Gershwin suffer from attacks by anti-Semites? I was surprised to learn that Virgil Thomson, the distinguished music critic–composer and WASP cultural Brahmin, whose own operas never enjoyed popular success, jealously and viciously lashed out at *Porgy and Bess,* deriding what he called its "gefilte fish orchestration!"

George Gershwin died at the age of thirty-eight. How many more artistic triumphs would have been his, and how much more would the world have been musically enriched, had he been able to live out his biblically allotted three score years and ten?

21 Audience Agape as Don José Leaves Carmen in Onstage Lurch; Cheapskate Impresario Evades Payment

I was press-agenting the New York City Opera's *Carmen* during its 1953 Chicago season when a surprising and unprecedented event took place at our Civic Opera House. Our Don José, the tenor David Poleri, was frustrated at what he considered to be conductor Josef Rosenstock's too-fast tempo. Suddenly, toward the end of the fourth act, just before he was to deliver a mortal stab to our Carmen, the mezzo Gloria Lane, David walked to the stage apron, angrily threw down his hat, and pointed at the hapless maestro. "Finish the damn opera yourself!" he shouted. With that he bolted from the stage. Another tenor, Walter Fredericks, was sitting in my front-row seat, which I had given him during the last intermission (I had a cold and feared I'd begin to cough). Fredericks rushed through a side door to the wings and began to sing. Gloria, desperate and thinking quickly, mimed suicide by stabbing herself with an imaginary dagger and falling to the stage floor. She was out for the next half hour until the house doctor finally brought her around.

The audience, agape and agog, probably was aware that it had experienced a happening unprecedented in opera history and exited the Opera House in a state of mixed excitement and delight. They had, they knew, a special story to tell their children and grandchildren. Among those present were two future general directors of the not-yet-born Lyric Opera of Chicago—Ardis Krainik, a teacher, and William Mason, our 1954 Children's Chorus soloist.

Harry Romanoff, the legendary night city editor of William Randolph Hearst's *Chicago American* right across the street from the Civic Opera House, never believed that this was anything other than one of my more flamboyant publicity ploys. I remember telling him, "Harry, yes, we love publicity, but we don't ever do anything like that even if it would bring a motherlode of press clippings!" The highly amused radio newscasters and wire services did their jobs well, and overnight the world was laughing at our bizarre incident. The New York City Opera's management and those of opera companies everywhere were not laughing, however, and David's career suffered a serious setback. The next morning he showed up at my office, apparently still unaware of the implications of his actions.

David was born near Philadelphia in 1921 and made his opera debut in 1949 in the title role of *Faust* in Chicago with Fortune Gallo's touring San Carlo Opera. I heard him for the first time in 1950 on WGN's weekly, nationally broadcast *Chicago Theatre of the Air,* which presented operas and operettas sung in English. I was thrilled by Poleri's startlingly beautiful and exciting tenor voice. Such celebrities as Jan Peerce and Richard Tucker were often featured on the program, and I could easily identify their gorgeous voices. This voice didn't sound like either of theirs, but I judged it to be of major caliber. Being an avid "tenor-phile," I waited anxiously for the program's end and the announcement of cast members both in Manhattan and Chicago.

The New York City Opera Company—one of my ongoing projects—was presenting its annual fall Chicago season (our city was then between resident opera companies), and I had only to wait until the next morning to tell its founding artistic director, Laszlo Halasz, about my discovery. He suggested an immediate meeting, which I arranged for the following afternoon. Poleri, to whom I'd introduced myself via telephone, had given a sensational audition in the old second-floor Opera House bar that adjoined my office. Halasz engaged him on the spot for the roles of Alfredo in *La Traviata* and Des Grieux in *Manon* for the company's next New York season. David was handsome, acted with flair, and possessed a manly stride that reminded me of another client, Italy's world-famed

Giuseppe Di Stefano. Also in 1951, Poleri was the Glyndebourne Festival's Don Alvaro in *La Forza del Destino;* in 1953 he was the Hermann in the Florence mounting of *The Queen of Spades;* and in 1955 he was Cavaradossi alongside Leontyne Price's Tosca in a pioneer NBC opera telecast of Giacomo Puccini's work.

The new Lyric Theatre of Chicago had planned to have Poleri appear in its 1954 inaugural season's *Taming of the Shrew* (Vittorio Giannini) as Lucentio, but Carol Fox, frightened by the news of one of his escapades (it seems he also took on a Cincinnati headwaiter who demanded he wear a tie), got out of the contract. In that year, however, he created the role of Michele in Gian Carlo Menotti's *Saint of Bleecker Street* in New York and also did the Italian premiere at La Scala, and in 1956 he debuted at Covent Garden as Riccardo in *Ballo in Maschera.* He then disappeared for the next few seasons because, he told me, of a severe respiratory illness that he treated by climbing mountains in Italy to restore his stamina.

In 1961 tenor Carlo Bergonzi became ill when he was our Lyric Opera of Chicago's Don Alvaro in *La Forza del Destino.* Suddenly, and between performances, he left for treatment in Europe. Whether in the United States or abroad, no tenor who knew the role was available. Strictly on a hunch, I called Poleri's parents' home in Philadelphia. *He* answered! He had just arrived from Europe that morning. I knew he had sung Alvaro at Glyndebourne and asked if he would fly to Chicago that evening. He would have to sing the role on the following evening, November 4. If all went well, I pointed out, he would have re-launched his American career. He agreed.

I met him at the airport that evening and whisked him to the Opera House, where our costumer, stage manager, and others were waiting for him backstage. David re-studied the score and libretto throughout the evening, ran through them the next day, and scored a resounding success that night. In a cast that included such stars as Eileen Farrell, Boris Christoff, Christa Ludwig, and Gian Giacomo Guelfi, Poleri did himself proud. He also saved our necks! We rewarded him with the tenor lead in the next season's *Prince Igor,* with Rudolf Nureyev in his American opera debut as the dancing Igor.

David and his wife, Ilse, once divorced, remarried in 1967 and flew to Hawaii for a second honeymoon that fall. Tragically, they died together in a between-islands helicopter crash on December 13. Although he was neurotic and unstable enough to have walked offstage in *Carmen* back in 1953, David Poleri should also be remembered as an important American artist who possessed one of the most superb tenor voices of his time. He had genuine star personality and an elegance and grace of bearing seldom seen on opera stages.

Hungarian born-and-raised Maestro Halasz, who auditioned David for the New York City Opera upon my urging so many years ago, was not only colorful but also the most perplexing eccentric with whom I worked in opera. Although I'm not a psychiatrist—just a theatrical press agent—I'm certain that the Laszlo I knew for a number of years was a prime subject for psychoanalysis.

If I were to ask Laszlo, for example, how he came down to the Opera House—by bus or subway—he was sure to answer "by subway" if he came by bus. He'd just be damned if he told you the truth. If he were to protest, "What do you mean, by bus or subway? Don't you know that I travel only by my chauffeured limousine" (which, of course, he didn't have) the reason for the lie might be understandable. That, however, wasn't the case. He wouldn't tell the truth; it was as if he would lose something precious by doing so. He was constantly—and unnecessarily—enmeshed in an ever-expanding tissue of lies. How many times did I hear the sobs of sopranos to whom he had promised the role of Mimi or Cio-Cio-San "next Monday night"? When the singer arrived at the dressing room she would find another artist whom he had previously engaged for that performance.

At the end of the first season we worked together he told me he was so happy with what I had done for him and the company that he was ordering the New York City Opera's controller to send me a bonus. "Danny," he said, "you'll be surprised at how much!" as he smiled and shook my hand. The bonus, of course, never came, and when I asked why the next time we met he appeared puzzled. Looking me straight in the eye, he blandly asked, "*I* promised you a bonus? You must be mistaken, Danny. I never did such a thing. You know that we are a poor company and can't afford bonuses. Besides, I know that you don't need the money. I'm sure that if you were shipwrecked on an island, you would soon find a way to survive! You see, I have great confidence in you, Danny!"

Almost everyone backstage disliked Laszlo, including the orchestra's members. On one occasion he went into a rage about something while conducting a rehearsal and threw his baton at a nearby musician, where-upon the orchestra refused to proceed. We called the Chicago Federation of Musicians' president Danny Garimoni (formerly the concertmaster of my old Oriental Theatre vaudeville orchestra), and he came over imme-diately to adjudicate the issue. When Laszlo insisted that the baton had somehow *slipped out of his hand,* the entire orchestra shouted, "*No,* you *threw* it!" He was forced to apologize, and the rehearsal continued.

Our staff was constantly embarrassed by his adamant refusal to pay the bills for services and/or materials during each Chicago season of the New York City Opera (stagehands, for example, would purchase necessary lum-ber and hardware). The funds to cover them had been previously allocated and were on hand. We had—for no good reason—become known as dead-beats, and it was assumed that we were *unable* to pay and on the verge of bankruptcy. After I received various complaint calls from suppliers, Laszlo and I were having lunch at Maurice's Restaurant close to the Opera House one day, and I decided to bite the bullet. "Laszlo," I asked, "why, since we have the money on deposit here, specifically for these purposes, won't you simply sign the checks and stop this ruining of our reputation?" "Danny, please try to understand," he confided. "I simply cannot bring myself to pay bills. I don't know why, but I just can't. Let them sue me, and if there is a court order, I'll have to pay—but not otherwise!" If I hadn't known it until then, it was apparent that I was dealing with a psychically complex situation and had no preparation—academically or otherwise—to deal with it.

In 1951 many of Laszlo's chickens came home to roost, so to speak, when the New York City Opera's abused artists revolted. The New York City Center trustees heard their testimony, and he was dismissed. Along with so many others who had worked with him, I did not mourn his going.

Some years ago, Halasz, who died in 2001 at the age of ninety-six, op-timistically sent me a copy of his repertoire, including Sergey Prokofiev's *The Love for Three Oranges,* which he conducted at every opportunity. Undoubtedly, he hoped that I would recommend him to Lyric's office of artistic administration. When we subsequently met at a New York state performing arts seminar I was giving we chatted amicably. I doubt that he remembered the strain in our relations of more than a half-century earlier—or, knowing him, he chose not to remember it.

22 Ardis Krainik, the Apple-Cheeked, All-American Girl and Award-Winning Savior of Lyric Opera

In the waning days of the truncated 1980 Lyric Opera of Chicago season (it had been cut from eight to five operas as a futile economy measure) I had been—in addition to my usual Lyric Opera duties and wide-ranging assignments for the Ford Foundation Theatre Communications Group and Canadian government—consumed with promoting our Italian Earthquake Benefit Concert on December 7. I was also trying to lift the morale of my colleague Ardis Krainik, whose relationship with General Manager Carol Fox was deteriorating. Despite Carol's progressively debilitating health, she still determinedly and disasterously held the reins of authority.

Ardis, then our artistic administrator, saw and understood the reasons for the company's deepening and dangerous economic crisis and knew what specific moves might save our existence. She was frustrated, however, by Carol's inability to make the necessary decisions, a continuing procrastination that could no longer be afforded. We were entirely out of money and in debt; reserve funds were exhausted. There seemed to be no chance that our board leaders, who were, understandably, upset, would sign notes for us at the bank. They had lost confidence in our administration. Two of our most prominent board leaders, fearing they might be held personally liable for Lyric's mounting debts, resigned.

In mid-1980 I highly recommended my friend Michael Manuel for the then unoccupied general manager position at the Australian Opera, where I had been an active consultant throughout the 1970s and launched a successful subscription campaign to open the stunning new Sydney Opera House. Michael, a Shavian-bearded Englishman, and Risë Stevens, retired from performing, were co-heads of the Metropolitan Opera's National Company, which I represented for two years. As it turned out, however, Michael didn't want to go down under.

Six months later, in early December 1980, Lyric Opera of Chicago's demise appeared imminent, and Ardis—who had been like a sister to me since 1954—asked me to find her another position. I called Sydney. The job there was still open. Within a few days Ken Tribe, the Australian Opera's management coordinator and one of my happy collaborators there, arrived in Chicago. He, Ardis, and I had a three-hour-long dinner meeting, after which he told me, "Danny, your views as to Ardis's qualifications and experience will certainly carry a great deal of weight with us." *And, as it turned out, they did.* Lyric's season ended on December 13, 1980. A few days later Ardis flew off to Sydney, and a week later she returned with a signed contact (*they* had signed it). She was supposed to show the document to me—and a lawyer—before signing and returning it over the weekend.

In the meanwhile, Archie Boe, the Sears, Roebuck CEO and Lyric's no-nonsense president, suddenly called an emergency board meeting for January 2, 1981. At the meeting he stated that Lyric would *not* close, and he declared that Carol Fox must retire and a new general manager must be appointed. With the exception of two board members who, if I recall correctly, abstained, the vote unanimously supported him.

The next day, January 3, Ardis was appointed as general manager of Lyric, and she and I shared the unhappy task of informing the Australian Opera of her change in plans. The news was not happily received, and the Australians were not able to settle on a new general manager for another year. I was somewhat embarrassed but am comforted because history has vindicated Ardis's decision to remain with Lyric, where she had been for twenty-six years. She became a great leader for our company (we changed her title to general director a few years later) and never regretted her decision. Under her management, Lyric Opera of Chicago achieved new levels of artistic distinction and a new level of fiscal responsibility. I am certain that *had* she left for the Australian Opera she would have made a major success there, too.

When Ardis took over Lyric's top job on January 3, 1981, the "emoluments pertaining thereto" were minuscule. The cupboard was indeed bare, and she asked for only a minimal salary. The next day, January 4, she asked me to promise to remain with Lyric for the next ten years—when she would be reaching retirement age. She knew that only a few weeks earlier I, too, had intended to depart as well. She was asking for a commitment very difficult for me to make. I was then a vigorous sixty-year-old at the peak of my audience-building successes in North America and abroad, besieged by arts managers and trustees everywhere who wanted my aid. Her belief in my indispensability was moving, however, as was her faith in my longevity potential. I promised to remain as her closest advisor for the next decade—to my great economic disadvantage.

Ardis's tasks were formidable, but she did everything right and did it so quickly! Having full authority, she corrected much that had gone wrong in the previous several years. Before the 1981 season's end she had saved Lyric hundreds of thousands of dollars in operating costs without any loss of artistic quality. She had a strong mentor in Artistic Director Bruno Bartoletti, her guide and friend for so many years. Those board members who so unhappily left us soon returned to the fold, as they had promised me they would. The entire staff and the company's supporting auxiliaries were galvanized, and fund-raising results, which had come to a halt, rebounded overnight!

All production plans for the 1981 season had been stalled by Lyric's financial crisis and had to be revived with dispatch. An unprecedented effort was immediately mounted to get our subscribers to return to an eight-opera season after the five-opera season of 1980, which had given a much lower cost to the subscribers. Over several intensive weeks I made about *two thousand telephone calls.* In a series of actions reminiscent of the First Hundred Days of Franklin D. Roosevelt's first administration, Ardis performed a management miracle—a feat of brilliant leadership. In summing up her first season as general manager, which ended on December 19, 1981, the *Chicago Tribune's* John von Rhein pronounced the artistic level "steadier than it had been in years." The *Sun-Times*'s Robert C. Marsh praised the initial Krainik season as "fine, well-realized and enjoying a 90–some percent attendance!" Ardis's administration, with Bartoletti's artistic input a major factor, gathered steam in the 1982 season, which ended with an astonishing $800,000 surplus! I can't recall any other season in Lyric's then more than three decades in which there had been *any* surplus at all! In my memory, *deficits* were the norm. Greatly increased fund-raising added to ticket income made the happy change possible.

By the end of the first season under Ardis's stewardship, Lyric's situation was greatly improved, the company was operating in the black, and a *Chicago Tribune* editorial praised her as Lyric's "Wonder Woman." Her appeal to the press went only so far, however. One journalist assigned to profile her for a national publication abandoned the commission because he found her story too bland in light of the voyeuristic trends in late-twentieth-century journalism. Apparently, none of his intensive research yielded any sexual peccadilloes in her past, and his desperate search for a colleague or competitor arts manager who would criticize her on any level came up empty-handed. Frustrated, he dropped the assignment. Later, a proposed biography was aborted for similar reasons, and a distinguished music critic captioned a portrait of her that hung in his office "Miss Pollyana."

The blonde, apple-cheeked, Wisconsin born-and-bred, youthful Ardis Krainik (she was twenty-five when we met) was everyone's idea of the all-American girl. She was pretty, had a lovely figure, and was athletic. She swam, rode horses, played tennis, and shot baskets with stagehands and opera singers alike on the empty stage of the Civic Theatre that formerly adjoined the Civic Opera House. On one occasion, diva Eva Marton, who had once captained a successful school basketball team in her native Hungary, beat Ardis *and* Plácido Domingo in an impromptu free-throw contest. Ardis came in second, while Plácido trailed them both! Ardis also took up skiing, which resulted in a broken leg; she hobbled about on crutches for many weeks.

A graduate of the Northwestern University School of Speech, Ardis had been working toward a master's degree in music when she came to Lyric as a clerk-typist in June 1954, five months before our first season and after she had just finished a year teaching speech and drama in Racine, Wisconsin, public schools. Possessing a lovely mezzo-soprano voice, she soon also became a Lyric chorister—then a part-time evening assignment—while holding her daytime office job with us.

By day Ardis filed and typed Carol Fox's letters and my publicity releases, using carbon paper to make extra copies in that era before photocopying. In an interview many years later she recalled those early days as "an entire season of hyperbole put forth by Danny Newman who gave us all instructions as to what to say on the telephone, underscoring that we were to talk about a fabulous newcomer named Maria Callas, who I'd never heard of. But, I was happy to be a Newman sales disciple." By night, under Maestro Michael Lepore's highly disciplined tutelage, she rehearsed with the company's chorus, mainly composed of the Polinaires, an excellent Polish American singing society. By our second season in 1955, and for the next several years, she graduated to singing *comprimaria* (supporting) roles and appeared with such stars as Maria Callas, Tito Gobbi, Renata Tebaldi, Giuseppe Di Stefano, Carlo Bergonzi, Birgit Nilsson, Ettore Bastianini, Richard Tucker, Giulietta Simionato, Mario Del Monaco, Eleanor Steber, Jussi Björling, and Anna Moffo.

After appearing with such opera-singer giants for five seasons Ardis was in thrall to grand opera. From that point on there was never any question that opera would engage her for the rest of her life. During those same years, however, she became increasingly valuable in the front office. By 1960 she had become our assistant manager and in 1975 she rose to artistic administrator before being named general manager in 1981. Although most of her time was sopped up by administrative problems, she was constantly growing in her understanding and knowledge of opera's artistic demands. Her mentors were, first, Maestro Lepore and then Maestro Bartoletti. For Carol Fox she became an indispensable right arm as the years progressed.

Overall, by the time Ardis succeeded to the company's top job she possessed enormous knowledge of the inner and outer workings of producing grand opera, from the big issues to the tiniest details involved in the exhaustive complexities of that collective art form. She knew the cost of every spotlight bulb; the going price (which she could usually somehow bring down) for services of the singer greats of the time; and various prices for building stage sets, whether in the United States or abroad, and for their shipping.

Ardis was a canny shopper and attributed that characteristic to her Bohemian background, a reference to her paternal heritage. She even eventually got around to cutting *my* part-time wages. Her father, Arthur, was a Manitowoc, Wisconsin, business executive. Her mother, Clara, forthright and of Norwegian extraction, always questioned why I remained loyal to a large collection of what she thought to be out-moded, wide-brimmed hats that included some from Vienna, Rome, and Paris—Habigs, Borsalinos, Barbisios, and Mossants. Her idea of a *proper* hat was American, a snap-brimmed little Dobbs. I still have a now somewhat mottled suede chapeau I purchased in Lyon in 1948. My only American hat is a huge Stetson, a gift from the millionaires of Midland, Texas, when I lectured there in the 1970s. That community's George W. Bush must have been just a lad then.

All of Ardis's sixteen years at Lyric's helm were successful, but 1989 was a banner one because of her international recognition as a prime mover in grand opera. On August 31 she startled the field by announcing that she was banning Luciano Pavarotti from Lyric Opera of Chicago after a relationship of sixteen years. His defections had mounted steadily as the decade progressed—during the 1980s the great tenor and star had canceled twenty-six of forty-one scheduled Lyric performances—and our good faith was being questioned in many quarters. Disaffection was growing among Lyric's faithful series subscribers. We had thirty-two thousand of them when, finally, Luciano notified us that he was cancelling *all* the *Tosca* performances in which he had been announced for the company's gala thirty-fifth anniversary season that fall.

From Luciano's standpoint, every cancellation was for a reason that made sense to *him*. Angry letters, however, poured in. I was especially vulnerable because I had been—with increasing difficulty—faithfully answering those plaintive letters and calls. When we learned in August 1989 that he was again cancelling—this time because of an "inflamed sciatic nerve"—we even offered to have him perform from a chair, but he refused.

Up to that point Luciano had canceled other opera companies' performances, but none rebuked him. Now, with the agreement of Lyric's board president William B. Graham, Ardis bit the bullet and fired the tenor! It was a business matter that had to be addressed, and she did not shrink when I told her to call Graham and get his go-ahead. Her prompt action unleashed an avalanche of approving media response the world over. For many weeks it was hot copy. Editorials lauded her, and one opera manager told the press, "She has taken the first bold step! We admire her!" That was in 1989, and as of the early twenty-first century Lyric—*without* Luciano's participation—has rarely fallen below a more than 100 percent season, even though those seasons have been increasingly longer ones!

The dust had not settled on Ardis's sensational response to Luciano's constantly recurring cancellations when she decided it was time to go public with her and Bartoletti's long-planned, long-term, and unprecedented "Toward the Twenty-first Century Artistic Initiative." The ten-year project was designed to produce and present seven important American operas of the twentieth century along with ten European twentieth-century classics works. *And* three world premieres would be commissioned as well! There would also be a major Ring Cycle over a four-year period under the musical direction of Maestro Zubin Mehta. All of this most ambitious program was to happen during the 1990s.

I am proud that every pledge we made in our "artistic initiative" announcement of October 8, 1989, was carried out on schedule! Only eight years after Ardis became the general manager of a virtually bankrupt and demoralized company, the economic strength, vigor, and artistic confidence of Lyric Opera grew to make her visionary and expensive commitment a marvelous reality. Undoubtedly, Maestro Bartoletti's in-depth understanding of—and wide experience with—contemporary as well as traditional opera provided Ardis with wise, authoritative, and invaluable guidance in conceiving and implementing the initiative. At every opportunity she expressed gratitude to the self-effacing and brilliant Florentine who made his American debut with Lyric in 1956 and became its artistic director and principal conductor in 1965.

Ardis shrewdly judged that the musical press would enthusiastically welcome the initiative, which was a rare long-term commitment for a major opera company. It would also create envy among her peers, the other members of the prestigious Association of International Opera Directors, many of whom—despite vast governmental subsidies—fell short of her accomplishments. Ardis was determined to get the maximum press coverage possible, nationally and abroad. She was confident that she was riding a good horse, and she was right!

Although I had a sore throat (the Pavarotti dismissal furor kept me on the telephone for weeks) I took Ardis to New York, where I had arranged in advance a series of individual press interviews with a large number of music critics and editors over several consecutive days and evenings. Over the years I had built good relationships with the highly specialized East Coast journalists. Now I called in my chips. Interviewers came to our hotel, one after another, for breakfast, lunch, dinner, and tea. A mother-lode of publicity resulted, no small recognition for an opera company located so far west of the Hudson!

Between the Pavarotti press bonanza of the months before and the excitement for our new initiative, Lyric Opera had reached new and higher levels of widespread attention, and Ardis Krainik became one of the the most admired opera leaders anywhere! For days on end—and nights, too—I had not stopped talking passionately to critics and editors, whether in person or on the telephone. When we returned to Chicago I was completely mute and needed throat-doctoring for months afterward. But it was worth it!

Ardis was the younger of the Krainiks' two daughters. She and her niece, Barbara Baule of Cedarburg, Wisconsin, were always close. Over the years Ardis had escorts rather than boy friends, but she never married, although perhaps she was married to her Lyric Opera of Chicago. An extremely knowledgable student of the Bible, she was aware that I was from a traditional Jewish background and loved to discuss biblical and theological matters with me. We must have been the only opera manager and theatrical press agent to regularly have such spiritual sessions. The biblically minded Ardis attributed my evangelistic prowess on behalf of Lyric and so many other arts organizations to my probable descent from prophet ancestors who fulminated against idolators on mountain tops in ancient Israel, much as I zealously denounced contemporary single-ticket buyers (nonsubscribers)!

Ardis, a mezzo-soprano, was soloist in the High Holy Days choir under Cantor Andrew Foldi at Chicago's Temple Isaiah, a prestigious Reform Jewish congregation. Foldi, a transplanted young Hungarian bass and a fine musician, had been the music critic prodigy of the *Chicago Times*. Later, in 1954, he joined our nascent Lyric Theatre and went on to become a highly regarded opera singer throughout the United States and abroad.

More recently, he was the director of Lyric's training affiliate, the Center for Young American Artists.

When I first knew her, Ardis was, like her parents, a Methodist, and then she became a Presbyterian. At some point she became aware of—then increasingly interested in—Christian Science. Eventually, she became a true believer in the teachings of Mary Baker Eddy and remained so for the rest of her life. Although Ardis, like many young women, had smoked and consumed the occasional cocktail, once she embraced "Science" she never again touched tobacco or alcohol. She became steeped in her new denomination's teachings and was a regular reader at Sunday services as well as the mezzo soloist at the central Christian Science Church. Her co-religionists much admired her, and she had many friends among them. As her career flowered she always pointed out that she was being directed in her various accomplishments by a higher power.

Ardis was like a younger sister to my wife Dina, and we were often together, just the three of us or with mutual friends. She was both likable and lovable and over the years built a legion of admirers and evoked friendship and loyalty from men as well as women. Many admirerers were Lyric Opera contributors, subscribers, and members of the company's several auxiliary boards. There is often an inherent adversarial relationship between the managements of many nonprofit musical organizations and their unionized musicians, stage crews, and other backstage employees, but under Ardis's benign influence acrimony declined considerably. One of her finest attributes was mothering a succession of young women who worked for her over the years as well as for other Lyric staff leaders. She was their confidant, confessor, and advisor, and her advice came with both compassion and wisdom.

Throughout the forty-three years we worked together we both in some sense acted in loco parentis for many staffers and artists who looked to us for help with all manner of needs and problems. Once our brilliant orchestra principal violist Rami Salamanov came to us, broken-hearted, after his valuable instrument had been stolen. He had found a high-quality replacement, but it would cost some thousands of dollars, and he didn't qualify for a bank loan. "Danny," Ardis said, "let's go to see Julius." The elderly Julius Frankel, a wealthy, European-born widower, loved Lyric and thought the world of Ardis. He treated us to lunch and gave us a check for the required amount. Rami, we promised, would make monthly payments on the loan. When Rami arrived with his first payment, however, Julius refused to accept it, saying that he now regarded his check as a gift! At Ardis's urging, Julius later became a generous production sponsor, beginning with our 1989–90 *Die Fledermaus.* Ever since Julius's death, the Frankel Foundation, headed by his faithful friend—and Ardis's admirer—Nelson Cornelius, has continued its regular and significant support of Lyric.

Early in her administration as general director Ardis and I often attended arts conferences together. She was especially grateful to me for introducing her to the many artistic directors and management officials with whom I worked closely through many years of consulting assignments. As a theatrical arts publicist I also had developed a wide acquaintanceship among critics in all of the arts disciplines, both in the United States and abroad. Ardis was eager to begin such direct relationships herself, and I was pleased to be able to make that happen for her. In later years she did everything possible to reciprocate. Although I amassed an extraordinary number of awards, the National Medal of the Arts was not among them. Ardis politicked on my behalf and wrote to the National Endowment for the Arts officials that "Danny has generated more income to arts organizations in our society than the combined contributions of the National Endowment, State and Municipal Arts Councils, and all of America's corporations and foundations combined. And remember, he does this in his spare time!" In May 1985 she presented me with Lyric Opera's highest honor, the Carol Fox Award, which I shared with our opera house landlord, James Kemper Sr. Her message to me in 1994 when we were celebrating our four-decades-long friendship was, "Imagine, forty years! Why that's a lifetime! And how happy I am that you have been an important part of mine. Such a team we are—you and me and Bruno. And how grateful I am. Thank you again for everything. Love, Ardis."

In 1997 when Ardis—cancer-stricken and mortally ill but still in control—asked me to prepare her obituary I tearfully did. It was the unhappiest request she had made of me since we met in 1954, when one of her first clerical tasks—in Lyric's original second-floor offices at 20 North Wacker Drive—was to type my flamboyant publicity releases. Ardis left us on June 18, 1997. I miss her greatly, for she was as much a sister to me as Bruno Bartoletti is my brother. After I had been a widower for a half-dozen years it was Ardis who emboldened me to woo and win the lovely Alyce. As always, the Krainik judgment was sound!

Like the late Carol Fox, Ardis received an astonishing number of honorary doctorates, was decorated by foreign governments, and was awarded high honors by local, national, and international organizations. She guided Lyric Opera in its purchase of the Civic Opera House portion of the 20 North Wacker Drive building and its subsequent $100 million renovation. She was a Northwestern University trustee, a former president of the Commercial Club of Chicago, and a board director of the Northern Trust Corporation.

In recognition of Ardis's many achievements, on Sunday, October 13, 1996, a galaxy of internationally acclaimed opera stars converged on the main stage of the Civic Opera House for the completely sold-out Ardis Krainik Celebration Gala Concert. Participants included June Anderson, Daniel Barenboim, Bruno Bartoletti, Richard Buckley, Vladimir Chernov, Barbara Daniels, Plácido Domingo, Renée Fleming, Mirella Freni, Nicolai Ghiaurov, Håkan Hagegård, Ben Heppner, Marilyn Horne, Kristian Johannson, Catherine Malfitano, Eva Marton, Timothy Nolen, Samuel Ramey, Michael Sylvester, Carol Vaness, Frederica von Stade, and Dolora Zajick. The event was featured on front pages, complete with color photographs, and an announcement was made that "henceforth, the main auditorium of the Civic Opera House would be known as 'The Ardis Krainik Theatre.'" It was the crowning accolade for the apple-cheeked girl from Manitowoc, who from her wheelchair basked in the acclaim.

23 Boyish Bruno Bartoletti Joins Lyric Opera Conductors Dimitri Mitropoulos and Georg Solti in 1956 to Become Artistic Director for Four Decades

High drama worthy of Victorien Sardou suddenly manifested itself in a backstage dressing room of Chicago's Civic Opera House when France's reigning diva, Régine Crespin, her journalist husband Louis Bruder, Maestro Bruno Bartoletti, and I were chatting about our respective World War II experiences as we waited for a staging rehearsal of *Tosca* to begin in 1964. Bruder had just begun to tell us how he was unwillingly pressed into the German army, even though as a native of Alsace-Lorraine he considered himself French. With the Germans in retreat in Italy in 1944 he decided to desert. He hid in the bell tower of a church in a small town near Florence, where a gaggle of sympathetic local teenage boys discovered him and brought scarce food and wine. Suddenly, Bruno—standing next to me—cried out, "Bruder, *I* was one of those kids!" Weeping, they fell into each other's arms. The town was Sesto Fiorentino, Bruno's birthplace, and in that very church he had celebrated his first communion. Soon we were all crying. Madame Crespin, our *Tosca*, was also our Ariadne of that season (1964); in 1963 she was our Amelia in *Ballo in Maschera*, Leonora in *Fidelio,* and Elizabeth in *Tannhäuser.* She would also lead master classes for Lyric Opera of Chicago's Center for American Artists.

Tito Gobbi was one of the world-renowned "big voice" stars of Lyric Theatre during its fabulous first two seasons in 1954 and 1955. As the company—renamed Lyric Opera of Chicago and under the sole general managership of Carol Fox—prepared for the 1956 season, the baritone became its shadow artistic director and advised Carol on casting decisions and repertory choices. He had her ear, and she had full confidence in his judgment. The conductors for the 1956 season included Dimitri Mitropoulos, Georg Solti, and a newcomer, Bruno Bartoletti, in his American debut. Like Solti, he was assigned to conduct four operas. Both Solti and Mitropoulos were world-famed, whereas Bartoletti, a twenty-seven-year-old Florentine, was comparatively unknown. He was at Lyric because Tito Gobbi told Carol Fox that he was the most brilliant young maestro in Italy. Tito told me that as well when he saw me leave for Midway Airport to greet Bartoletti upon his arrival from Italy.

I encountered a very thin young man who looked like a teenager, hungry and self-effacing. Indeed, if universities offered courses in self-effacement he could well be the professor. He was the last man in the world to thrust himself forward, to the despair of Carol Fox, even when in later years he became Lyric's artistic director. Carol wanted him to be instantly famous if he were "her" conductor. She even resented that Bruno's wife, Rosanna, did not push him forward like other conductors' wives who so often shamelessly promoted their husbands' careers. Although Bruno has a deservedly high opinion of his abilities, his public stance continues to be one of exemplary modesty. When we first met, I knew no Italian and he knew no English. He did know Spanish, however, and I had some high school dalliance with its Castilian version under the tutelage of a Swedish-born instructor (Bruno once told an interviewer that he also communicated with me via pantomime). At any rate, we managed to communicate as best we could until, with quick intelligence, he began to speak English. Although many years have passed I still don't speak Italian. (Once, I spent a week being treated for pneumonia in a provincial hospital near Venice, and only through my wife Alyce, who does speak that language—and six others—was I able to communicate with the dedicated doctors and nurses who pulled me through.)

While still a youngster, Bruno rose to be chief flutist of the Florence Opera and for that city's annual Maggio Festival, where the famed Artur Rodziński frequently conducted. The maestro, long plagued by heart problems, fell ill one day during the first act of a dress rehearsal for Pyotr Tchaikovsky's *Pique dame*. Long an admirer of Bruno's inherent musicality, seriousness, and precocity, Rodziński had him brought to his dressing-room couch during intermission and handed him the baton. "Today you are the conductor," he said. The rest of the rehearsal went very well. The youthful Bartoletti had won his conductorial spurs and has presided over opera orchestras internationally ever since. Among his ports of call have been Buenos Aires, Rome, Milan, Turin, Genoa, Naples, New York, San Francisco, Tokyo, Munich, Berlin, Bologna, Venice, and Copenhagen.

He made his American debut at Lyric on October 23, 1956, conducting *Il Trovatore* with Jussi Björling as Manrico, Herva Nelli as Leonora, and Ettore Bastianini as Count Di Luna. The next day's *Chicago Tribune* carried Claudia Cassidy's strong thumbs-up review. He "crackled with talent," she said and added, "From start to finish, this fiery young Italian named Bartoletti knew precisely what he was doing in the pit, conducting Verdi both supple and exact, with a flexible, authoritative lyric line." The scholarly Irving Sablosky of the *Daily News* reported in a rare burst of exuberance that Bruno was "the season's lyric find; small, wiry, with a starving artists' face, conducting with a combination of fury and pleading gentleness that drew from the Lyric orchestra its most integrated sounds of the season. The strings sang with beguiling Italian clarity and candor, the brass discovered unsuspected mellowness, and Verdi's blood-and-thunder climaxes were taken full-scale, with absolute authority. The chorus responded to Bartoletti with a new command of color and shading, and the cast seemed to work under him with complete freedom and assurance."

Considering that maestroes Mitropoulos and Solti, both superstars, had conducted earlier that season, Bruno's immediate triumph was all the more remarkable. He followed with *La Traviata* featuring Eleanor Steber, Renata Tebaldi, Jussi Björling, and Tito Gobbi and *La Bohème* with Björling, Tebaldi, and Bastianini. For the next forty-five years he would be an ornament of successive Lyric seasons, entrusted with the company's artistic direction for decades to come.

An unrelenting atmosphere of crisis plagued us during the years that we of Lyric Opera were pouring our energies—and company funds—into producing the ill-starred world premiere of John Milton's monumental literary work *Paradise Lost* as an opera. Although Bruno conducted it brilliantly, grand opera is a collective art form and in this case every artist involved did not reach his demanding standards. Two years alone were lost when composer Krzysztof Penderecki apparently lost his muse. In the fall of 1978, opening night at long last only a few weeks away, we sequestered him in the room next to my office in the sixth floor of the Civic Opera House, where he desperately struggled to finish the opera. Bruno, who was to conduct the premiere, was down in the house, intensively and bravely rehearsing the already completed portions of the work with our orchestra. It was tortuous going because of the work's avant-garde style and densely textured complexities. As Penderecki would finish a page we rushed it down to Bruno. Penderecki told me that he was astonished by Bartoletti's quick mastery of the score's inherent difficulties and how he instinctively and with consummate skill and clarity taught it to the instrumentalists.

Milan's La Scala had entered a partnership arrangement with Lyric whereby we would give the world premiere of *Paradise Lost* on November 29, 1978, and they would give the work's European premiere on January 21, 1979. Because of Penderecki's fame the Italians wanted the composer himself to conduct on that occasion and also to do a concert version for the new pope, John Paul II, at the Vatican. Although he *did* conduct all the Italian performances, Penderecki told me he would much rather have Bruno conduct in Milan because he could never reach Bruno's level of conducting. Penderecki well knew the musical minefields his score contained.

Bruno is an Italian version of the self-made man, a Florentine Horatio Alger. He prides himself on being a son of proletarian parents whom he supported generously in their old age. He would never, he told me in the 1950s, permit their standard of living to be lower than his and his wife's. For several decades the Bartolettis have divided their time between a spacious apartment hotel suite in central Chicago and their eighteenth-century Tuscan farmstead in a grove of weathered olive trees that adjoins an orchard of cherries and apricots. The home has a view of the medieval town of Fiesole, which in the summer hosts a *scuola di musica* for talented but impoverished youngsters. When I wrote the brochure for its fund-raising drive in 1982 its board consisted of Claudio Abbado, Bruno Bartoletti, Riccardo Muti, and Mstislav Rostropovich.

The house, which is entered through a courtyard, is furnished and decorated with the restraint and inherent modesty that characterizes this fine and refined family. Their Vicolo San Marco home is close to the Florence city limits, and their neighbors have included Harold Acton and Barbara Munchausen, a close relative of the German "tall tale teller." The home was lovingly and expensively renovated and enlarged during the second half of the twentieth century, and there the Maestro, a traditional pater familias, presides over his growing family.

Bruno was born in 1926 in Sesto Fiorentino on the fringes of Florence—that great, historic center of art treasures on the banks of the Arno River—as social and political upheaval and accompanying economic hopelessness were creating fascism as well as communism in the chaos that followed World War I. Bruno's was a working-class family—when work was to be had. Widespread unemployment was the norm for many in the north and the south of Italy. Bruno's father, Umberto, was a skilled but often unemployed iron worker. Umberto's blacksmith brother Gino was the father of Bruno's beloved cousin Enrico, a brilliant and popular theologian whose candidacy for the papacy had been quite credible before he died at the age of fifty-nine.

I first came to Florence in the 1950s to savor its wonders, but the devastation and deprivation caused by the Arno River flood of 1966 brought me closer to its unfortunate citizens, especially Bruno and Rosanna, as I became active in organizing Lyric Opera's considerable efforts on behalf of that stricken city. Journalists who have written that Bruno has the appearance of a starving artist were unaware that he was indeed at least half-starved for some years. He was a spindly lad through the war years, grew up impoverished, and was poor during his student years at Florence's Luigi Cherubini Musical Conservatory.

Sparked by Bruno's inspiring dedication and unrelenting hard work, the Bartoletti family has risen to eminence—even prosperity and increased social standing—since World War II. Bruno and Rosanna's daughters, Chiara and Maria are, respectively, an art historian and a teacher of the classics. Their husbands, respectively, are Stefano Merlini, professor of constitutional law, and Giovanni Poggi, a pediatric physician. Their burgeoning brood of grandchildren now includes Arianna, Margherita, Filippo, Livia, and Niccolo. Bruno is as tender with them as he is with the flowers in his garden and his orchestral musicians (never forgetting that he was once one of them). Bruno's brother Luigi is a renowned doctor of gastroenterology, and his sister Anna is an administrator for the American pharmaceutical firm Eli Lily. Rosanna Bartoletti, a retired teacher, in Lyric's early days was the children's qualified tutor during each Chicago opera season.

For the past few hundred years it would be fair to say that kindness—to hardly mention compassion—has been rare among orchestral conductors. Many have devoutly believed that instilling fear is an indispensable strategy for getting the best possible results from musicians. Some of this traditional blood-letting has been curbed by the rise, during the past half century, of orchestra committees (composed of the formerly helpless instrumentalists) and unions. Maestro Bartoletti, however, possesses perfect pitch in human relationships as well as music. Where many opera and symphony musicians still seek to ameliorate the unhappy conditions in which they so often work, Bartoletti enjoys such remarkable affection and trust from his musicians that they demanded—at a time when they were conducting a bitter contract negotiation with our management—he be given a lifetime contract! I have assisted hundreds of opera and symphony orchestras yet never heard of another such demand from musicians. In Bruno's case, the unusual amity extends to colleague conductors, administrators, stage directors, singers, designers, prompters, and all who contribute to the quality of the colorful theater life he so cherishes.

Bruno is fun-loving and a charmer extraordinaire at dinner parties. Many times when, across a crowded room, he expertly mimes our shared memory of a certain arts biggie voraciously consuming pounds of peanuts we fall into helpless laughter that puzzles those around us. He also possesses a typical male Italian reaction at the approach of gorgeous young women—*bella regazza!* Hearsay has it that he once fell off a La Scala rehearsal platform when pleasurably disconcerted by the passing of a luscious eyeful. Asked to confirm that it happened he denies it, but he is clearly pleased by the rumor!

Bruno's attachment to American ways (and all things American, including McDonalds french fries) began during the waning days of the war, when the U.S. Army asked him to make music for its soldiers, which meant that he often accompanied opera and concert singers and was rec-ompensed not only with fees but also with scarce and much-appreciated food.

My beloved parents of blessed memory gave me no brother. I have, however, long had one—younger by seven years—in Bruno. I was the first person he met in the United States more than a half century ago, and we formed an immediate bond. He invariably introduces me as his brother, while Rosanna and Alyce are veritable sisters. Some of Bruno's admirers insist that his family name—at least the last part of it, *toletti*—derives from the beautiful medieval Spanish city of Toledo and that his ancestors migrated from there to Italy some five hundred years ago. "Maybe" he replied when I asked.

Bruno is a versatile musicologist, conductor, administrator, and ar-tistic director with an extensive depth of experience on many musical levels. Considering that he is steeped in Italianate opera heritage and an acknowledged master of its beloved classics of the nineteenth and early twentieth century, he has an astonishing understanding of—and affection for—the repertory of the later twentieth century. A man of wide-ranging and eclectic musical tastes, he is familiar with the music of every era and committed to a wide range of musical specialties. Among the nontra-ditional works he has conducted are those of Béla Bartók (*Bluebeard's Castle*), Luciano Berio (*Opera*), Alban Berg (*Wozzeck, Lulu*), Benjamin Britten (*Serenata, Billy Budd, Peter Grimes, Death in Venice, War Requiem, Midsummer Night's Dream, Illuminations, Phaedra*), Luigi Dallapiccola (*Il Prigonero, Fly by Night*), Paul Dessau (*Die Verurteilung des Lukullus*), Al-berto Ginastera (*Don Rodrigo*), Hans-Werner Henze (*The Stag*), Umberto Giordano (*Madame Sans Gens, Fedora, La Cena Delle Beffe*), Leoš Janáček (*Makropoulos Affair, Katya Kabanova*), Krzysztof Penderecki (*Paradise Lost*), Ildebrando Pizzetti (*Assassination in the Cathedral*), Sergey Prokofiev (*The Love for Three Oranges, Angel of Fire*), Gioacchino Rossini (*Tancredi*), Dmitri Shostakovich (*The Nose, Lady Macbeth of Mtsensk*), Richard Strauss (*Elektra*), Pyotr Tchaikovsky (*Eugene Onegin, Pique dame*), and Kurt Weill (*Mahagonny, Der Lindberghflug*).

Given this extensive repertory of nontraditional works, many of Bruno's younger fans tend to think he is primarily a conductor of contemporary scores. He's just as much at home, however, conducting such staples as

Madama Butterfly, La Bohème, Tosca, Carmen, L'elisir d'amore, Cav & Pag, Lucia di Lammermoor, La Gioconda, Otello, Tales of Hoffmann, Andrea Chénier, Gianni Schicchi, Il Tabarro, Suor Angelica, Un Ballo in Maschera, Maria Stuarda, Il Due Foscari, Macbeth, Attila, Nabucco, Girl of the Golden West, Salome, Barbiere di Siviglia, Falstaff, Manon Lescaut, Turandot, La Cenerentola, Rigoletto, Boris Godunov, Sonnambula, and *Khovanshchina.*

Once, when Bruno had just conducted a symphonic program to acclaim, I asked why he so rarely took on such assignments. Why did he so obviously prefer the opera world? He answered that opera was *theater* and he loved life around the theater and its challenges. For relaxation he studies symphonic scores, reads voraciously, and attends concerts and art exhibits as often as possible. I introduced Bruno to Saul Bellow, and they became fast friends; he has read all of the Nobel Prize–winner's novels in their Italian translations. Bruno also passionately cheers for his favorite soccer team, Turin's Juventus. His tastes in entertainment are indeed catholic.

When John von Rhein, the *Chicago Tribune* music critic, hailed Maestro Bartoletti's twenty-fifth anniversary as Lyric's principal conductor and artistic director in his Sunday, January 21, 1990, article "Unsung Opera Hero," he wrote, "Over the years, no conductor has brought to Lyric a wider range of scores or a more important list of first performances. . . . Characteristically, he'd rather talk about Lyric's eminence than about what he has done to help the company achieve that status. Free of megalomania, he sees opera as a collective effort involving many talents and is far more interested in the success of the whole than in personal glory. That is Bartoletti's way."

Since his Chicago debut on October 23, 1956, Bruno has conducted more than six hundred Lyric Opera of Chicago performances. As artistic director he has supervised a few thousand more. His prolificacy is exceeded in the field only by James Levine at New York's Metropolitan Opera, which operates almost all year. Bruno, an artistic director of the old school, feels responsible for all the elements involved—casting, orchestral, choral, scenic design, and costuming. He sees the whole picture—not just from a conductor's perspective—and is sensitive to all opera's aspects, whether musical or visual.

Since retiring from Lyric he conducts abroad nonstop. Long retired as Florence Opera's intendant, he continues to conduct and record there.

Bruno has enjoyed great success as conductor of Benjamin Britten's *Death in Venice* in Genoa. In Chicago, he did all of Lyric's *La Bohème* performances in 2001–2 and in 2002–3 all of its *Cavalleria Rusticana* and *I Pagliacci* performances and has returned to conduct in each fall–winter season to date. Conductors are famously long-lived. When just two years shy of his eightieth birthday, Bruno conducted in Lyric's fiftieth anniversary season that began in the fall of 2004. He musically directed all performances of the Franco Zeffirelli staging of *Tosca,* with Aprile Millo, Neil Shicoff, and Samuel Ramey as the starring triumvirate. He is one of the few maestroes of our time who can so perfectly wring all the blazing emotional juices out of those high-voltage, verismo music dramas.

His recordings also continue to be classics. These include *La Gioconda* (Decca) with Montserrat Caballe and Luciano Pavarotti; *Manon Lescaut* (Angel) with Caballe and Plácido Domingo; *Ballo in Maschera* (Decca) with Renata Tebaldi and Pavarotti; and *Trittico* (London) with Mirella Freni, Leo Nucci, and Lorenzo Giacomini. Among his recordings for Decca are Puccini's *Il Trittico* (*Il Tabarro, Suor Angelica,* and *Gianni Schichi*), with Mirella Freni performing all three leading soprano roles. Her cast colleagues were Giuseppe Giacomini, Juan Pons, Leo Nucci, Roberto Alagna, and Elena Suliotis. *La Nazione*'s review mentions Bartoletti's "elegance, ever-changing depth of colors, dynamic balance, his strongly personal and poetic imprint!" His *Cavalleria Rusticana* CD (Nuova Era) evoked the following review: "A passionate edition, vibrant and completely captivating with Bartoletti leading the wonderful Orchestra della Toscana. He gives a deeply felt reading of the score, vivid and passionate in its colors, both red hot and languid in its contrasts!" He has also done *Tosca* with Domingo and Raina Kabaivanska and *Mefistofele* on video. Bruno holds the Sarah and A. Watson Armour III Distinguished Conductor Award and Italy's Grand Ufficiale della Repubblica and Cavalieri di Gran Croce medals.

On the occasion of Bruno's twentieth anniversary with Lyric, Thomas C. Willis, the *Chicago Tribune* music critic, wrote on November 28, 1976, that "the slight, dynamic Florentine has comparatively little recognition. For a man marking his twentieth year of service to Chicago Music, Bartoletti is definitely under-appreciated." Willis attributed this to Bartoletti having "no visible desire for the limelight." Bartoletti's utterances, Willis said, "reveal tact as well as determination." He added, "'When I first came here,' the maestro said, 'we had the best stars, but the visual aspects of the performances were sometimes weak. Now, we are a theatre, balanced on all levels.'" In the many ensuing years of Bartoletti's artistic direction the new singers he nurtured became not only Lyric regulars but also world-renowned stars. He made Lyric the home of stage directors and designers of a caliber befitting a company of major stature, which Lyric was fast becoming. Among the regisseurs engaged were Liviu Ciulei, Virginio Puecher, Yuri Lubimov, Hal Prince, Giorgio de Lullo, Eduardo Filippo, Frank Galati, and Robert Falls. I had successfully lobbied for the engagement of the latter three Americans.

Also at the conclusion of the slender Florentine maestro's first twenty Lyric Opera years, Donald Palumbo, Lyric's renowned chorusmaster, observed, "In Maestro Bartoletti's hands, we always feel that we're being faithful to the composer, to the librettist, to the style of the opera. He always reminds us that if we trust the score, everything seems to unfold as the composer intended. Tempo, rubato, fermatas, and dynamics all seem natural, almost inevitable." William Mason maintains that "no one in the history of Lyric Opera has affected it more profoundly or positively than Maestro Bartoletti, a man of great culture and knowledge. His talent and taste at the helm have been pivotal and inspiring in Lyric's artistic success. He's been the artistic moral compass for the company as it has progressed. Lyric Opera will always be Bruno's company." "I love to make music with Bruno," said Plácido Domingo. "He works with you, breathes with you, and supports you in what you're tying to do—and he does this at the very highest artistic level. He inspires with his sense of history and style that is so rare these days."

"Playing under Maestro Bartoletti," Everett Zlatoff-Mirsky, retired concertmaster of Lyric Opera Orchestra, recalls, "I learned the emotional and theatrical architecture—the dramatic ebb and flow—of the great operas. He has been the most important influence of my operatic life." Philip Gossett, a noted Rossini-Verdi scholar and former dean of humanities at the University of Chicago remembers the Rome Opera's *Otello* (Rossini) and *Due Foscari* (Giuseppe Verdi) at New York's Lincoln Center, "Bruno was the guiding genius behind that visit. He has shown exquisite and catholic taste, offering audiences important European masterpieces and significant American works." Gossett also thanked Bruno for what he has "done and continues to do for us individually, for Lyric Opera, for the city of Chicago, for the world of opera in the second half of the twentieth century."

When in 1973 interviewer Linda Winer asked Bruno to justify Lyric's awarding its American Bicentennial commission to Krzysztof Penderecki, who is Polish, he responded, "Don't forget, this is the city that commissioned *The Love for Three Oranges* from Russia's Prokofiev!"

Opera-goers throughout the Midwest are contemplating, as I write this in mid-2005, Lyric Opera's fifty-first international season, with its exicting new production of Puccini's *Manon Lescaut* with Kaita Matilla, Vladimir Galouzine, and Christopher Feigum and stage direction by Olivier Tambosi. Bruno Bartoletti, of course, is the conductor.

In the 2005–6 season, Maestro Bartoletti successfully defied the traditional belligerent opera-goers of Parma by his several virtually nonstop weeks of brilliant conducting, emerging as the hero of the usually grudging Parmesans. In an unlikely but nonetheless authentic happy turn of fate, Parma loves Bruno Bartoletti!

24 Maria Callas and Renata Tebaldi: Two Donnas, Both Prima!

The new Lyric Theatre (later to be known as Lyric Opera) of Chicago started in the mid-1950s by attracting the important star power that had been bottled up in Europe during World War II. It would be years before the impoverished opera companies on that side of the Atlantic could again afford to pay the costs of producing grand opera in a grand manner—even with their government subsidies. Compensation for singers, directors, designers, and choreographers, however, *was* within the reach of Lyric's management. There were practically no indigenous important American competitor companies except the San Francisco Opera—which offered very short seasons, not all that well-attended—and the Metropolitan Opera. The Met was the dominant player, and its new manager, Rudolf Bing, felt that he held all the cards through his virtual monopoly. If you were a foreign opera star who wanted to work in the United States, you had to agree to the Met's maximum fee of $1,500 per performance—and not a penny more!

Maria Callas was delighted to give Bing his comeuppance when Lyric's Carol Fox—whose feisty spirit she admired—offered her $250 more per performance. Maria signed up for both the 1954 and 1955 seasons, and soon afterward the world's other greatest diva, Renata Tebaldi, signed on for 1955. Among the other big-time artists Lyric snared during its first two seasons were Ettore Bastianini, Carlo Bergonzi, Jussi Björling, Anita Cerquetti, Mario Del Monaco, Dorothy Kirsten, Giuseppe Di Stefano, Tito Gobbi, Gian Giacomo Guelfi, Alicia Markova, Birgit Nilsson, Nicola Rossi-Lemeni, Tullio Serafin, Giulietta Simionato, Léopold Simoneau, Ebe Stignani, Richard Tucker, Astrid Varnay, and Vera Zorina.

Madame Callas enjoyed enormous success in her 1954 debut season at Lyric Theatre in the title roles of *Norma, La Traviata,* and *Lucia di Lammermoor.* When she appeared in Lyric's *I Puritani, Il Trovatore,* and *Madama Butterfly* during the 1955 season, New York opera-lovers were in open revolt because they had never even heard Maria. The provincial (from a New York perspective) Chicagoans, however, were having a field day—or two seasons of field days! So Bing came, reluctantly, to Chicago after having enraged the diva by refusing her salary demands—like an Amonasro brought to Egypt in chains, his entire artists' fee structure in jeopardy, and he capitulated after attending Maria's performance in *Il Trovatore.*

Knowing Bing would have to surrender and that the courtly Viennese would kiss her hand, I planted every news photographer in the American Midwest in Maria's small dressing room—with her gleeful agreement, of course. After the curtain calls I rushed her there, and we all waited for Bing. We didn't have to wait long. Soon there was a knock on the door. "Who is it?" she archly called out. "RRRudolf Bing"—the *R* rolling and Teutonic—came the reply. With malicious sweetness she beckoned, "Oh, do come in!" I raised my arm to signal the waiting photographers, and every Speed-Graphic camera came to eye-level. The door opened, Maria extended her hand, and Bing crossed the threshold, kissing that hand on cue. Flashbulbs lit the room, and pictures of what I then called "the greatest surrender since Grant accepted Lee's sword at Appomattox Court House" hit the world press the next morning along with Bing's announcement that Maria Callas would sing at the Met in the 1956 season.

It was assumed that we would be sharing Maria's services with the Met in the coming years. Fate intervened, however, when—following our final 1955 performance, *Madama Butterfly*—a federal marshal named Stanley

Pringle handed her a little piece of paper—the famous subpoena—in the wings of the Civic Opera House just after the last of her many curtain calls. I, of course, just happened to be there with all the photographers to catch for posterity that scene more dramatic than even Sardou might have dreamed. Maria protested with shrill screams of defiance to the hapless minion of the federal courts and even cited celestial immunity. "I am an angel, you can't do this to me!" she screamed. She must have envisioned herself floating above the rest of us, as in a Marc Chagall painting. By morning Maria had taken leave of Chicago and, as it turned out, of Lyric, too. She maintained, however unreasonably, that we ought to have defied the federal courts for her and somehow protected her in this matter. The press on every continent ran juicy stories about Maria's backstage showdown with Pringle, accompanied by those incredible spitfire photographs.

What was all this about? The other shoe was falling, finally, in an ongoing lawsuit concerning Edward Bagarozy (the plaintiff and Maria's former manager) versus Maria Callas (the defendant) over her breach of contract. We helped her stave off that litigation for two years; in 1954 we even brought her into the country via Canada, thus avoiding the subpoena of the New York court where Bagarozy had instituted his suit. In 1955, however, he filed anew, this time in federal courts, which have jurisdiction in Chicago.

Had Maria been served upon arrival to rehearse for the 1955 season she would undoubtedly have immediately fled the country and Chicago would not have experienced her *I Puritani*, *Il Trovatore*, and *Madama Butterfly*. Before she arrived, however, we privately appealed to friends in high places and received a "stay of execution." She wouldn't be served until she *finished* her contract with us, and that's the way it was. Everyone gained thereby. Lyric kept its centerpiece attraction, the public was able to continue experiencing the performing genius of a fabulous and unique artist in *three* outstanding operas (seven performances in all), *and* Maria received all her fees and the kind of rhapsodic press reviews that most opera singers dream of but rarely receive.

To understate matters, she left in a huff. We would not see Maria again until 1974, eighteen years later, when we convened the Verdi International Congress under our Lyric auspices and—for the first time—not in Europe. She accepted our invitation to appear on a blue-ribbon panel of celebrated international critics, musicologists, and scholars and artists to consider solutions for the artistic problems in opera. Deliberations took place in the Civic Theatre adjoining the Civic Opera House and before an audience of opera enthusiasts, many of whom came from great distances to Chicago. By the time of the Verdi Congress, Maria and Carol Fox, both now long gone (Maria died in Paris on September 16, 1977), had made up and become friendly again. Over the years Maria sent greetings to me via mutual friends, and we had a warm reunion between the sessions.

When it came Maria's turn to speak you could have heard a pin drop. She made the astonishing statement that opera's artistic problems could *all* be solved by eliminating all baritone arias from composers' scores. The "offending baritone arias only impeded the flow of the operas' storylines!" Was she joking or did she really mean it? I think that most of us there thought she meant it. I saw her onstage, in the wings, in 1954 as she attempted to stop Tito Gobbi, the great baritone and—mind you—her close friend, from taking a solo curtain call after his rendition of the senior Germont's two glorious arias in the second act of *La Traviata.* "Not in *my* opera!" she screamed in the wings, grabbing his arm before he shook her off and bounded out in front of the curtain to terrific applause. She sulked in her dressing room for a very, very long time before going on in the third act. Maria went after applause-hungry tenors, too. According to one apocryphal tale she is said to have kicked dramatic tenor star Mario Del Monaco in the shins repeatedly on one occasion to discourage *him* from bounding out for well-earned cheers!

That Maria harbored other eccentric ideas was emphasized over lunch at my club one day in 1965 when she spoke of taking on roles that were clearly way outside her voice category. She insisted that a good singer should be able to perform *any* role in the opera repertoire, from contralto at the bottom to coloratura at the top. To prove her point, and with perverse logic, she said, "Danny, you're a writer. Well, what kind of a writer would you be if you could only type A, B, C, D, and E on your typewriter, and not F, G, H, I, J, K, and all the other letters of the alphabet?" Discretion being the better part of valor, I quickly changed the subject!

Perhaps I am a romantic, but I was touched by Maria's devotion to her elderly husband, an Italian industrialist who never left her side (I chuckle when I write "elderly" because when I met Giovanni Battista Meneghini he was nearly three decades younger than I am now). The three of us were at lunch one day at the old Covenant Club after a color photograph session at Tribune Tower. Over dessert Maria told me that when she had been poor and unrecognized, he, a man of substance and great connection in the opera world, had believed in her talent and backed her career. Then she said, eyes brimming with love and gratitude, "He married me." She would never permit anybody, she added, to hurt him or fail to show him proper respect. (I'm not sure what evoked that line of thought; maybe somebody at the theater that morning had addressed him as "Mr. Callas.") As she went on and on about how wonderful Meneghini was, he sat there. He spoke no English yet seemed, somehow, to grasp that she was declaring her love for him and, like me, was more than touched. Theirs was not, as some thought, a marriage of convenience. She really loved him—or so she insisted to me. I believed her, and I saw that he *adored* Maria. Meneghini, I'd been told, was regarded as the Henry Crown of Italy, having supplied the concrete for the *autostradas* after parlaying his inherited brickworks into a twelve-factory industrial complex.

Maria was so devoted to her Battista that one evening she decided to use the kitchen of their Ambassador East Hotel suite and cook a meat pie for him, probably according to an old Brooklyn recipe of her mother's. Her culinary effort, however, ended in disaster when either the pie or the oven (I never found out which) caught fire. No one was injured, but a lot of smoke was curling through the hotel's corridors and the fire department had to be summoned. But then a hotel that caters to international celebrities must expect to have some bizarre occurrences.

At any rate, the Meneghinis ate out that night at their favorite dining place—not the elegant Pump Room downstairs but the humble O'Connell's hamburger joint at the nearby intersection of Rush and State Streets. Although certainly not fancy, it had the virtue of being very economical, and Maria was somewhat frugal, which—in her defense—she told me was due to the privations she had endured in wartime Europe. On the afternoon of her arrival in Chicago to begin rehearsals for her American debut in *Norma* in 1954, for example, I invited some important press people to her Ambassador East suite and suggested that she order wine and finger sandwiches from room service for the event. Maria staunchly resisted before finally giving in. Neither Carol Fox nor I had an expense account in the early seasons of Lyric Theatre, and when either of us dined with the Meneghinis we paid the check ourselves. Neither Maria nor Battista ever reached for it.

As I now write about Maria Meneghini Callas—as she was known in those pre–Aristotle Onassis days—a half century has passed since I first worked with her. Although she was then a celebrated opera singer, there has since arisen a worldwide cult devoted to her. A new generation knows her only through those remarkable recordings of the 1950s and via the approximately fifty books that have been written about her life and sensational career.

Thirty-some years ago a Greek-immigrant journalist, Arianna Stassinopoulos, now the political commentator Arianna Huffington, asked me to join her in a radio program devoted to her just-published *Maria Callas: The Woman behind the Legend*. The book featured extracts from a treasure trove of personal letters that Maria had written to a close family friend in New York who then made them available to Stassinopoulos. I have also lectured many times about Maria's American debut and my passionate press agentry in her support. When, many years later, Terrence McNally's excellent drama *Master Class* about her postcareer pedagogic efforts was produced, I gave some Callas-oriented lectures in tandem with those performances. And when Faye Dunaway was doing a national stage tour of that play she came to see me to extract some of my "Maria memories" in order to add authenticity and depth to her performance. Some years ago a British TV producer and his camera crew journeyed from London to Chicago to record my memories of Callas for BBC's internationally televised version of her life. How could I not be pleased when he told me that I was the most articulate person he had ever interviewed? I still receive and respond to letters and calls from Maria's present-day aficionados, including a few who demand to know why Lyric Opera of Chicago doesn't engage her more often!

The November 1, 1954, occasion of Callas's American debut in *Norma* brought immediate worldwide attention to the aborning Lyric Theatre. The Chicago Civic Opera House was jammed not only with opera enthusiasts from far and wide but also with critics, musicologists, and other musical pundits. Maria, Giulietta Simionato, Mirto Picchi, and Nicola Rossi-Lemeni fairly burned up the stage in Vincenzo Bellini's searing masterwork replete with passion, intrigue, tragedy, and violent vengeance. Maestro Nicola Rescigno conducted both superb performances of that truly grand opera, with soaring choruses, magnificent orchestral accompaniment, and thrilling vocalism. Maria delivered the virtuoso pyrotechnics demanded of Norma in spades! Her American career and Lyric's initial season skyrocketed together, all the way up to the highest reaches of the operatic firmament! The wire services were on hand to cover it, as were publications such as the *New York Times, Time Magazine, Newsweek,* and *Life Magazine.*

As Lyric's press agent I exploited Maria's recent La Scala triumphs and succession of Angel Records hits for the debut. Angel, in fact, sponsored our opening night festivities, which we called the Angel Ball and which followed the *Norma* premiere. "La Divina," as Roger Dettmer, Hearst's *Chicago American* music critic took to calling her, followed up with a terrific *La Traviata* with tenor Léopold Simoneau as her Alfredo and Tito Gobbi as Papa Germont. Maria was so completely credible as the "woman who has gone astray" that you forgot you had seen a dozen other sopranos in that role. She made you think *La Traviata* was an original work and wonder how it would end!

At the dress rehearsal of *Lucia di Lammermoor,* her third and final assignment of the season, with tenor Giuseppe Di Stefano as Edgardo, I sat next to a distinguished visitor, Georgio Polacco, the Chicago Civic Opera's principal conductor of the 1930s, who had come from New York for the occasion. As Maria's stunning "Mad Scene" progressed he kept muttering, almost under his breath but nonetheless audible to me, *"fe nom enal"* (phenomenal). And he was right! She literally stopped—*stopped*—the show's premiere two nights later. The house went wild at the scene's conclusion. I clocked the ovation at thirteen minutes, and Maria deserved every moment and minute of that roaring applause. She had perfectly realized what Gaetano Donizetti and his librettist Salvatore Cammarano must have hoped for in their *protagonista.* It was an interpretation of derangement so dazzling that one could say, "Here is the ideal synthesis of the vocal and the theatrical that epitomizes lyric drama!"

The *Chicago Tribune*'s Claudia Cassidy captioned her review, "Which is mad? The Callas *Lucia* or her frenzied public?" She went on, "Near pandemonium broke out, a roar of cheers, a standing ovation. I am sure they wished for bouquets to throw, and a carriage to pull in the streets. Myself, I wish they had both. She is a superb singer in the grand style, a lyric actress of enormous talent. . . . Lucia's first act, spun like silk, sometimes with an edge of steel . . . the 'Mad Scene' sung with a beauty and purity of coloratura and fioriture that can set susceptible folk roaring with joy!"

Without question, Maria worked very hard. She was the first to arrive for rehearsal and the last to leave. I importuned the press to cover the *Norma* dress rehearsal with their photographers so we could have big, beautiful picture layouts the next day. Carol, however, was nervous. She feared that her high-powered star, reputed to possess a high-voltage temperament, would blow a gasket if a flashbulb popped at a delicate moment. All my theatrically educated instinct told me that the only thing that might make Madame Callas unhappy would be if flashbulbs *didn't* pop.

In fairness there were many other reasons to be nervous. Opera on a grand scale was being put together—a vast jigsaw puzzle requiring a profusion of complicated and expensive elements to be perfectly prepared and then revealed at exactly the right time and in the right place. If any one of those components wasn't just right, the whole painstakingly constructed thing could come crashing down! Maria's cooperation where publicity was concerned was total. I had rightly judged that in addition to having considerable artistic strengths she possessed the rare ability to detect every possibility for good publicity, even before a sophisticated press agent such as I did. I tested her and did not find her wanting. I even went so far as to use pictures of her two years earlier when she weighed 210 pounds as part of a before-and-after, full-page layout in the *Daily News*. The "after," of course, showed her at the 132 pounds she had achieved through dieting. She happily gave a lengthy interview to reporter Patricia Hancock and advised all overweight women to carry out *her* diet system. In her case, she stated, losing weight also required exorcising a tapeworm that she blamed for her past obesity (I never understood all this). Readers, she said, who followed her instructions would attain sylphlike figures not unlike her own!

Maria's father, George Kalogeropoulos, who was estranged from her mother, came to Chicago for his daughter's American debut. She introduced us, and we were together a great deal for the next several days. He was terribly proud of her. He was tall, slim, and perfectly turned out for the premiere. Kalogeropoulos reminded me of my late, elegant friend, the eminent pianist Rudolph Ganz, not only in his impeccable full-dress attire but also with a wide and impressive red sash across his chest, for all the world like an ambassador at an imperial ball. In fact, he was then a pharmacist on Riker's Island. La Divina was born in New York City on December 2, 1923, and baptized as Maria Anna Sophia Cecilia Kalogeropoulos. She was a teenager when her mother, Evangelina Dimitriadis, took her to Greece, where World War II soon made their lives extremely difficult. Nevertheless, Maria's vocal training and early performances began in the shadow of the Acropolis.

In her second Lyric season, 1955, she was merely marvelous, with Giuseppe Di Stefano and baritone Ettore Bastianini in Bellini's *I Puritani.* She was also sensational as Leonora in *Il Trovatore,* with Jussi Björling the Manrico, Ebe Stignani as Azucena, and Bastianini and Robert Weede alternating as Di Luna. In her third and final opera of that season—*Madama Butterfly*—she came a cropper, however, not mainly in the opinions of the public or the press but in her own estimation. She never quite believed in herself as the dainty Cio-Cio-San. Even though we brought in the famed retired Japanese "Butterfly," Hize Koyke, to painstakingly coach her, Maria thought herself not credible in the role. She had never attempted it, and she never appeared in it afterward, although she did make recordings as Cio-Cio-San.

I pause to explain a bit more about the Callas-Bagarozy imbroglio. In the spring of 1947 the European opera manager Ottavio Scotto engaged me to promote the opening of the proposed new United States Opera Company, to be headquartered in Chicago and expected to tour widely. (The old Chicago Opera Company, which I represented, had announced closure after its 1946 season.) That spring, about twenty European opera singers, many of great renown, and a few brilliant newcomers came to New York and on to Chicago to begin rehearsals. One of the newcomers was Maria Callas, seven years before her American debut with Lyric. She alone of the group did not immediately come along to Chicago but remained in New York for coaching by Bagarozy's wife, a voice teacher. Maria, he told me, had lived in their home, and while there she evidently signed a management contract with Bagarozy, under which he would receive a healthy percentage of her income for years to come.

Unfortunately, the elderly Scotto had vastly underestimated the costs of his ambitious project, and the United States Opera Company never opened. It was a catastrophe for the stranded artists who had come to Chicago from Europe. Among them were important international stars such as sopranos Carmen Gracia, Mafalda Favero, and Hilde Konetzni; dramatic soprano Anny Konetzni; mezzo-soprano Cloe Elmo; lyric tenors Nino Scattolini, Galliano Masini, and Franco Beval; dramatic tenor Max Lorenz; baritone Danilo Checchi; and basses Nicola Rossi-Lemeni and Heinz Rehfus.

With the all-out press support of *Tribune* critic Claudia Cassidy and the cooperation of Herb Carlin, the Civic Opera House's manager, I helped promote a fabulous benefit concert for the stranded artists. Although the performance was well attended, the revenue was only enough to get the singers back to New York City. They had to then pay their own way back to Europe. Maria, however, was able to go directly from New York to Italy, where her career soon blossomed. Her contract with Bagarozy was never implemented. When she began to be successful he claimed his share of her fees, but he had no way to collect as long as she didn't come to the United States. When we announced in 1954 that she was coming to Chicago's new Lyric Theatre, he began legal action. Although she told me she didn't know Bagarozy, she was forced to settle the suit later when she signed with the Metropolitan—for how much I don't know.

When Renata Tebaldi, Callas's great rival of that era, came to Lyric for the 1955 season we worked out rehearsal schedules so the two donnas, both prima, would never be in the Opera House at the same time. The ongoing, worldwide publicity about their feud fascinated journalists as well as the public. In many ways it was a natural competition. Callas performed a wide range of taxing roles that featured astonishing feats of vocal prowess. In doing so she was aided by uncanny theatrical instincts and guidance of the master stage director Luigi Visconti (and later by his young associate Franco Zeffirelli) and by Tullio Serafin, one of that generation's conductor giants. Tebaldi, whom Arturo Toscanini had chosen as soprano soloist for his return to La Scala concert in 1946, had a voice that poured like rich cream, effortlessly, exquisitely, and with ravishing tone. Her acting, although always dignified, did not approach Maria's unique flair and unerring dramatic validity. Audiences were either for Callas and against Tebaldi or vice versa. There was no middle ground! In Italy, volunteer claques always engaged in extended sessions of shouting brava at their respective idols' performances. Those in the Callas camp never missed a chance to hiss when Tebaldi sang, and, of course, the Tebaldi-faithful returned the "compliment" at all Callas performances! It was said that Maria would never dare appear at the San Carlo Opera House in Naples, considered exclusive Renata territory.

Renata arrived in Chicago on a late October day in the fall of 1955 via the New York Central's crack Twentieth Century train, after traveling from Europe by boat. I greeted her at the La Salle Street railway station, a huge bouquet of roses in hand and leading a corps of news photographers and a delegation of Renata Tebaldi's already burgeoning American fan club. Like the Queen of the Night (the Day and the Twilight, too), Tebaldi swept grandly down the steps of her Pullman car followed by her retinue: her mother, her secretary, and her personal maid. Her personal effects included thirty-seven pieces of expensive luggage (yes, I counted), a number duly recorded in the next day's newspapers. She also brought two mink coats, one sable coat, three mink stoles, a wardrobe of high-fashion evening gowns, and all the costumes required for her roles in *Aida* and *La Bohème.* In those days it was the norm for major opera singers like Callas and Tebaldi to bring their own costumes with them, no matter how they clashed with the other artists' costumes or the stage sets. Mario Del Monaco's wife Rena, a voice teacher, made him a new set of costumes each year for his roles (she would also stand in the wings during his performances and sing along with him throughout, requiring the harried stage manager to constantly caution her to modulate her tone).

Renata checked into the Whitehall Hotel on the morning of her arrival and immediately invited the press corps to a lovely brunch in the hotel's dining room. She spoke no English, but with that dazzling smile she didn't need to. Besides, her English-speaking secretary, Linda Barone, was on hand to interpret. Naturally, what was on the mind of the reporters was the purported hostility between Callas and her. When they pressed Renata about it she said—with obvious sincerity—"No company needs a *prima donna assoluta* [absolute prima donna]. There is room for everybody!" From that point on all of us in the room felt certain that the much-publicized feud was very much one-sided. One night when Renata was performing Mimi in *La Bohème,* Maria decided to attend and swept grandly down the center aisle—immediately recognized by the audience, which cheered her lustily. Thus, even before the curtain went up Norma had upstaged Mimi!

When, at the first rehearsal for her Chicago debut in *Aida*, Tebaldi, who was in the neighborhood of six feet tall, made no murmur of protest when confronted with a substitute tenor, Doro Antonioli, who was short, the management loved her! That love affair continued shamelessly for many years. Renata's Aida and her Mimi were both triumphs in that 1955 season, and over the years she appeared with our company often, interpreting central roles in *Tosca, La Forza del Destino, Otello, Andrea Chénier, Adriana Lecouvreur, Falstaff, Madama Butterfly,* and *Fedora*. She even appeared in a dress rehearsal of *Manon Lescaut* in 1968 with the youthful Plácido Domingo. After that appearance the Asian flu immediately felled her before the opera's opening night. She remained ill for many days, and we were forced to bring a replacement soprano from Italy for the *Manon Lescaut* performances. Although more than thirty-five years have passed, I still recall my painful task of obtaining Renata's signed release from our contract while she was still ill, unable to rise from her bed.

I revered Maestro Tullio Serafin and with him had the great privilege of being involved in publicizing the productions of three opera companies. At the height of the fevered furor between the competing camps of Callas-ites and Tebaldi-ites, he was often asked, "Maestro, who do you *really* think is the greater star, Callas or Tebaldi?" And, he told me, "I always tell them what my dear friend Maestro Toscanini once said, in a similar connection: 'Le stelle? Le stelle sono *soltanto* nel cielo!'" (The stars? The stars are *only* in the heavens!).

The "Familia Bartoletti" arrive in Chicago for Lyric Opera's 1964 season. *Left to right:* Bruno, Rosanna, Maria, and Chiara Bartoletti. (Photo by Mike Rotunno; courtesy of Lyric Opera of Chicago)

Maestro Bartoletti's friends, Saul Bellow and Alfredo Kraus, were on hand to help him celebrate his twentieth Lyric Opera anniversary in 1976. In his 1956 American debut season in Chicago he conducted four operas, and his conductor colleagues at the time included Dimitri Mitropoulos and Georg Solti. (Photo by Robert W. Gedman; courtesy of Lyric Opera of Chicago)

With only days remaining until the world premiere of the avant-garde Penderecki opera *Paradise Lost*, its orchestral score was still incomplete, yet Bruno Bartoletti bravely continued to rehearse his Lyric Opera of Chicago musicians in the Civic Opera House. Somehow the opera opened on schedule in Chicago, at La Scala, and (in concert form) at the Vatican, where it was presented for Pope John Paul II. (Courtesy of Lyric Opera of Chicago)

In the fall of 1955, Danny Newman greeted Renata Tebaldi as she arrived on the Twentieth Century Limited to make her Chicago debut with Lyric Theatre in the title role of *Aida* and then as Mimi in *La Bohème,* one of the beloved diva's many memorable appearances with the Chicago opera company. Their warm relationship continued for the next thirteen years. (Courtesy

On November 17, 1955, Maria Meneghini Callas and technical director Monte Fassnacht were in the stage wings of the Civic Opera House moments after the final curtain for *Madama Butterfly* when U.S. marshal Stanley Pringle attempted to serve the imperious diva with a federal subpoena. She ignored his efforts. (Courtesy of Lyric Opera of Chicago)

Callas is jubilant as Rudolf Bing, who had refused to provide the fees she demanded at the Metropolitan Opera, "surrenders" in her dressing room after her triumph as Leonora in *Il Trovatore* at Lyric Theatre in 1955. (Courtesy of Lyric Opera of Chicago)

Callas chats with her collaborator in opera and recitals, Giuseppe Di Stefano, during a 1955 rehearsal break backstage at the Civic Opera House before a performance of *I Puritani*. (Photo by Quinn; author's collection)

Tito Gobbi, one of the twentieth century's most revered singing actors, is especially remembered as the bone-chilling Baron Scarpia in *Tosca* and was one of Lyric Opera's most prolific stage directors. (Courtesy of Lyric Opera of Chicago)

Tito Gobbi and Giulietta Simionato, baritone and mezzo-soprano, were Lyric Opera audience favorites from the 1950s through the 1970s. Here they are Falstaff and Dame Quickly in the much-praised 1958 production of Verdi's masterwork *Falstaff*. (Photo by Nancy Sorensen; courtesy of Lyric Opera of Chicago)

Roger Dettmer, the bon vivant arts critic for Hearst's *Herald-American* and later the *Tribune*, was an original Lyric Opera of Chicago booster, especially in its first two seasons, 1954 and 1955. (Courtesy of Roger Dettmer)

Two of Danny Newman's closest friends in the opera world, the Bulgarian bass Boris Christoff and Swedish tenor Jussi Björling, were both opera and recital stars of magnitude. They appeared in Lyric Opera of Chicago's 1957 production of Verdi's *Don Carlo*. (Photography by David Lannes; courtesy of Lyric Opera of Chicago)

Alyce Newman and Zubin Mehta enjoyed a "Ring Cycle" cast party on March 11, 1996, at Chicago's Casino Club. (Author's collection)

Tenor Plácido Domingo joined Alyce and Danny Newman at the opening night cast party for Lyric Opera's *Girl of the Golden West* on October 17, 1996. Domingo sang the leading tenor role in that Harold Prince–staged production. (Courtesy of Lyric Opera of Chicago)

José Carreras, Pavarotti and Domingo's "Three Tenors" partner, is greatly admired by Lyric Opera of Chicago audiences for his stunning performance as the king in the *Masked Ball* (1976). (Courtesy of Lyric Opera of Chicago)

Krzysztof Penderecki, one of the twentieth century's most successful composers, in 1978. (Photo by Stuart Rodgers; courtesy of Lyric Opera of Chicago)

Luciano Pavarotti, chair of the December 7, 1980, Lyric Opera of Chicago Italian Earthquake Benefit Concert, did not forget to promote his new *William Tell* recording, taking aim at the apple on Danny Newman's head. (Photo by Carmen Reporto, as published in the *Chicago Sun-Times.* Copyright 2005 Chicago Sun-Times Inc. Reprinted with permission)

Danny Newman didn't need a smoke-filled room in which to reveal—not surprisingly—his nominee for the opera world's highest office in 1976. Luciano Pavarotti grins and happily bears it. (Courtesy of Lyric Opera of Chicago)

Renata Scotto, for almost three decades a Lyric Opera leading soprano and James Levine's primary prima donna for many Metropolitan Opera years, arrived in Chicago for her 1988 performances as Mimi in *La Boheme* and was met by Danny Newman for her Lyric Opera debut, also as Mimi, opposite Richard Tucker's Rodolfo, in 1960. (Courtesy of Lyric Opera of Chicago)

Lyric Opera gave a *Don Carlo* post–final performance buffet on December 3, 1957. To the right of the food-laden table is Carol Fox (wearing corsage) and behind her are Sirio Tonelli and Danny Newman. (Photo by Bill Knefel, as published in the *Chicago Sun-Times*. Copyright 2005 Chicago Sun-Times Inc. Reprinted with permission)

Dina Halpern, Judge
Abraham Lincoln Marovitz,
and Cindy Pritzker in the
Civic Opera House's Grand
Foyer, September 12, 1984,
on the occasion of Danny
Newman receiving the Bronze
Star. (Author's collection)

Norman Pellegrini, the veteran
radio producer, anchor, writer,
and raconteur, and Danny
Newman have been profes-
sional associates for more than
fifty years. Here, they attend the
WFMT radio Lyric Operathon,
which set new fund-raising
records. (Courtesy of Lyric Opera
of Chicago)

The eclectic Nobel Prize–winning author Saul Bellow encouraged the writing of this book. The close friends shared a life-long love of Yiddish language and literature and Chicago's ethnic lore. (Courtesy of Lyric Opera of Chicago)

In the Graham Room at Lyric Opera of Chicago, soprano Felicia Weathers, Lyric general manager Carol Fox, and artistic director and principal conductor Bruno Bartoletti pause after a rehearsal of the Virginia Puecher–staged, Luciano Damiani–designed *Angel of Fire* (1966). (Courtesy of Lyric Opera of Chicago)

25 Giuseppe Di Stefano, Dapper, Dashing Bon Vivant and the Tenor Darling of Opera Lovers Everywhere!

The Metropolitan Opera, on its annual post–New York season national tour, stopped briefly in Chicago for a series of performances each year between the demise of the old Chicago Opera Company (as I've said, I went down with *that* ship!) in 1946 and the emergence of a new resident company, Lyric Opera, then called Lyric Theatre, in 1954. During one of those Met visits, all of which I publicized, I received an enthusiastic call from Francis Robinson, the company's handsome and elegant press agent. The sensational Italian tenor Giuseppe Di Stefano, Francis confirmed, would arrive the next day to prepare for his Chicago debut as Alfredo in *La Traviata.*

Francis, preferring not to leave New York City, had subcontracted his Association of Theatrical Press Agents and Managers (ATPAM) agreement to me. We were fellow ATPAM members and good friends, having been on the road together in advance of legitimate plays. Francis well knew of my love of the tenor voice, and he spared no superlatives in praising the Sicilian-born super-*tenore.* Di Stefano, a passionate performer if ever there was one, was gifted with a marvelous lyric vocal instrument along with exquisite Italian diction. The year before he had taken La Scala by storm and had just begun to set New York audiences to shouting all-out bravos.

I had heard the tenor only on Angel Records and was fairly salivating at the opportunity to hear him in person. Because I was simultaneously handling a half-dozen other performing arts projects as well, I was unable to meet him at the airport but arranged for news photographers to cover the arrival. I got to our backstage door in time to greet him before he checked into the then-fashionable Bismarck Hotel, where I booked so many top-level musical artists. I'll never forget how Giuseppe burst through the stage door. A paragon of masculine vitality, he was darkly handsome, perfectly coiffed, and resplendent in a camel's hair designer coat that had a huge sash. He wore an open-throat silk shirt and a gorgeous velour hat. His extensive retinue included an internationally connected manager, Vladimir Lubarsky; a secretary who had previously served the Polish tenor Jan Kiepura; a piano accompanist; a masseur; and various acolytes. Impressed, I said to myself, influenced by Gilbert and Sullivan, "Why, he's the very model of a modern major opera star!"

My high expectations were dashed, however, when the following evening he came up short as Alfredo, not sounding anything like his own high-powered entrance through our Civic Opera House stage door had promised! Fortunately, a few nights later he did electrify the audience as Rodolfo in *La Bohème*. I was to learn via future Met visits and then with a half-dozen years with Lyric Opera of Chicago that consistency was not Giuseppe's long suit. Most of the time he was terrific! And he also cut a fine figure onstage, striding about with superb macho confidence. I was to become one of his most avid enthusiasts. After his first, disappointing Chicago performance, I called Francis Robinson and complained. My comments led to some coolness between us for some weeks, but I called back with the highest praise for Di Stefano immediately after his second and *vastly* improved performance.

Giuseppe ("Pippo" to intimates), whose beautiful lyric voice so thrillingly thrust up into the tenor stratosphere, was ecstatically welcomed by postwar opera aficionados everywhere. They felt that in him they'd found the answer to their prayers—a new Tito Schipa or a new Beniamino Gigli. He obviously enjoyed his rapid rise from stark poverty to being an impeccably groomed, dapper, dashing bon vivant; a gourmet, fancier of beautiful women, and devotee of fast sports cars; and the darling of opera lovers.

The only child of Salvatore and Angelina Di Stefano, a policeman and a dressmaker, Giuseppe was born near Catania, Sicily, on July 2, 1921, but was raised mainly in Milan. He had no childhood musical training except as a chorister in a rural church when he was fourteen (ironically, considering his later rakish predilections, he even entered a seminary). He graduated to the choir loft of Milan's Duomo Cathedral at the modest wage of 5 lira per week and was amazed when friends began to insist that his voice was becoming one of extraordinary quality. They introduced him to the proper teachers, and at seventeen he entered and won two vocal competitions in Italy. Eventually, Maestro Roberto Moranzoni—who had conducted at the Chicago Civic Opera House in the 1920s and whom I had publicized in the mid-1940s—was to teach Giuseppe the art of "interpretation."

World War II interrupted, however, and Giuseppe joined the Italian army's infantry in 1941. While in uniform he would sing at the drop of a hat, and his prescient, opera-loving regimental commander is said to have observed, "You may be a lousy soldier, but as a tenor you will one day be a glory for our country!" Thus he was not sent to the Russian front and went on to vindicate that officer's good judgment. He was captured but escaped to Switzerland, where he soon became a professional singer at a radio station in Lausanne.

After the war—in 1946—Giuseppe made his opera debut in *Manon* at Milan's Teatro Reggio Emilia and began to enjoy meteoric success. On February 25, 1948, he made his Metropolitan Opera debut as the Duke in *Rigoletto* and went on to perform eleven other traditional roles there. In 1947 he began to make recordings of Sicilian folk songs and then recorded highlights from *La Bohème* with Licia Albanese as his costar. Eventually, he would make those historic Angel recordings of *Tosca* with Tito Gobbi as Scarpia, Maria Callas as Floria, and himself as Cavaradossi. Over the years Giuseppe probably made more recordings than any other Italian vocal artist. He sang throughout Italy and was even victorious with the formidable, opera-haughty audiences of Parma's Teatro Reggio with *La Sonnambula* and *L'Amico Fritz*.

By 1947 Tullio Serafin had arranged Giuseppe's La Scala debut in *Mignon* with Antonio Guarnieri conducting and with Mafalda Favero and Cesare

Siepi as his cast colleagues. Later that year, with Giulietta Simionato and Siepi, Di Stefano appeared at Scala in *Mignon*. He was a huge success in Milan as he had been at the Met for four successive years. He—predictably—fell out with general manager Rudolf Bing by failing to arrive for rehearsals on schedule. The irate impresario cancelled all of Di Stefano's future Met contracts. A difficult, demanding, and vengeful boss, Bing also sought to bar him from all U.S. stages. So Giuseppe returned to La Scala's top-drawer leadership of Antonio Ghiringhelli and Victor de Sabata, who were thrilled at the turn of events that gave them back their protégé, to become their prize leading tenor for the next decade.

Giuseppe married his Maria in 1949, and they had three children. The Di Stefanos graciously "loaned" their Italian nanny, Luigina, to Lyric's general manager Carol Fox and her husband, C. Larkin Flanagan, to care for their infant daughter Victoria in the late 1950s. Luigina, not only a devoted caretaker, also taught tiny Victoria to speak Italian before she had begun to learn English!

When the Lyric era began in 1954 Giuseppe was one of the greatest in a roster of great stars, essaying the principal tenor roles in such operas as *Lucia di Lammermoor, Tosca, I Puritani, La Bohème, Madama Butterfly, La Gioconda, Adriana Lecouvreur, Turandot, I Pagliacci, Carmen, Un Ballo in Maschera,* and *Fedora*. Included in our Lyric Opera family circle during those years was Remy Farkas, the artist and repertory director of Angel Records, who was married to Maria De Stefano's sister—they must have been among the world's most beautiful women!

One of Giuseppe's most ardent fans was Steve Bedalow, who in later years and with no previous managerial experience presented him in several well-attended recitals that I publicized on a pro-bono basis. My files for 1963 contain my press release stating that "Di Stefano will make his only Chicago recital appearance of the past five years when he appears at Orchestra Hall on Monday evening, November 11, in a program entitled 'An Evening of Italian Song.'" I have also uncovered publicity materials—produced on my manual typewriter—for his Prudential Hall Recital in November 1958.

It was hard for enthusiasts, including myself, to accept that Giuseppe Di Stefano seemed by the mid-1960s to disappear from the rosters of major opera companies. Theoretically, he had years of good singing left in him.

Many said that the reason for his career decline was his devil-may-care, vocally profligate approach to his art, which contrasted sharply with that of his friend Jan Peerce, who, although seventeen years older than Giuseppe, always carefully husbanded his vocal resources, wary of additions to his repertoire. "Yes, it is a magnificent work, but is it right for *me?*" Jan would ask himself. Giuseppe seemingly thought that *every* opera was right for *him.* Jan, now of blessed memory, who admired Pippo's abundant vocal gifts, said, "He was one of the finest tenors of his time or any other." Jan had no success, however, in urging Giuseppe to be firm about saying, "This I can do, this I *can't* do." In *Bluebird of Happiness,* Jan writes that he failed to convince Di Stefano of that statement's wisdom and that he went on to sing "every opera under the sun, even *Otello.*" Jan explains, "If you drive a car, it doesn't mean that you can drive a taxicab, let alone a big Mack truck." When asked whether he had abused his voice, Giuseppe said:

> I wanted to enjoy life. I didn't want to walk around with a scarf around my throat if it became a bit cold outside. Yes, I smoked a lot, and it's true I used to gamble, and I would stay up late and sometimes drove around all night. So, of course, critics wrote: "He wasn't in shape to go onstage, he was undependable." And they could always find some people in the opera to whisper about me, people who were jealous. *I* was never jealous of anybody myself. I never had to go around saying that I had the greatest voice. Let people today judge me by my recordings.

Between 1954, when Lyric Opera of Chicago began, and 1960, Giuseppe Di Stefano performed in eighteen major productions with our company. I spent a good deal of time and effort keeping track of him during those memorable seasons for he was apt to disappear even in mid-rehearsal and keeping tabs on eccentric tenors was just one of the multiple duties of a company press agent. At one dress rehearsal, for some reason, he decided not to wear his costume even though we made production photographs only on those occasions and there was only *one* dress rehearsal for each opera of the season. He misbehaved, however, with such aplomb, and even disarming charm, that we were always quick to forgive him.

Pippo is not a tippler, but he never refused an opportunity to make a wager. His fascination with games of chance had caused him to ask for performance fees a year ahead of time from certain opera company managements. Roulette was his favorite way of losing money. When he wandered off (nobody knew where) between acts at one rehearsal I began to call all the gaming places in central Chicago. Undoubtedly, by the time he finished his first season with us he knew where every gambling house was located in the city *and* its environs! And so did I!

Another weakness was his admiration for lovely women. One day in the mid-1960s when he no longer performed with us, he startled me when he suddenly emerged from a chauffeured car as I was passing on Madison Street just east of the Civic Opera House. I knew the beautiful, elegantly accoutered woman with him. When he spied me he asked imperturbably and in a conspiratorial whisper, "Danny can you keep a secret?"

Giuseppe is as proud as he is tempestuous. When he and the martinet-maestro Herbert von Karajan did not see eye to eye at La Scala on the proper interpretation of the role of Rodolfo in *La Bohème* (a matter of transposing the first-act aria), the star tenor set a unique record by accepting a $10,000 fee for *not* performing! With characteristic panache, Pippo immediately contributed that amount to charity. Although possessing a ravishing pianissimo in the late 1940s and early 1950s, he began to take on heavier roles in the 1960s to the dismay of some critics who thought he was sacrificing the pristine purity of his voice in order to perform more demanding elements of the tenor repertoire. A critic, in Pasadena, California, however, must have made him very happy by praising him because "he forewent the chandelier-shattering way to easy applause."

By 1966 Giuseppe's years in the world's big opera houses had ended. He then entered the then-thriving operetta field with ease and success, racking up a hundred performances in Berlin's Theater des Westens as Prince Sou Chong in Franz Lehár's *The Land of Smiles* and then seventy North American performances in 1967. As that year ended he had sung that same role fifty more times at Vienna's Theater an der Wien. Things somehow went awry, however, soon afterward when he tackled another popular Lehár work, *Der Zarewitsch*, in 1968. His contract was canceled after only sixteen performances, and—aside from a Johann Strauss *Ein Nacht in Venedig* venture almost a decade later—he has eschewed operetta.

In 1974, when Lyric Opera hosted the first International Verdi Congress convened outside Europe, famed opera singers, musicologists, music critics, and aficionados from many countries came to the week-long sessions in Chicago's Civic Theatre (then adjoining the Civic Opera House).

Among them were Maria Callas and Giuseppe, who were taking a break in their unfortunately not very well received recital tour of venues in Hamburg, London, Paris, Tokyo, and North America's principal cities. Maria seemed to be chipper, but Pippo was quieter than usual and not in one of his best moods. Maria, at least, had the pleasure of telling off the world's baritones in a bizarre speech to the congress (chapter 24), but he had no role in those proceedings.

One of Giuseppe's most consistently delightful personal traits is a never-failing and devilish sense of humor. In 1979 we were celebrating Lyric Opera's twenty-fifth anniversary with a lavish gala concert that was preceded by the Chicago Historical Society's "Hundred Years of Chicago Opera," an exhibit that had opened in its impressive museum the day before. Principal Lyric artists of the past quarter century—many of them already retired—were coming from all over the world. I awaited them with a platoon of press photographers in the lobby of the museum, which had a huge, glassed-in entry hall. I was able to see all the artists and out-of-town music critics as they arrived in limousines and cabs, and, seeing me with my complement of photographers, visitors came straight to me. I was busy hugging divos and kissing divas (many of whom I hadn't seen in years) and getting them photographed when in strode Pippo. (This was at the time that many know-it-all opera cognoscenti were saying that his career decline was caused by never having developed a "proper vocal *technique*.") Seeing me, and knowing that I was a year and a half older than he, still passionately practicing my profession, Giuseppe looked into my eyes and very earnestly asked, "What is it, Danny, your *technique?*"

Indubitably, in his first Lyric Opera seasons (1954–60) he was one of the most exciting singers I have heard or cherished. Even though he gave me many anxious moments long ago, he has been a good and true friend through the years. These days Pippo, jaunty as ever, resides in Santa Maria near Lake Como and also, for part of the year, at his home in Kenya, where in 2005 he was viciously attacked by bandits and has been undergoing a slow recovery from the attack's effects.

26 Baritone Tito Gobbi, Lyric Opera's Godfather Who Made the Huge Civic Opera House Shrink to Intimate Size

Claudia Cassidy, the legendary Chicago music and drama critic, once wrote that Tito Gobbi was "Lyric's godfather at its christening" and that "he struck one of its deeper roots." I loved her descriptions of his starring characterizations in his and Lyric's 1954 debut season. His Scarpia in *Tosca*, she wrote, was "evil, carnal, sinister, ruthless, yet of obsidian elegance, the aristocrat of style, that silky, dark baritone supple as a rapier." Just days earlier in the role of the elder Germont he had helped Maria Callas send Lyric soaring via her Violetta in *La Traviata*. Also that season there was the bubbling delight of his Figaro in *Barbiere di Siviglia*. Claudia Cassidy praised "the putty-nosed clowning, the brilliance, opulence and blitheness in masquerade, deftly spun of wit and knowing slapstick. Tito's Figaro was young, debonair, with a flick of malice, too—a true singing actor to toss off 'Largo al factotum,' and to make the huge Civic Opera House suddenly shrink to intimate size." His exuberant, ego-maniacal Figaro remained the standard by which opera aficionados of that time were to judge Gioacchino Rossini's singing barbers.

Gobbi—handsome, charismatic, and the best actor of his era in the opera world—was a precursor of a more modern theatrical approach for singers. He used his voice to develop character in the manner of Konstantin Stanislavsky's actor disciples. During Lyric's first decade he was also its "shadow" artistic advisor and greatly influenced Carol Fox, the company's founding general manager, in the choice of artists and selection of repertoire (chapter 23).

On a mid-October afternoon I greeted Tito Gobbi at Midway Airport on his first arrival to Chicago, and I continued to greet him for the next quarter of a century. He was most often accompanied by his wife Tilde and their daughter Cecilia, who is now a lovely matron with a grown daughter. I quickly interviewed our new star because I had received only a limited amount of advance publicity material from his European manager, the cigar-chomping S. A. Gorlinsky, who also represented Tito's frequent costar, Maria Meneghini Callas. At the time, Gobbi's English was quite limited, so I put what he told me into my own words and released the results to the press. He was delighted with them:

My Unpromising Debut in Grand Opera!
by Tito Gobbi, as told to Danny Newman

I had left my law studies in 1937 at the university in Rome to study voice. My teachers there must have thought I had promise because I was given a scholarship stipend of one thousand lire a month and the right to attend La Scala rehearsals and performances. Please understand that I had never appeared on the opera stage or done any public performing whatsoever. One evening, in formal attire, I attended a performance of *Orseolo* by Ildebrando Pizzetti. Sitting in my assigned box seat, little did I realize that I would be appearing on that very stage before the evening was out! For, I had hardly seated myself to await the beginning of the overture, when an opera company official excitedly rushed into my box and dragged me backstage with him despite my protests. It seems that somebody was needed to enter upon the stage at a certain cue, sing one line—all on one note—and then, exit. The regular comprimario had failed to appear. I protested that I had no experience, that I wasn't ready, that I needed to have rehearsals, that I was afraid, etc. However, I was assured that it was a snap, that all my fears were groundless, that when the moment came, one of the assistant conductors would push me out onto the stage, and I would then sing my one note and retire from the field with honor.

Meanwhile, somebody daubed evil-smelling makeup all over my face with a dirty rag, and I was forced to don a costume that was obviously several sizes too big for me (I was an unbelievably spindly lad at the time). The moment came—or at least the assistant conductor in charge of Tito Gobbi thought it had. He pushed me out onto that huge stage, fiercely whispering, "Sing!" Always respectful of my superiors, I obeyed. I sang. This was a mistake! My mentor, nervous himself, had bade me begin on the wrong cue, and world-famed basso Tancredi Pasero was still in the middle of his great aria! Yet, I sang out my one note. The basso, cut off before his time, stopped and stared at me incredulously. The conductor, who was the *Orseolo* composer Pizzetti himself, had a desperate look on his face (I shall never forget it; it haunts me still), and his baton was poised like a sword to run me through.

The prompter, almost apoplectic with rage, hoisted himself on one elbow out of his prompter's box and screamed at me for all to hear: "Oaf! Lout! Villain! You have ruined us! You have ruined us all!!!" I fled into the wings, tearing off my costume, scraping off the makeup with my handkerchief, and rushed out the stage door, into the dismal night, shouting back to my "colleagues" of La Scala: "To hell with your opera! I am going back to law school!"

And he did, winning the degree of Doctor of Jurisprudence. However, despite this unpromising beginning, Tito Gobbi remained in the field of grand opera.

How I Became the Pride of Parma
by Tito Gobbi, as told to Danny Newman

Parma, a city near Milan in the north of Italy, is famed for its population of hard-hearted opera aficionados. There you find a special breed of opera fan. He is opera-wise and knows that he is. He thinks that no one in the world knows as much about singers as he does. He is known to become violent and to throw things when displeased by vocal artists. Thus, even seasoned opera stars fear to sing for the hypercritical ears of the Parmigiani. For example: A new tenor singing one night at the Parma Opera House committed the unpardonable sin of cracking on his high notes! The audience didn't just boo. It *whistled* its supreme contempt! Next morning, the unhappy tenor hailed a porter at the railway station, and instructed him to carry his luggage to the train for

Milan. The porter picked up the bags and was about to start toward the train when he stopped abruptly, turned, and looked sharply at the defeated singer. "Aren't you the tenor who sang last night?" he asked. Shamefacedly, the humiliated singer admitted: "Yes, it was I." "Then, carry your own bags," the porter-critic hurled dismissively at him and angrily stalked away!

This is how, in 1946, *I* made *my* debut there: I drove a new car—a custom built Alfe Romeo—into that opera-intoxicated town. As I parked in front of the hotel, word spread that the new baritone had arrived. A crowd gathered, ostensibly to admire the car, but they had really come to look over their new potential victim, despite there having been some good reports about him.

But one could clearly see, in their sullen demeanor, their real feelings in the matter, which were: "*We* haven't passed on him yet!" I strolled past a butcher shop, and the proprietor—a huge, surly man—called out to me: "Are you the new baritone for *Barbiere* tomorrow night?" I politely replied: "Yes, why?" He then said threateningly: "You should have come here with a special voice instead of a special car." I protested: "But you haven't heard me yet!" He ignored this, saying ominously, "*We'll see tomorrow!*"

On the following night, not without trepidation, I began to perform for an audience that sat with folded arms like judges in a criminal court. Perhaps prodded by this pressure, I sang quite well. However, there was practically no applause at the end of the individual arias and in the places such audience response normally comes. I thought that my goose was cooked. However, at the very end of the performance, I was surprised by a tremendous ovation, lasting many minutes. Afterward, practically the entire audience, it seemed, followed me to the restaurant where I was to have supper. All their former intransigence just disappeared. They seemed to love me! I asked them why they had applauded so sparingly except for the final ovation. They said that they hadn't been sure that I could keep up such a high standard, and until they were sure—that is, until the very end—they were not going to give me the satisfaction of a big hand. One of the spokesmen shrugged his shoulders and said by way of explanation of the strange folkways of the Parmese, "That's the way we are."

The next morning on my way to the restaurant, I passed the butcher shop again. The proprietor, who had been lazing in the sun, bolted into the shop immediately upon seeing me. I passed on, not wishing to rub salt in his wounds. I had hardly seated myself at my table when the front door burst open, and the hulking butcher roared: "Where is the special baritone with the special car and the special voice? Here is a special sirloin for him!" He was carrying an enormous steak such as I had not seen since before the war. It was duly broiled, and I ate it with good appetite and great satisfaction. I felt I had earned it!

Like many non-Italian operagoers, I first savored the youthful, handsome Tito Gobbi, who was theatrically gifted and had a supremely expressive voice, when I publicized his widely distributed Italian-made movies, *Rigoletto* (conducted by Tullio Serafin) and *Il Barbiere di Siviglia* (with costars tenor Ferruccio Tagliavini and basso Italo Tajo), at Chicago's World Playhouse during the 1940s. Over his twenty-eight Lyric Opera of Chicago seasons Tito performed principal baritone roles in forty-six productions and was stage director of twelve works, including *Il Barbiere di Siviglia, La Traviata, Tosca, Aida, La Bohème, Rigoletto, Il Tabarro, Un Ballo in Maschera, Girl of the Golden West, Andrea Chénier, Otello, I Pagliacci, Le Nozze di Figaro, Adriana Lecouvreur, Don Carlo, Falstaff, Gianni Schicchi, Simon Boccanegra, Fedora, Nabucco,* and *Don Giovanni.*

Born on October 24, 1913, Gobbi died in Rome on March 5, 1984, less than two years after his final Lyric assignment, staging *Tosca* in 1982. Although he was a star in major opera centers the world over, many years of sustained success came in Chicago and London. My London relatives regarded me in awe when Tito left a telephone message for me at their home when I was in town on a consulting assignment for the Royal Opera House.

Lyric has presented a proud procession of grand opera's most celebrated artists, but none received the affection and regard that Tito enjoyed. We honored his memory in 1984, and I eulogized him from the stage of the Civic Opera House on the opening night of *Barbiere,* a production he had originally staged for us. When I asked Tilde and Cecilia to rise from their first-row seats the applause was thunderous. Our printed program contained a large selection of photographs of Tito in some of his favorite roles. In addition, our WFMT good music radio station and its Fine Arts Network presented two hours in "Celebration of Tito Gobbi," a program lovingly planned by Ardis Krainik and WFMT's president Ray Nordstrand, program director Norman Pellegrini, and his associate Lois Baum. They even sent two staff interviewers to Europe to tape remarks of Tito's old colleagues, including tenor Carlo Bergonzi. Tilde and I corresponded until a few weeks before her death; she had lost her sight but still wrote—or scrawled—letters to me, which were, somehow, legible. She was highly cultured, the daughter of a distinguished musicologist and sister of Franca Christoff, wife of bass Boris Christoff. Wise and witty, she was a tower of strength for her Tito. Tilde was his never-wrong, ever-sensitive life partner who provided total love and dedication.

For me, Tito proved a space-grabbing gold mine. He instinctively understood what was required. He'd spend hours at his dressing-room makeup mirror, for example, posing for photographers to carry out the "Master of Make-Up" theme I used over and over to get the large picture layouts that were the envy of my publicist colleagues. Tito delighted in altering his appearance, a cute, turned-up nose for Tonio, a slightly different up-turned nose for Gianni, or a hawklike beak for Scarpia. He loved when I took him to a barbershop to observe at firsthand a working barber's technique so he could shave Dr. Bartolo authentically in *Barbiere.*

Tito was highly sophisticated, and I think my old-fashioned "stunt" press-agentry amused him, but he lent himself to it as if it were serious business. He didn't mind the intrusion of photographers at rehearsals as long as the pictures were run in newspapers or magazines. He was, however, incensed by a picture that appeared in the early edition of the *Chicago Tribune,* one taken at the dress rehearsal of *Nabucco,* the season-opener in 1963. It was a huge photograph. Because of the camera angle, his brother-in-law Boris, portraying the high priest, Zaccaria, appeared to be a giant, whereas Tito, in the title role, was the size of a pygmy. When Tito saw the picture in that evening's early edition of the *Tribune,* he called me at home and demanded that I do something about it. I grabbed a cab, rushed down to the *Tribune*'s picture desk, and convinced the editor to switch pictures (they had many other good shots) in time for the morning editions. They did so, Tito was assuaged, and Boris never said anything to me about the matter.

I was always very careful to search out the roomiest and best-appointed living quarters for the Gobbis, especially after visiting them at home in their palatial Via Asmara apartment in Rome that had a living room with enough space in which to stage a chamber opera. Tito was the scion of a wealthy family that owned eight cars until the 1929 economic depression struck. He was a motoring enthusiast extraordinaire. He was superbly educated and held a jurisprudence degree from the University of Padua; in addition, he painted, sculpted, and was an engaging conversationalist on a wide range of subjects. Tito's reaction was instant when I told him that our failure to arrive at a contract with musicians would cause us to forego the 1967 season: "Chicago, without Lyric," he said, "would be a maimed city!" I later used his powerful statement to headline a fund-raising brochure for Lyric.

Tito and Sam Wanamaker were the emcees for Lyric's lavish 1979 twenty-fifth anniversary gala. Gobbi returned to Lyric for the last time in 1982 to stage our successful revival of *Tosca* with Grace Bumbry/Eva Marton, Ingvar Wixell/Siegmund Nimsgern, and Plácido Domingo/Veriano Luchetti. Time and time again he celebrated his birthday with us, and photographers recorded that he always blew out the candles with one breath—as one might expect from the greatest Scarpia of all time! He gave master classes for our young singers, and for many years he headed the Rosary College extension opera training program at Florence's lovely Villa Schiffanoia. Gobbi had one regret about his otherwise satisfying Chicago career—not performing *Wozzeck*. He considered that role one of his greatest. Geraint Evans did it twice at Lyric, in English.

I came to like Tito the most in the latter days of his career when he had retired from singing to become a stage director. A man of culture and high intelligence, he had mellowed and become more reflective. He had by that time seen it all, done it all, and was philosophical about life. I remember him with much affection and great respect.

A brief tale of two Titos follows: The Yugoslav consul-general and I greeted the Balkan bass Miroslav Cangalovic when he arrived in Chicago to rehearse for his Lyric debut as Colline in our 1956 *La Bohème* with Renata Tebaldi and Jussi Björling. The diplomat confided that he never missed one of Tito Gobbi's performances. "I can understand that," I responded. "Tito *is* a great star." His response was unexpected: "Yes, but that's not the real reason I love him so much. You see, Mr. Newman, Yugoslavia is a communist country and not very popular here. So your Civic Opera House is the only place in this country where I can publicly yell my head off with "BRAVO *Tito!* BRAVO *Tito!*" Little had Gobbi known he'd been made a surrogate for the tough dictator Josef Broz Tito!

27

Saving Roger Dettmer's Life; or, Hell Hath No Fury Like a Tenor Panned!

Music critic Roger Dettmer arrived on the Chicago scene as the 1950s began for his first important job, at the *Chicago Herald-American*. On his first day I appeared in his office on the second floor of the Hearst Building and introduced myself as the press agent for the New York City Opera Company, which had been presenting fall seasons in Chicago each year since the 1946 demise of the old Chicago Opera Company, of which I had been the publicist. Dettmer's experience as a music critic (he later also covered the theater beat) was at that point on the thin side. He was, I believe, hardly older than his mid-twenties and had been cutting his critical teeth as a music reviewer at the Cincinnati Zoo's outdoor summer opera, where roaring lions and trumpeting elephants could be heard along with arias. Roger greatly admired soprano Dusolina Giannini, whom he had heard there. She was the celebrated sister of composer Vittorio Giannini, whose *Taming of the Shrew* and *Harvest* were produced by Lyric Opera of Chicago in 1954 and 1961.

I would regularly visit the *Herald-American* offices to cajole journalists during that period. Some were friends and others were mentors, including

Managing Editor Lou Shainmark, City Editor Harry Reutlinger, Picture Editor Vern Whaley, Chief Photographer Tony Berardi, Drama Critic Ashton Stevens, Movie Critic Lucia Perrigo, Labor Editor Meyer Zolotareff, and Feature Writer Ann Marsters. I was often in the city room in the evening, sitting beside the worldly wise and colorful night city editor Harry Romanoff as he cunningly worked the telephones and assumed various identities. On the floor above was the *Chicago Herald and Examiner,* the *Herald-American*'s sister daily and also a Hearst publication.

I saw Roger almost daily, and we became warm friends. We even developed an affectionate form of greeting in the manner of such contemporary "Dutch comics" as Smith and Dale, whom I handled in vaudeville. I would become "Krrrrausmeier" and address Roger as "Dettmeier." More than a half-century later we still do so, but by telephone. We were also good next-door neighbors for many years. Although Roger has long been retired and now lives in Annapolis, Maryland, we continue to correspond. I always thought that he was somewhat hypochondriacally inclined because he seemed to complain a great deal about various ailments. Now, so many years later, I ask him to forgive me for my doubts. He really *does* suffer from some of the health problems I once thought he imagined.

Roger, a talented writer, was one of those critics who is at their best when either praising or damning artists and the works under review. The problem with doing that is that most performers and most musical events are neither marvelous nor horrible. Most are somewhere in the middle, and Roger didn't quite know how to deal with those. He apparently had neither the style nor the patience to handle the majority of cases before his critical court. As I once told him, "Roger, you are like a singer who has thrilling high notes, gorgeous low notes, but no middle range!"

He warmly and even enthusiastically welcomed the opening of our new resident opera company in 1954 and became best friends with Lawrence V. Kelly, who along with Nicola Rescigno and Carol Fox founded Lyric Opera. Roger wrote a great deal about Lyric Theatre of Chicago before its February 1954 "calling-card" performance of *Don Giovanni* with Eleanor Steber, Léopold Simoneau, Nicola Rossi-Lemeni, Bidú Sayão, Irene Jordan, and John Brownlee. He raved about the show and heavily promoted the company's first season, which opened on November 1, 1954, with the American debut of Maria Meneghini Callas in the title role of *Norma.*

Roger immediately deified her as "La Divina." When Maria was also fabulous in the title roles of *Lucia di Lammermoor* and *La Traviata*, Roger was happy as can be. Maria was sensational, and he went all-out for her as he knew how to do so well. The next season, 1955, saw him all-out praising Maria in another three operas, *I Puritani, Il Trovatore*, and *Madama Butterfly*. Roger was probably at his happiest and most inspired to affirmative articulation during those seasons, for we not only had Maria but also a collection of some of the world's other most talented opera luminaries.

When, after our second season in 1956, Kelly and Rescigno seceded from the young company and left Fox in sole charge of the renamed Lyric Opera of Chicago, Roger's enthusiasm waned somewhat. In 1957 (I'm leading up to how it came about that I saved Roger's life), Lyric began to do three performances of some of its productions; for the first three years—with rare exception—it had done only two of each work. At any rate, one of the operas given *three* performances in our 1957 season was *Don Carlo,* with tenor Brian Sullivan engaged for the title role on November 22 and 25, and Jussi Björling, who had already been the Rodolfo, Des Grieux, and Cavaradossi of that season's *La Bohème, Manon Lescaut,* and *Tosca,* as the Carlo in the final *Don Carlo* performance of November 27. Roger took violent exception to Sullivan's rendition of that role and even questioned the printed program's accuracy in stating that he was a member of the Metropolitan Opera's artistic roster. The insinuation was that the tenor on Lyric's stage must have been an impostor!

Roger's penchant for extravagant statement, in this case not affirmative but negative, almost cost him his life. About fifteen minutes before curtain time on the following night, when we were presenting a *Lucia di Lammermoor* performance with Anna Moffo in the title role and Giuseppe Di Stefano the Edgardo, I noticed that Brian Sullivan was lurking at the head of aisle 4, where Roger usually entered the house. All my finely honed "hell hath no fury like an opera singer panned" instincts told me there was big trouble ahead. Knowing Roger usually showed up not more than five minutes before curtain on the nights he wasn't reviewing, I realized that I had—at most—only ten minutes to avert a catastrophe the full dimensions of which I hadn't yet realized.

When I greeted Brian and asked why he was there (he hadn't asked me to provide a ticket), he replied, clearly, deliberately, and chillingly—teeth

clenched—"I am going to *kill* Dettmer!" I heard with dread his next statement: "I really mean that . . . *I am going to kill him!*" Brian Sullivan was a
strapping and—at that moment—enraged Irish American; Roger Dettmer is thin and frail. I shuddered at the thought of the potential beating
in store for him. Then, too, I noticed an ominous bulge in Brian's coat
pocket. It might have been his gloves or a rolled-up muffler, but I feared
it was a revolver. I desperately kept talking to Brian, attempting to soothe
him, and pointed out that we still had the death penalty for murder in
Illinois. As I talked I kept him walking along with me through the aisle
6 door and then backstage. We walked and talked until we were out the
stage door and onto Wacker Drive.

Perhaps the cold evening air brought Brian to his senses and—heaven
be thanked—he became more morose than belligerent. I walked him down
Madison Street the four blocks to the Morrison Hotel at the southeast
corner of Clark Street, talking all the way, and up to his Tower Suite (which
I obtained at only $7 a night for our principal singers from the hostelry's
owner, William Henning Rubin, my friend of many years). I entered the
suite with Brian and remained with him until the performance was well
into the first act. I left him, finally, as he was dozing off on the couch and
then returned to the Civic Opera House in time for the beginning of the
second act. As I remember that bizarre, almost tragic evening I recall being
asked years later to give the eulogy at that kindly hotel owner's funeral,
when I spoke of his exemplary generosity in giving our opera singers incredibly low rates for the Morrison's high-up luxury accommodations.

The story has a sequel. Despite Roger's low opinion of Brian's performance in *Don Carlo,* Carol Fox thought well enough of the tenor to engage
him for the next season in the role of the Pretender, Dimitri, for Nikolay
Rimsky-Korsakov's version of Modest Musorgsky's *Boris Godunov* with
the fabled Bulgarian, Boris Christoff, in the title role. Brian took his assignment very seriously. During the off-season in Chicago and between
his appearances at the Met he had learned the part thoroughly, including
the original Russian text we were using. The production opened on November 17, 1958, and was a smash. Christoff's powerful performance was
lauded to the skies, and Brian, too, was highly praised by Roger Dettmer
and other critics. On my rounds of the singers' dressing rooms just before
the second performance of *Boris* five nights later, I looked in on Brian,

who was at his dressing table and applying theatrical makeup. I noted that he had taped Dettmer's fine review to the upper-left-hand corner of the mirror. I stood in back of him, and—seeing my reflection—he gestured to the review and said with an absolutely straight face, "Y'know Danny, this Dettmer is really a *very* perceptive critic!"

28 The Great Jussi Björling of the Seamless Voice (and a Bone-Crushing Arm-Wrestler as Well)

It was an evening in early October. We were about to open our 1957 Lyric Opera of Chicago season with Mario Del Monaco, Renata Tebaldi, and Tito Gobbi in Verdi's *Otello* with Tullio Serafin conducting. The telephone rang in our second-floor office in the Civic Opera House. Anna Lisa Björling, wife of the great Swedish tenor Jussi, was in great agitation and asking for me. She and Jussi had just landed in New York on a flight from Stockholm and had intended to fly on to Chicago the next morning. While Jussi was off to find their baggage, she was handed a cable from Sweden informing her of the sudden death of Jussi's brother, Gosta, of heart failure. She predicted that if she told Jussi he would take the next flight home. She asked me to tell her what to do.

Both Jussi and Anna Lisa were my good friends. I had worked with him over the previous decade with three different opera companies and in a number of recital appearances. I asked if she thought that—if he did go home—he would come back for at least part of the Chicago season. She said she didn't think so. Jussi was set to appear in *four* operas with us—*half* of our entire 1959 season: *La Bohème,* with Anna Moffo's and conductor Gianandrea Gavazzeni's American debuts; Tullio Serafin conducting *Manon Lescaut,* with Renata Tebaldi and Cornell MacNeil; Bruno Bartoletti conducting *Tosca,* with Eleanor Steber; and Georg Solti conducting *Don Carlo,* with Anita Cerquetti and Boris Christoff. I didn't have to underscore to Anna Lisa what Jussi's departure would have done to our season—only our second since undergoing the tortuous metamorphosis from the two original Lyric Theatre years. To make matters worse, our finances were still precarious. Somehow I was confident that she would make the right decision. "Anna Lisa," I told her, "I can't decide for you, and to be fair, it would obviously be in Lyric's interest for me to tell you, 'Don't let him leave.' But you, Anna Lisa, must decide for yourself." There was a long pause, and then she replied, "I've made up my mind. Tomorrow morning we'll fly on to Chicago, and only when we're in the hotel there will I show him the cable. Then, I think he'll stay." In her excellent book *Jussi Björling* (1996), written with biographer Andrew Farkas, Anna Lisa describes our 1957 telephone conversation pretty much as I have recounted it here. I was also praying, however, that she was somehow hearing the subtext of my tremulous speech: "For heaven's sake, Anna Lisa, get Jussi to Chicago! We must have him here!"

Jussi's glorious, silver-trumpet sound was totally unique in its perfection from the bottom to the top of his range. Unlike virtually all other tenors, his voice was seamless. He never had to shift "vocal gears" as other, even very great tenors did. His voice had the same incredible consistency throughout. A true aficionado can immediately identify his surging, clarion sound. Once, when I was riding in a cab with four Finnish music academics after a seminar I gave in Helsinki, the driver turned on the local good-music station, which was just then playing a classical opera recording of a wonderful tenor. All four professors—and the driver—pronounced the singer to be Nicolai Gedda, the marvelous Russian-Swedish tenor whom I handled in a 1970 *La Traviata* in Chicago with Montserrat Caballé and Piero Cappuccilli. To me, however, the sound was unmistakably that of Jussi, and I said so. When the recording ended the announcer vindicated me.

In Chicago, Claudia Cassidy wrote as far back as 1948 that "the timbre of Björling's voice was burnished, secure and of a tonal splendor unique in contemporary music." By 1951 she was, if possible, even more enthusiastic: "The beautiful voice, as shining in stratospheric brilliance as it is poignantly veiled in shadow, has been polished to technical perfection. His standards of interpretation are the highest, being informed, imaginative and patrician. In performance he is both generous and eloquent, but he has an instinctive serenity, a rocklike inner reserve. He is a vastly popular singer who maintains the aristocratic art of song." When, during that same year, the widow of Enrico Caruso heard Jussi sing "Vesti la giubba" from *I Pagliacci,* she presented him with one of her late husband's opera costumes, declaring to the blond Norseman, "You have the old Italian School of Singing. You're the only one worthy to wear his mantle, to bear Rico's crown!" Her comment brings to mind the mistaken stereotypes of Scandinavian singers being cold and lacking passion. Those notions are further discredited by one of Jussi's leading ladies, the American soprano Regina Resnik, who described his performance with her in *Manon Lescaut,* "If anybody left his heart and his blood on the stage that day it was Björling as Des Grieux. I have never heard singing as passionate from any other tenor!"

Jussi, somehow, never looked quite as right in opera costumes as he did in his white tie and tails in recital appearances. On the concert platform he was both handsome and dignified, the very model of an artist at ease with his art. Particularly in the early stages of his career, his acting was not quite convincing. Anna Lisa says that to pretend to be somebody else was contrary to his straightforward, honest nature, and that led to him being self-conscious in costume and makeup. Over the years, though, even his severest critics had to admit that his stage deportment had improved considerably. Moreover, from the standpoint of the majority of opera aficionados, if you could sing like Jussi Björling, who cares?

He possessed a powerful physique and a barrel chest. Had there been an Olympic category for arm wrestling Jussi would have undoubtedly come up with the gold medal. He was world-class in that sport. His strength was so phenomenal that he once inadvertently broke a hapless competitor's arm in two places. I usually greeted him with a hug rather than a handshake because his clasp was bone-crunching.

Jussi fought alcoholism all through his adult life, and Anna Lisa has written about that with great love and understanding. The myriad stories about his insobriety, however, are only partially justified. In truth, what was remarkable was his capacity to restrain the urge most of the time. He never canceled any performance I publicized, and I never, ever, saw him inebriated. He often seemed to sublimate his inherited weakness by quaffing soft drinks. Because he carried no coins in the pockets of his costumes, I observed him on several occasions fumbling for a nickel in front of the backstage Civic Opera House soft-drink machine (yes, almost sixty years ago a bottle of cola cost just 5 cents). Often, I would provide the nickel.

Considering how much an uninflated dollar bought in that era, opera stars earned a good living, but it is hard to believe how small their recompense was compared to present fees. I believe that Jussi earned $560 per performance at the Met, while Ezio Pinza got $550 and Zinka Milanov $300. A first-class postage stamp cost 3 cents. It must be remembered that, economically, Europe was still on its knees after the war, and singers couldn't earn much there. America, even without governmental subsidies, was comparatively flush. I recall a press conference that I arranged for Ljuba Welitsch, the "Bulgarian Bomb Shell" on the day she arrived to fulfill her first Chicago recital engagement. Seductively draping herself across the carpeted floor of her Bismarck Hotel suite, the celebrated diva engaged in banter and badinage with reporters. When asked what she hoped to find in America, she replied without hesitation, "Loff and high fizz" (love and high fees). Artists of that era constantly importuned me to conduct a little espionage for them as they desperately sought to discover how much Lyric's management was paying their colleagues. It took constant diplomacy and artful dissembling on my part to fend them off. "Listen, Riccardo," I would say, "Please understand that what you're asking for is classified State Department information, and I work only in the Post Office!"

When Jussi died in 1960 he was only forty-nine. Many people were astonished, thinking he must have been much older because he had appeared in the United States since he was a teenager with the Björling Family Singers. Jussi was a third-generation Björling tenor. His singing blacksmith grandfather was named Lars Johann; Karl David, his singing-prizefighter father, joined his four sons—Olle, Jussi, Gosta, and Kalle—to augment the Björling Quartet, which toured internationally. Jussi's versatile father was also a uniquely gifted voice teacher who so perfectly grounded Jussi in the principles of proper vocalism that his rock-solid technique was universally held to be ideal in all respects.

Jussi enjoyed a distinguished career at Sweden's Royal Opera House, performing the standard repertoire in Swedish before a growing demand for his services in opera houses the world over forced him to re-learn those works in Italian and other languages. He told me that once he began to sing, for instance, the role of the Duke of Mantua in its original Italian he lost all desire to return to performing in his native tongue. Experts agreed that his diction and style in Italian, French, and German were authentic and impeccable.

Over many years of work in the opera field I've observed—not always with amusement—how some wives of celebrated singers seem to feel they must prove that they are indispensable to their spouse's career success. I recall one such woman planting herself in the wings and singing along with her husband while the stage manager desperately sought to shush her. In another case, a spouse would point out imagined slights to her husband and then pick fights with the "offenders." I always imagined her regaling him thus, "You see, Filippo, without my protection you are a doormat in this backstage jungle! Fortunately, *I* am here to fight for you."

Happily, there were exceptions, one of whom was the lovely Anna Lisa Björling. The wise Tilde Gobbi and the compassionate Sarah Tucker also provided sensitive support and serenity for their talented husbands. Anna Lisa was herself a fine professional vocal recitalist and an occasional opera artist. Whenever I saw her, however, she was in her role as loving wife, and if I were a critic I'd have given her a rave review! I deeply appreciate what she wrote about my friendship with Jussi and herself:

> We grew to like Chicago, the audiences, and our professional associates, particularly Danny Newman. Once when Jussi was passing through Chicago, he unthinkingly wired ahead to Danny, asking him to meet his plane, which arrived at pre-dawn, but Danny was there. When Jussi saw him waiting, he began to cry. Danny asked, "Jussi, why are you crying?" Jussi replied, "You came to meet me so early in the morning." Danny protested, "Jussi, you sent me a telegram!" Perhaps Jussi didn't realize that a cable from him meant a command performance to Danny.

Writing about Jussi Björling is more than a thrill. I have been enthralled by tenors since my childhood. Throughout the late 1920s and into the 1930s and 1940s I had heard the impassioned artistry and vocal magnificence of such masterful cantors as Gershon Sirota, Mordecai Hershman, Josef

Rosenblatt, Shavel Kwartin (opera diva Evelyn Lear's grandfather), and Pierre Pinchik. In the 1950s, it was Moshe Kusevitzky, the fabulous cantor of Warsaw, then in the United States, who was the world cantorate's Jussi Björling. It was thus preordained that I would become involved with virtually all major opera and recital tenors of my time (which is turning out to be a *long* time!), including Carlo Bergonzi, Franco Corelli, Mario Del Monaco, Giuseppe Di Stefano, Plácido Domingo, Giuseppe Giacomini, Alfredo Kraus, Lauritz Melchior, Luciano Pavarotti, Jan Peerce, Léopold Simoneau, Set Svanholm, Ferruccio Tagliavini, Richard Tucker, Jon Vickers, and Ramón Vinay—and, via the old 78-inch recordings, Enrico Caruso, Francesco Tamagno, Beniamino Gigli, and Josef Schmidt. I'm rather like Rosalinda in *Die Fledermaus,* who faints dead away upon hearing Alfredo's top A! Indeed, William Mason, Lyric Opera of Chicago general director since 1997, says that "tenors were always Danny's favorites, and they had great admiration for him, too. He counted Jussi Björling and Richard Tucker among his friends, and whenever a new tenor was making his debut, Danny was always at the first stage-orchestra rehearsal so that he could pass judgment!"

All the tenors I have mentioned were superb. They belonged to an exclusive, charmed circle, and each offered something special. While listening to any one of them, I would think, "There can't be anyone greater!" If you had to vote on which offered the most qualities you admire in a singer, you'd have to give the prize to Jussi, especially in the *lyric* tenor category. Jussi personified perfection. There are endless reams of review superlatives written about his greatness by the most perceptive music critics of his generation. Yet I doubt that any could—or did—succeed in describing in words the effect that Jussi's performances had on the public, especially those who, like me, were super-smitten. That is why I have chosen not to reproduce an endless succession of vast redundancies of those rave press notices. Those who had the privilege of experiencing the miracle of the essential Jussi over and over again know that what we felt, and what we remember, is beyond articulation no matter how gifted the writer.

29 Kiril Kondrashin Gives Puccini Lessons, and Adventures with the Russians

Kiril Kondrashin, the noted Soviet conductor of the Moscow Philharmonic, came to widespread international attention when he conducted for the young Van Cliburn's 1958 Tchaikovsky Piano Competition triumph. In October of that year, Kondrashin made his American opera debut with Lyric Opera of Chicago, conducting Renata Tebaldi, Giuseppe Di Stefano, and Cornell MacNeil in *Madama Butterfly.* Both Tebaldi and Di Stefano told me that no Italian conductor had revealed to them the nuances of the Puccini score as had the great Russian maestro.

Kondrashin arrived accompanied by his interpreter, a handsome, personable young man named Nikita Sanikov who some of us speculated was a KGB agent sent to make certain that the conductor did not defect while in America. Josef Stalin was still ruthlessly running his "evil empire" as President Ronald Reagan later designated the dictator's vast domain. Kondrashin certainly seemed to be walking on eggs when interviewers asked about his homeland. Although Sanikov insisted that he had never been outside Russia, his English was virtually perfect and colloquially midwestern in accent, thus confirming what we had read about the extraordinary efficacy of the Soviet language training for foreign-service candidates.

Kiril and Nikita (we were quickly on a first-name basis with each other) were unquestionably open in their admiration for the many conveniences of everyday life in the United States. They couldn't get over, for example, the ease with which we made long-distance telephone calls. Because my European actress-wife Dina Halpern spoke some Russian, they gravitated to our home time and again, where they admired her and her electric appliances. They couldn't get over our refrigerator, ordinary to us but wondrous to them.

Because it limned some of the excesses of unbridled capitalism, Upton Sinclair's pre–World War I exposé of conditions in Chicago's meatpacking industry had long been a staple of Soviet education and indoctrination, so my guests insisted on being taken to the sites of the stockyards even though most of them had been moved to Sioux City, Omaha, and Kansas City. I could, and did, however, take the Russians to the old Stockyards Inn, where they devoured huge succulent steaks evidently not yet easily available, even to privileged artists, at home. When Kiril complained that the radio in his hotel room played only pop music from the top to the bottom of its dial, I obtained an FM radio and showed him how to tune it to the three excellent FM music stations we then had in Chicago. Our radios played the classics, too, and we Americans were not entirely *nye kulturna!*

In the weeks the four of us were together, my wife and I had come to feel close to "the boys," and we spoke freely about many things. When the subject verged on what was apparently dangerous ground for them, however, they understandably dissembled. Once, when I mentioned anti-Semitism, Kiril responded with what seemed standard party-line parroting. He said, via Nikita's interpreting, "Such a barbarous thing as anti-Semitism is impossible in the Soviet Union. Impossible!" And this at a time when Stalin's increasingly paranoid persecution of his country's Jewish citizens had become well known throughout the world! I could only conclude that Kiril had made this patently preposterous statement to demonstrate his Soviet loyalty in the presence of Nikita, thus giving more credence to our original suspicion that Nikita was indeed Kiril's KGB watchdog. I retaliated the next day, however, when I took the boys for a several-hour ride through Chicago's wealthy northern suburbs, Evanston, Wilmette, Winnetka, Glencoe, Hubbard Woods, Highland Park, and Lake Forest. They were goggle-eyed at the thousands of luxurious private homes with impeccably groomed grounds. "Workers' housing!" I insisted.

The Russians had arrived well in advance of the *Butterfly* rehearsal period and in good time to attend our gala 1958 season premiere performance of *Falstaff*. I arranged for them to be invited, of course. Kiril, being a conductor, brought his formal clothes from Russia. Nikita, however, had neither full dress nor tuxedo. Besides, he told me, he had serious ideological misgivings about donning such "imperialist and bourgeois" raiment. I didn't try to convince him and left him to his inner struggle. Finally, he decided to go for it all—white tie, tails, and top hat, all of which I rented for him at Gingiss Brothers. He couldn't look at himself enough in the full-length mirror there. He was a very good-looking, strapping young man, and in his opening night finery he was a knockout. I think the premier event was a defining moment for him in appreciating our "decadent" but very attractive way of life. From that point on, our ways became increasingly acceptable to him. At any rate, my wife and I enjoyed looking on as Kiril and Nikita quaffed champagne and danced into the wee hours after the performance.

After Kondrashin's engagement ended and the boys were preparing for their return trip to Moscow, a strained and unhappy moment came when I suggested that we exchange home telephone numbers and addresses so that we could keep in touch. There was a long and painful pause as they looked at each other and away from us. Finally, Kiril said, "I'm sorry." I understood. It would be dangerous for either of them to receive messages or mail from the United States.

Kondrashin's *Madama Butterfly,* with Renata Tebaldi, Giuseppe Di Stefano, and Cornell MacNeil as the starring triumvirate, was the kind of success of which we opera management people dream. The *Chicago Sun-Times* critic Robert Marsh wrote of Kondrashin, "He knows how to evoke the most delicate—and fiery—of orchestral hues, blending instrumental colors into textures as fine as Japanese silks. He paced the opera so that it sang all the way, with the voices supported by their accompaniment rather than vying with it for attention." The *Tribune's* Claudia Cassidy observed,

"The eloquent Russian's sweeping, almost languishing approach had its Puccini splendors." Donal Henahan, who would become chief music critic of the *New York Times,* stated in his *Chicago Daily News* review that the Russian maestro "lovingly handled the singers" and was in "command every moment." Chicago audiences had seen many fine *Butterfly* productions by earlier companies in the city's turbulent opera-company history, but everyone present for this event seemed to feel they had experienced the opera for, somehow, the first time. At the celebratory cast supper afterward, Tebaldi, Di Stefano, and MacNeil joined the rest of us in heartfelt praise for Kiril Kondrashin, and he was obviously deeply moved by our enthusiastic hosannas.

A few years later our doorbell rang. It was Kiril. He had begun to get permission for more foreign appearances and was on his way to one of them. During our happy reunion we took him into the kitchen and to our refrigerator. We all laughed. In succeeding years there were a few more visits. In 1978—twenty years after his Chicago *Madama Butterfly*—he managed at long last to defect from a still-repressive Soviet Russia and became music director of Amsterdam's prestigious Royal Concertgebouw Orchestra. Unfortunately, his new life in the free world was a brief one. He died in 1981 at age sixty-seven.

30 Plácido Domingo: Tenor, Conductor, Impresario, and Dominant Personality of the Opera World

Having given the greater part of my professional life to the passionate pursuit of "committed" (subscribed) audiences for the performing arts, I see only good in that concept and its promulgation. It is good for the involved opera, theater, ballet, and orchestra organization; good for the artists; and good for the subscribers, who—through the discipline of regular attendance at elegant and exciting entertainment events—become ever more knowledgeable, discerning, discriminating, and sophisticated, ever more perfect audience-instruments for our artists to play upon. Heaven forfend that a major star who has been featured in the advance subscription brochure should—for whatever reason—fail to appear on the promised series date!

Suddenly, I was almost plunged into the volatile vortex of just such a painful situation in 1984 and emerged only by the proverbial skin of my teeth. Plácido Domingo, who began with us at Lyric Opera of Chicago as a promising and fast-rising tenor in our 1968 *Manon Lescaut*, had, a half-dozen years later, risen to international fame and superstar status. He had, well ahead of time, contracted to be the Don José for all our 1984 *Carmen* performances, thus covering the great majority of our subscribers, some of whom had been recently recruited. Too late in the game (subscriptions had already been sold), a conflict was revealed (perhaps a slip-up on the part of his staff), whereby it had become very important for him to back out of our final *Carmen* date on November 30.

Ardis Krainik, whom I had known since the company's 1954 inception (she was then a chorister and office typist), had in 1984 been general director for only three years and had not yet developed the confidence to take on a blockbuster tenor as she did in 1980 when she fired Luciano Pavarotti for repeated cancellations of contracted appearances. Usually, powerful artists are able to get opera companies to back down in scheduling conflicts. Over my many Lyric years I was asked to take on various unpleasant perilous tasks, whether salving the wounds of prima donnas and principal baritones attacked by critics or assuaging the hurts of disaffected contributors for whatever reason. Contending with Domingo's attempted November 30 defection fell my lot, too. I wrote a long, carefully considered letter to Plácido, fully explaining our subscription system's intricacies and pointing out why so many hard-won subscribers might regard his absence not only as cause for no longer buying series tickets but also as a reason to stop contributing—another body blow! I reminded him that it was our thirtieth-anniversary season, and it must not turn into "gall and wormwood." "Plácido," I implored, "it's not just Lyric's honor that is at stake—it's *your* honor, too!" I called upon his personal loyalty to Bruno Bartoletti, Ardis Krainik, and myself. Later, I had good reason to learn that some of what I wrote did get through to him.

By now I have worked with Plácido off and on for some forty years, and I know him to be a fine, sensitive, and conscientious person. We pressed him hard in 1984. When he didn't respond to my letter right away, I went to New York and bearded him in his Met dressing room. To my delight, he finally gave in and agreed to do the November 30 date, thus forcing his managers to somehow get him out of the other commitment. Our *Carmen*, staged and designed by Jean-Pierre Ponnelle, came off beautifully, with Teresa Berganza and Alicia Nafe alternating in the title role and Michel Plasson conducting. Plácido, patriotic Spaniard that he is, caused quite a stir when he demanded we remove atmospheric graffiti vilifying the king of Spain that had been scrawled across one of the sets. Fortunately, it proved a tempest in a sangria pot, and—needless to say—on *this* matter *we* capitulated!

A few years later there was a lovely dinner party in a posh private club atop the Chicago's lofty Prudential Building. At that event, which was attended by both artistic and board leaders of Lyric and the Symphony, Plácido told those assembled that I had taught him the great importance of subscription to the opera field, lessons that I know have been of value to him in his present-day role as general director of two major opera companies, one in Washington, D.C., and the other in Los Angeles, while he continues his performing career.

For me, Plácido Domingo is head and shoulders above other leaders of the opera world. Since 1968 I've publicized twelve seasons of his appearances at Lyric Opera of Chicago, including in *Andrea Chénier, Tosca, Carmen, Otello, Lucia di Lammermoor, Samson et Dalila, La Fanciulla del West, Fedora,* and *Idomeneo.* I was also with him for several concert events in the 1980s and 1990s at Chicago's Civic Opera House and the historic Auditorium Theatre.

Many opera tenors are necessarily conscious of their limitations and therefore carefully control the range of their repertoire. Plácido, however, is clearly and uniquely free of such considerations. As of last count, he essays 122 roles—and every year that astonishing number grows while he thrives on each new challenge. As of this writing, he has garnered eleven Grammy Awards (plus two in the Latin division) and has made more than a hundred recordings (ninety-eight of them full-length operas!). His *La Traviata, Otello,* and *Carmen* films have been major theater releases, and he's made more than fifty videos. Filmed at the original settings, his *Tosca* telecast from Rome was seen by more than a billion viewers in 117 countries. He has had twenty season-openers at the Met, surpassing Enrico Caruso's seventeen. Plácido has conducted at the Met, Royal Opera House, Covent Garden, and the Vienna State Opera.

I've always been amazed at Plácido's physical and emotional stamina; his travel schedule and work regimen are unbelievable. Yet he handily handles everything with unmatched aplomb. To his administrative tasks he brings a wealth of practical knowledge derived from his vast association with opera company operations everywhere. He told me some thirty or more years ago about the workload he had with his parents' Zarazuela troupe in Mexico as its youthful stage manager, carpenter, electrician, costumer, scene-shifter, prompter, chorister, publicist, and ticket-seller—*and,* he said, "I also swept the stage!" Undoubtedly, such a background provided perfect basic training for his future career, more important, I think, than any university arts management course could have been. Plácido's experience seemed familiar as he recounted it to me, for I underwent a similar and variegated grounding in the theater and its complexities at a similar age.

Although marriages in general—in our time—are certainly not as long-lasting as they once were, the union between Marta Ornelas Domingo and her Plácido is still going strong after more than four decades. Their two sons, Plácido Jr. and Alvaro, were born, respectively, in 1965 and 1968. Plácido is quick in interviews to lovingly praise Marta, always pointing out that she gave up her promising soprano career in order to become his "helper in all things" as he puts it. Marta, a native of Mexico, studied voice and languages and began to appear in Mozartian and German lieder concerts at the Opera Bellas Artes of Mexico City. There in 1961, the same year she and Plácido met, she won the highest award for her Susanna in *Le Nozze di Figaro* opposite Cesare Siepi's Figaro and Teresa Stich-Randall's Countess.

Plácido and Marta married in 1962 and were off to Tel Aviv to appear together with the Opera Company of Israel, where for the next several years they performed in virtually the entire standard repertoire of the opera tradition within that company's always strained economic circumstances. In one Israel Opera Company photograph, the Domingos are costumed as Mimi and Rodolfo for a staging of *La Bohème.*

After almost three years the Domingos, enriched with much professional opera experience, returned from the Middle East. In the 1950s and 1960s I attended a number of performances at Israel Opera. When asked why that company's presumably "grand opera" staging wasn't more grand, I suggested that, costs of producing big-time operas being what they are, the Israelis, who were constantly threatened by the seven hostile Arab nations surrounding them, could either afford a first-class army and air force or a first-class opera company but not both! Then, the events of 1967 (i.e., the Six Day War) underscored my point!

Marta's soprano roles have included those of Despina, Rosina, Rosalinda, Micaela, Marguerite, Tatiana, Donna Elvira, Lauretta, Maddalena, and Nedda. In later years, mothering chores honorably acquitted, she began a new career, stage direction, and made her debut at the Teatro de la Opera in Puerto Rico. She has staged productions for the opera companies in Seville, Los Angeles, Bonn, Liege, Washington, D.C., St. Petersburg, and New York (the Met).

It was in 1985 that Plácido put his burgeoning career on hold to begin a long—and in vain—vigil outside a collapsed structure in Mexico City where four members of his family were trapped during an earthquake and perished. Broken-hearted, his anguish evoked sympathy the world over. Because the news of that terrible event had reached him backstage at our Lyric Opera of Chicago where he was in rehearsal, I saw firsthand how this sensitive man was devastated. He could not return to Lyric that fall, and the 1985 season had to continue without him.

One can hardly write about Plácido Domingo's fabulous and multifaceted career without reference to his part in one of the most sensational box-office attractions in modern show business history, the Three Tenors. With his two co-superstars Luciano Pavarotti and José Carreras and conductor greats Zubin Mehta and James Levine, the attraction fascinated even greater audiences than had the huge numbers that turned out for Buffalo Bill's historic Wild West shows a century earlier. The Three Tenors even out-grossed all big-time sports spectaculars. Under the management of a latter-day P. T. Barnum, Impresario Tibor Rudas, and with the advantage of sophisticated electronic amplification, the Three Tenors performed in huge outdoor venues in New York, Tokyo, London, Los Angeles, Vienna, Gothenberg, Munich, Dusseldorf, Melbourne, Modena, and Barcelona. In Paris, in front of the Eiffel Tower, they performed for an audience of 150,000 in addition to an estimated billion television viewers in more than a hundred countries.

Although music purists contest the value of such wholesale introductions to great music to a new and previously unreached public and often point out the imperfections of high-decibel amplification, listening to the marvelous tenors—under *any* circumstances, whether in conventional opera theaters or the vast expanses of a football field—is an occasion for special aural pleasure. For someone who enjoys tenors as much as I do, a

Three Tenors concert is like being served a top sirloin, a New York strip, and a filet mignon—all at the same meal!

I've always been in awe at the startlingly wide range of Plácido's repertoire choices for opera appearances and recordings and his consistent willingness, busy as he is (and no person in the musical world is busier) to study and master difficult scores that I'll guess very few managers are after him to perform a second or third time. A short list will indicate his unalloyed artistic idealism—and he has encompassed more roles than any other opera singer, ever. Some of the esoteric assignments have been in Ruperto Chapi's *Margarita la Torenera,* Jean-Philippe Rameau's *Hippolyte et Aricie,* Jules Massenet's *Hérodiade,* Giacomo Meyerbeer's *Le Prophete,* Gian Carlo Menotti's *Amelia Goes to the Ball,* Anton Garcia Abril's *Divinas Palabras,* Gomes's *Il Guarany,* Giacomo Puccini's *Le Villi,* and Saverio Mercadante's *Il Giuramento.*

Plácido says that he considers himself fortunate because—thanks to his art—he has been able to see much of the world and bring "a little joy to millions of people." I've always admired the seriousness with which he regards his responsibility to audiences. Before his April 16, 1985, recital in the Auditorium Theatre he was so ill that the opening curtain had been held up for some ten minutes and the management was reconciled to canceling the performance. He had such misgivings about disappointing the public, however, that at the last minute he asked me to go out on that hallowed stage and say he *would* perform and do the best he possibly could. I followed his instructions, and somehow—although handicapped—he managed to thrill his listeners with a succession of Gaetano Donizetti, Gioacchino Rossini, Giuseppe Verdi, Puccini, and Massenet arias in the first group and then—after intermission—to enchant them with Spanish songs by Amadeo Vives, José Serrano, Federico Moreno Torroba, Pablo Luna, Gerónimo Giménez, and Manuel Fernández Caballero. I'm sure that his throat was hurting at the end, but he was happy. He hadn't let 'em down! Unquestionably, Plácido Domingo is the dominant personality of the opera world of our time. I fervently wish him to enjoy continued good health and incredible vitality.

31 *Paradise Lost* Composer Krzysztof Penderecki and Pope John Paul II

Beginning in 1972, Lyric Opera began to make plans for participating in the then-upcoming 1976 American Bicentennial celebrations and controversially commissioned the noted Polish avant-garde composer Krzysztof Penderecki (*Ksheesh*-toff Pen-der-*etz*-kee) to create an ambitious new opera. His *Devils of Loudon*—based on John Whiting's dramatization of Aldous Huxley's account of witchcraft, exorcism, and sexual hysteria in baroque France—evoked much excitement in the musical world, as had his *Losmogonia* oratorio. That work, commissioned for the twenty-fifth anniversary of the United Nations, impressively expressed metaphysical speculations about a future in which man dared confront the fundamental questions of time, space, and eternity.

Many American musicians took a dim view of Lyric's prestigious commission going to a foreigner, especially considering that the prestigious assignment would commemorate the two-hundredth anniversary of the nation's founding. Carol Fox and Maestro Bruno Bartoletti took that complaint into consideration, but they felt it not appropriate to be parochial or narrowly nationalistic on such an occasion. America's Bicentennial deserved to inspire an opera by one of the world's finest contemporary composers. Among those discussed were England's Benjamin Britten, Germany's Hans Werner Henze, and Italy's Luigi Dallapiccola.

In finally settling on Penderecki, Fox and Bartoletti were hearkening to critics who had been disappointed in the 1950s and 1960s when Lyric did not embrace composers of contemporary and "progressive" works. Unquestionably, Penderecki was highly regarded internationally as a creator of both operatic and symphonic repertoire in those categories. *Devils of Loudon* had been a recent sensation in the world of the musical avantegarde. Perhaps onto the scale also went the fact that Chicago is one of the largest centers of Polish-born population anywhere, including Warsaw and Kraków. Other reasons for Penderecki's selection were what was then a too-short list of established American composers as well as Carol Fox's well-known preference for Europeans in the opera field.

Penderecki came to Chicago in January 1973 for the official announcement. By mid-1974 there had also been meetings with Carol Fox and Maestro Bartoletti in Milan, New York, Salzburg, Florence, Madrid, London, and Kraków. It was finally decided that the new opera would be based on a monumental work of Western literature. Penderecki had long been intrigued by the operatic possibilities for Dante's *La Divina Commedia* and Milton's *Paradise Lost.* The final choice was the latter classic, for which there would be an English libretto with Hebrew elements. Bartoletti would conduct, producer-director Sam Wanamaker was to be the regisseur, and poet-dramatist Christopher Fry would fashion the libretto. By 1975 the Czechoslovakian stage designer Josef Svoboda and choreographer John Butler had also come on board.

As it turned out, however, our composer couldn't deliver the score on time for the 1976 deadline. He seemed to have lost his muse. Troubles multiplied. Sam had other contractual commitments and had to withdraw, and the next two years brought—to put it mildly—a plethora of changes in artistic personnel along with overwhelming technical problems. Directors, designers, and writers came and went while elaborate and costly stage settings were constructed only to be jettisoned. Panic set in at one rehearsal when the three-story-high towers on both sides of the proscenium, containing all our choristers—who were tightly packed in and stacked three stories high—wobbled and came close to toppling! In addition, Carol Fox's continued declining health made it increasingly difficult for her to deal with the ominously mounting difficulties. Her right hand, the resourceful Ardis Krainik, was constantly pursuing Penderecki at various places here and in Europe to remind him of his obligation to us. Even through the most stringent years of communist rule in Poland, Penderecki enjoyed special "national treasure" status, which enabled him to leave and reenter the country at will. Thus, he pursued an incredibly busy international career while maintaining residences in both Kraków and New Haven, Connecticut, where for many years he was an ornament of the music faculty of Yale University.

In that chaotic atmosphere the costs of production were going through the roof. Finally, we came perilously close to our much-troubled world-premiere presentation, which had been rescheduled to the fall of 1978. The harried composer had come to Chicago to finish the score. At the same time, Maestro Bartoletti was entering the six final rehearsal weeks with the cast principals and orchestra in the Civic Opera House. As Penderecki frantically strove to complete the work we rushed each page down to Bartoletti's orchestra rehearsal in the pit. We had installed Penderecki in the room adjoining my press office on the sixth floor of the Opera House. I was to see that he continued to work without pause. On October 16, 1978, my FM radio was softly playing WFMT's classical music programming while I used two fingers to type publicity releases on my manual typewriter. Suddenly, there came an important news announcement from Rome. Karol Wojtyla, the archbishop and cardinal of Kraków, had just been named the new pope: John Paul II.

During the years we worked together I came to know that Penderecki, although greatly influenced by German culture, was first a patriotic Pole. Sensing he would be very pleased by the news, I opened the door between us and announced, "Krzysztof, *now* you have a *Polish* pope!" Startled, he looked up from his score and asked, "What are you saying?" "Karol Wojtyla, archbishop and cardinal of Kraków, is the new Pope," I replied. He seemed incredulous, so I urged him to listen to the still-ongoing broadcast through the open door. As he did so he began to exclaim, almost hysterically, "A Polish pope, a Polish pope!" over and over. He grabbed my arm and asked, "Danny, do you know what this means? We Poles have dreamed of this for over a thousand years!" And he began to laugh, and cry, and then sob heart-wrenchingly. Then he suddenly stopped and declared he couldn't possibly work any more that day. I must get him a bottle of whiskey immediately. I sent out for one, and he continued to cry and exclaim over and over, "A Polish pope! It's wonderful! Wonderful!" And so it went for hours as he drank, laughed, babbled, and cried. No more completed pages of the *Paradise Lost* score went down to Bartoletti that day. I felt guilty and didn't tell my Lyric colleagues that I had unwittingly halted the composing for some hours just weeks before the world premiere.

Somehow despite the cumulative anguish of those six long years we opened in late November 1978 and presented all planned seven performances for our large and loyal subscribed audience. We also broadcast the world premiere via an international radio syndication that reached as far as Australia. Under the unhappy circumstances we were greatly relieved to have—at long last—the opera open! Because we had presented *Paradise Lost* in partnership with Teatro alla Scala, we moved the entire production—lock, stock, and barrel—to Milan for eight performances in January and February 1979. There was also a private concert version for Pope John Paul II at the Vatican.

La Scala provided its orchestra for the opera's Italian run, but Penderecki insisted that it bench its chorus and Lyric's entire choral complement be brought over—which it was and at great expense. The Chicago cast principals, including Arnold Moss, William Stone, Ellen Shade, Joy Davidson, Frank Little, and Paul Esswood, also were heard in Milan. Although Penderecki conducted, he told me beforehand that he would never be able to do so on the level of Bartoletti's magical mastery of the formidable complex and avant-garde score. Carol Fox, then seriously ill, made the trip to Italy and was deeply moved by the pope's personal greeting.

The negative economic impact of that project on Lyric Opera of Chicago was considerable, and that coupled with Carol's continued decline in health, which led to her unhappy retirement at the end of the 1980 season (cut down to just five operas instead of the usual eight), caused an almost fatal economic crisis for the company. Fortunately, under Ardis Krainik's leadership, which began in January 1980, the company righted itself and soon began to flourish again (chapter 22).

Although many years have passed since the troubled birth of *Paradise Lose*, other opera companies continue to avoid tackling its massive staging—and orchestral *and* choral—complexities. From time to time, symphony orchestras perform parts of the score, the Adagietto-Adagio and the Prelude, Vision, and Finale. Undoubtedly, the huge costs involved in doing the entire opera—and the perceived failure of its original production—have discouraged would-be producers, even in central Europe where Penderecki is one of the most revered of contemporary composers. His more recent operas—his third and fourth—have been *The Black Mask* at the 1986 Salzburg Festival and a 1990–91 opera buffa created as a burlesque in the spirit of Gioacchino Rossini and based on Alfred Jarry's *Ubu Rex*. Astonishingly prolific, Penderecki has composed a number of symphonies and concertos in rapid succession, including works for flautist Jean-Pierre Rampal, violinist Anne-Sophie Mutter, and cellist Mstislav Rostropovich. Some of his most universally respected early works are *The Threnody for the Victims of Hiroshima,* the *St. Luke Passion, The Entombment of Christ, The Resurrection of Christ, Magnifcat,* and the Violin Concerto written for Isaac Stern, as well as the *Te Deum* he dedicated to Pope John Paul II.

For some time now I haven't seen Penderecki or his lovely blond wife Elzbieta. Although not in any Lyric Opera connection, they became friends of my late wife Dina, who was also from Poland. When I lost Dina, I received a beautiful letter of condolence from Elzbieta. When, every once in a while through the years, Krzysztof is in Chicago he stops by to say hello, and I have seen him in New York and Montreal when we were both working in those cities. He is a charming and handsome man, and it is startling to find that his beard has turned white.

32 The Great Luciano Pavarotti, Faithful Lyric Opera Star, Turns "Serial Canceler" and Ardis Krainik Reacts

Tenor Luciano Pavarotti was at the apex of a great grand opera and concert career when, on August 30, 1989, Ardis Krainik, general director of Lyric Opera of Chicago, responded to the famed tenor's cancellation of his long-contracted appearance for the company's thirty-fifth anniversary season premiere production of Giacomo Puccini's *Tosca* by informing him that Lyric could not consider him for any future engagements. Specifically, in her "shot heard 'round the world" she said, "We are now unwilling to risk one more cancellation by Mr. Pavarotti."

Ardis stated that Pavarotti had conscientiously carried out his Lyric performing obligations from 1973 to 1980. In mounting crescendo from 1981 onward, however, he canceled a great number of his contracted Chicago performances. That created continuing dissatisfaction among Lyric series-ticket subscribers and, finally, cumulative rage among them as well. I had been their faithful ombudsman through the years and received a torrent of angry calls and letters. Ardis, too, was the unhappy target of constant and bitter complaints. Many subscribers knew us personally and would stop us in the street to voice their anger ("You're not going to let him get away with this stuff, are you?" "You're suing him, aren't you?" And on and on). Although we always had a heavy complement of star power in our annual seasons, Luciano had become a special favorite of our audiences, and they felt cheated when he didn't show up as promised.

Luciano's recurring defections in the late 1980s must be viewed in the context of Lyric's out-sized subscribership. For many years some 90 percent of its seats were occupied by series-ticket-holders and only 10 percent by individual purchasers. The number of subscribers and length of seasons regularly increased throughout the 1990s, although Luciano was already gone. Because subscribers are a central source of the contributed money that is our lifeline, the staff is always, and understandably, devoted to their satisfaction.

No one at Lyric wanted to cause Luciano hurt. We greatly admired him as the unique artist he is and considered him a friend. Breaking off relations with him was necessary in defense of our subscribers, from whom we subsequently received a flood of commendatory letters. *Not one* said we hadn't done the right thing! Although they didn't want to then go on record, other opera managements—sometimes also victims of costly Pavarotti cancellations—hastened to praise our action privately.

To be fair, Luciano was definitely not disappointing our subscribers because of whim or petulance or "temperament." Once, for example, his father, whom he adored, was ill. A baker and tenor-aspirant, Luciano's father still sang at weddings. "If you think *I'm* a good tenor, you should hear my *father!*" Luciano would state with pride. Another cancellation was because one of his three daughters was gravely ill with myasthenia gravis, a weakening of the muscles. His 1989 cancellation of *Tosca*, the final straw for Lyric's management, was caused by the singer's "persistent" illnesses.

During the years I worked with him—and that was before his "Three Tenors" era—I always admired his patience with the many people who came tearing at him, wanting all sorts of favors. Overall, I thought he maintained a good balance in that abnormal atmosphere and managed somehow to treat most supplicants in a kindly fashion.

In 1980, before the 1981 through 1989 series of cancellations that ended Luciano's long-time Lyric affiliation, he had been unable to appear in one of his scheduled *Masked Ball* performances. On that occasion, however, he literally talked himself hoarse in his zeal as general chair of the Italian earthquake relief benefit event that Lyric Opera was fostering. On the morning of December 10, 1980, my telephone rang, and an unsteady, croaking voice painfully identified itself as Luciano's. "Danny," he said, "I cannot sing tonight. I cannot even talk. Tell Carol and Ardis." I told them, and they—thunderstruck—immediately began to seek a replacement. As for me, I lived in dread that entire day because I would have to go on-stage and give the audience the bad news. When the time came, I bravely and stentorially announced, "To replace Luciano Pavarotti, who is unable to perform this evening, our sister company, the Metropolitan Opera, has loaned us its distinguished tenor, Carlo Bini!" "Give us our money back!" one man shouted, undoubtedly an unreliable single-ticket-buyer type. Whereupon hundreds of people—our subscribers, of course (God bless them)—immediately and ferociously hushed him. I'd like to think they were thus trying to reward my courage. At any rate, Bini, knowing in whose shoes he was treading, did himself proud with his portrayal of King Gustavus II (we were doing the Swedish version of *Ballo*). Our subscribers' not unkindly acceptance of their Luciano loss that night should be viewed, however, in light of the fact that he had never canceled a Lyric performance before that season.

That 1980 *Ballo* also reminds me of the bitter feud between Luciano and Renata Scotto. It had begun the year before at San Francisco Opera, when the outraged tenor claimed the diva had insulted him in a television interview. When Luciano arrived in Chicago a month ahead of the *Ballo* rehearsals for one of his Chicago vocal recitals that we were sponsoring, I had dinner with him in his Drake Hotel suite. "Danny," he coyly asked, "who is our Amelia for *Ballo?*" I knew that he knew the answer so I said straight out, "Now Luciano, you know damn well that Renata Scotto is doing it." Whereupon he said, "Oh, *no,* I will never appear with her again!"

I said nothing more on the subject, but the next morning I reported the conversation to Carol Fox, who would soon be entering her final season as Lyric's general director. Carol, gravely ill, hit the ceiling and screamed that she would replace him. (How do you replace a Luciano Pavarotti? I thought.) She began to talk about a rising tenor whom I knew couldn't—so to speak—shine Luciano's shoes and ordered me to ready a big publicity campaign to establish him. I quickly punctured that balloon and told her what I believed—that Luciano, despite the game he was playing with us, was a thorough professional who would surely honor his contract. He did. Stage director Sonia Frisell, however, must have despaired when her two "lovers," Gustavus and Amelia, never uttered a word to each other during the entire rehearsal period! That the Luciano-Renata *Ballo* was somehow vastly successful was, under the circumstances, a miracle. It won all-out press enthusiasm that matched the public's appreciative applause.

In the fall of 1981 the recently named Pope John Paul II made his first visit to Chicago, and I brought Luciano and our tenor Frank Little to sing for him at Holy Name Cathedral. We came to rehearse the day before, and Luciano engaged the priests in philosophical and theological discussion. "Why," he asked, "if my actions are predestined by our Creator, am I responsible for my sins?" I was called to the telephone at that point and didn't hear the clerical response. On the next day, as we approached the cathedral, Luciano was more nervous than I had ever seen him, and I asked if everything was all right. He said, his voice quavering with emotion, "Danny, do you realize that I will be singing for *Il Papa?*" His nervousness increased, and when he began to sing "Ave Maria" he faltered momentarily. Then he recovered in a second and went on to sing flawlessly. Undoubtedly, there *is* a big difference between an opera performance and rendering a sacred song in church.

When in the mid-1980s my late wife, the actress Dina Halpern, underwent serious oncological surgery, Luciano sent what must have been a florist's entire stock of long-stemmed roses accompanied by a boldly handwritten note: "To Dina, from Luciano Pavarotti with loving wishes for your recovery." When the flowers were delivered, every nurse from the floors above and below Dina's room came running! Although most Americans were not operagoers, Luciano's fame, enormously increased via phenomenal recording sales and radio and television exposure, put him on the same level with the rock stars who ruled—and still rule—the entertainment roost.

By the advent of the 1970s, after Pavarotti's career had reached sensational status and when the touring Met brought him to Minneapolis (where I was then advising the Minnesota Orchestra, Guthrie Theatre, Minnesota Opera, and other Twin-Cities arts projects), I rushed to the cavernous Northrop Auditorium to hear him for the first time. I reveled in his thrilling and astonishing ability to toss off nine consecutive high Cs with incredible ease and panache in *Daughter of the Regiment*. The great Alfredo Kraus, the young Rockwell Blake, and a very few other tenors could also pull that off but not with that ringing Pavarotti power!

Luciano's mass popularity was underscored for me when in the 1970s I delivered him to a record autographing session that had been scheduled for only a few hours. When we arrived at mid-morning a few thousand of his aficionados were already lined up around the block, and more of them kept coming despite a driving rain. The few hours stretched into the entire day and early evening (the rain never stopped), and he—good naturedly—kept signing. On another record autographing occasion when Luciano's new recording of *William Tell* was featured, he posed for photographs as Rossini's protagonist-archer shooting the apple off his little boy's head—and I was the boy. Fortunately, it was a charade and I escaped unscathed!

One woman had literally built a shrine to him in her home, and I always informed her when he was to arrive in Chicago. I saw to it that Luciano was always greeted and cheered by fans, and I was head cheerleader. Of course, I always called the newspaper and TV assignment editors, so photographers and camera crews were invariably on hand. Those "arrivals" developed a circuslike atmosphere, and it was a lot of fun for all of us! Sometimes our close friends Bob and Flo Weiss would be on hand to whisk him to their suburban home for dinner and an overnight stay. On other occasions I would take him directly to his hotel, where baskets of succulent food sent by other good friends awaited the always hungry Luciano. Of course, that didn't happen when Luciano was dieting; at those times I alone benefited from his friends' largesse.

Opera tenors are not known for admiring other tenors, but Luciano was an exception. He was, for instance, an all-out fan of Richard Tucker, of whom he said, "A phenomenon. His voice is beautiful, shimmering, silvery, powerful, youthful, and vibrant. His technique is as close to perfect as one can get!" After a Met matinee broadcast he telephoned Tucker in his dressing room to tell him, "You are the master of us all!"

Luciano is a native of Modena, Italy, where he and Mirella Freni, world-renowned soprano, were both born in October 1935. Neither of their mothers had enough breast milk and so brought their hungry infants to the same wet nurse. Mirella complained to me that "Luciano got all the milk!"

We all know of Luciano's decades-long struggle with his considerable weight and of his recurring attempts to avert the perils of excessive caloric intake only to relapse after achieving encouraging initial success. During periods when he was succeeding he would prepare dinner for us both, conscientiously cooking a diet meal for himself and a regular one for me. He is an excellent chef, and the food was of gourmet quality. I would be voluble in my praise, while he was silent about his own austere repast. Preparations for those meals began early in the day at provisioners' shops where he would carefully select the Italian ingredients necessary. Back in his kitchen, he would lovingly—never hurriedly—pursue his cookery. Once I when I brought Bess Winakor of the *Chicago Sun-Times* to dinner Luciano was gallant and charming. Moreover, his pasta was smashing.

Luciano had been an excellent all-around athlete in his day, thin and superbly muscled (he proudly showed me a photograph of him attired in his school's soccer team uniform). He had gained a lot of weight by the time I met him in the early 1970s but was still a skilled and graceful tennis player. I would delight in watching him and Ardis Krainik as they exchanged more than spirited volleys over the net at the suburban estate of Lee A. Freeman Sr., who was a Lyric Opera board leader. After Luciano became an enthusiastic equestrian we arranged to provide him with a super-sturdy steed whenever he felt the urge to ride. Antonio Cagliarini, a Gucci executive, often played tennis with Luciano and won his long-term loyalty by managing to always lose the match. Luciano once presented me with a lovely "Gucci exclusive" cravat—undoubtedly with the advice of Antonio—and generously inscribed its package "A Little Thing for a Great Man!" He also never let my important birthdays or anniversaries go by without a loving telegram. Luciano is certainly a terrific tenor and good man, and I wish him health and happiness as he approaches retirement.

33

Tempestuous, Controversial Carol Fox, Who against All Odds Founded Lyric Opera of Chicago

In late February 1954 Lawrence V. Kelly called to introduce himself and ask me to meet him and his friend Carol Fox for lunch at the Swiss Chalet of the then-elegant Bismark Hotel. I was very much aware that they had, under the aegis of a new opera-producing entity Lyric Theatre of Chicago, just presented their two calling-card performances of *Don Giovanni* at the Chicago Civic Opera House, reviewed enthusiastically by the city's music critics, including the *Tribune*'s brilliant Claudia Cassidy, the *Daily News*'s erudite Irving Sablosky, and the Hearst *Chicago American*'s aesthetic Roger Dettmer.

I was also aware of Lyric Theatre's arrival on the Chicago musical scene because the colorful Harry Zelzer, a well-established local concert manager whose Allied Arts Corporation I represented to the press, was bitterly opposed to its emergence and had lost no time in conveying his feelings on the matter to me. Seven years had passed since the demise of the Chicago Opera Company—which I represented—the last of the half-dozen resident companies that had opened and closed since the founding of the first, the Chicago Grand Opera, in 1910.

Zelzer expected to someday head a new Chicago Opera but had expected to do so when *he* got around to it. He assumed that no one else had the know-how, enterprising spirit, or backing to tackle such an undertaking. As he saw it, the young upstarts (Fox was twenty-seven and Kelly was twenty-four) had no right to poach on his "entitlement." I should mention that a triumvirate founded the Lyric Theatre. Partnered with Fox and Kelly, the chief financial officer and managing director, was the thirty-eight-year-old, American-born, and Italian-trained artistic director, Nicola Rescigno, with whom I worked as press agent during the old Chicago Opera Company's 1946 season, when he conducted the Chicago opera debuts of tenor Richard Tucker and soprano Patrice Munsel in *Lucia di Lammermoor.*

Fox and Kelly said they called me because I had the background they lacked—years of practical experience in the opera and theatrical field, promotional savvy, and press contacts in the entertainment world. They had learned of my work with the Chicago Opera Company and the Chicago seasons of New York City Opera and the Metropolitan Opera and that I had also handled a few hundred musical recitals and concerts in Orchestra Hall and the Civic Opera House. They told me about their exciting artistic plans for a brief—but world-class—fall opera season. I liked both of them immediately, and I loved the prospect of Chicago getting a new, first-rate opera company that could pass muster with the high standards of so intuitively astute and demanding a critic as Claudia Cassidy, who for seven successive years decidedly turned thumbs down on the efforts of the visiting New York City Opera Company and was not all that enthusiastic about some of the Met's touring offerings.

Carol and Larry (as they asked me to address them) were intent on getting my full-time, year-around services and offered an attractive contract. Because I had many other on-going projects, however, I felt that I couldn't accept their offer. In addition, I told them that it made no sense for them to enter into such an expensive commitment because the season wouldn't begin until nine months later (scheduled for November 1, 1946) and would run just four weeks (until November 30). Their over-generous offer bespoke the limitations of their business sense, a factor that would characterize the new company's artistically brilliant but very brief life—the fall seasons of 1954 and 1955. Finally, they reluctantly agreed that I would work with them part time, and I resolved to myself that I would give them much more time than they could pay for.

They had no operating capital. For the launching of such an ambitious project, there should have been a war chest of funds, not only for production costs and ticket-sales advertising but also to cover the certain deficits even if all tickets were sold, especially because no subscription audience existed and neither did the contributors it would have generated. Subscription would only begin—in a very limited way—for the 1955 season. With so few funds for advertising we would be overwhelmingly dependent on free space (publicity) in the press and on the radio (TV was not yet a factor). There were then five daily Chicago newspapers. Fortunately, their music critics—who were also feature writers and interviewers—were well disposed to our project and to myself. Cassidy in particular wisely understood the significance of the star power Lyric Theatre was out to attract, especially when we announced that the fabled Maria Meneghini Callas would make her American debut in *Norma,* the initial season's opening production, in November 1954.

Throughout the 1954 and 1955 seasons our world-class singers poured into Chicago, including such luminaries as tenors Carlo Bergonzi, Jussi Björling, Giuseppe Di Stefano, and Mirto Picchi; sopranos Rosanna Carteri, Anita Cerquetti, Dorothy Kirsten, Eleanor Steber, Teresa Stich-Randall, Renata Tebaldi, and Astrid Varnay; baritones Ettore Bastianini, Tito Gobbi, Gian Giacomo Guelfi, and Robert Weede; mezzo-sopranos Giulietta Simionato and Ebe Stignani; and bass Nicola Rossi-Lemeni. La Scala's Maestro Tullio Serafin came, too, while the brilliant Michael Lepore was chorus master and Ruth Page headed the ballet, which offered such luminaries as Alicia Markova, Vera Zorina, Sonia Arova, and Oleg Briansky.

I was able to get newspaper photographer coverage of our stars' arrivals at Midway Airport (this was, of course, before O'Hare Airport) and for every dress rehearsal, a first in Chicago's arts history. To my press-agently joy, I was also able to obtain a succession of big picture layouts, with picture editors kindly supplying extra prints. Lacking funds, we—of course—commissioned no new productions during that period. *All* stage sets came from the old opera warehouse at 2559 South Dearborn Street, where what remained of the productions of several failed opera companies were stored, although fire and flood damaged most of them through the years. Costumes for Lyric's initial seasons came almost entirely from our backstage storage areas. At that time the Civic Opera House, its contents, and warehouse were owned by the 20 North Wacker Drive Corporation, which rented the house and its adjoining Civic Theatre to any tenant who could afford it.

Chicago's opera-lovers, of whom there were not all that many (a half century later their numbers are more than ten times as great), enjoyed Lyric Theatre's two short but artistically exciting seasons. The economic picture, however, was disastrous. In desperation, Larry Kelly had tapped the singers' withholding taxes to cover operating expenses, but those deficiencies would have to be made good. Carol, between the 1955 and 1956 seasons, fell out with Rescigno and Kelly, the main issue apparently being Rescigno's wish to have his powers and compensation spelled out in a written contract. Evidently, she saw that as a threat to her primacy in the founding triumvirate. Kelly took Rescigno's side.

The company had achieved overnight, worldwide recognition even though the public was unaware of the severity of the money problem. This had changed the partners' thinking. Previously—as dear friends—they felt no need for legal clarification of their respective roles. In fact, the program for two performances of the "calling card" *Don Giovanni* contained no staff titles. However, for the initial season, fall 1954, I named Carol as general manager and Larry as managing director.

Mayor Richard J. Daley asked Judge Abraham Lincoln Marovitz to adjudicate their mounting argument. (Lyric had brought international attention to Chicago, for which Daley was grateful.) The imbroglio ended with Carol Fox remaining the sole operating head of the company, which changed its name to Lyric Opera of Chicago. She and her backers formed a board of directors of prominent businesspeople under the presidency of Thomas I. Underwood. Members of the new board undertook all financial obligations of the now-defunct Lyric Theatre entity, including the missing withholding taxes. Larry and Rescigno left Chicago immediately to found the Dallas Civic Opera.

Although Larry and Carol remained angry with each other for the next five years, I'm happy I was able to bring them together. In the fall of 1961 I received a frantic long-distance call from Larry, who said he desperately needed the great Peruvian tenor Luigi Alva for a Dallas Civic Opera performance that week. Alva had somehow signed agreements for the same period with both Dallas and Chicago, and because Lyric's contract was signed first it legally took precedence. Would I, Larry asked, plead his case with Carol, who hadn't spoken to him for six years? I always liked Larry and wanted to help him. I thought fast and told him to fly to Chicago immediately and meet me backstage before our performance that night. I would find a way to bring him together with Carol. When he arrived that evening I rushed him to the dressing room she was using for an office, pushed him in, and closed the door on them. As I had hoped, about fifteen minutes later they emerged, their faces tear-stained but smiling. They had reconciled.

Even though Carol risked that Luigi Alva might not return to Chicago in time for his next Lyric performance, she agreed that he could go to Dallas with Larry the next morning. The gods were on everybody's side. Alva was a big success in Dallas and did get back to Chicago on time. Carol and Larry became fast friends again, and she even urged me to go to Dallas to establish a subscription audience for him, which I subsequently did by getting my Ford Foundation sponsors to assign me there. Larry Kelly was one of the most charming people I have known. He died young, unfortunately, and is buried in Calvary Cemetery in Evanston, Illinois.

Carol was a "brand-buyer." She wasn't out to discover young singers and directors; she sought to create a world-respected opera company *as soon as possible.* Thus, her talent "searches" shrewdly zeroed in on the era's star power—already acknowledged and established top talents. The fact that she signed the fabulous Maria Callas—Europe's most publicized and successful soprano diva—for both the 1954 and 1955 seasons of the new Lyric Theatre, snatching her from the Metropolitan Opera's Rudolf Bing, is only the beginning of the story. Along with Callas came a number of the world's other most in-demand opera singers.

Carol's strategy, however, also had drawbacks. When Joan Sutherland made her sensational Vancouver Festival North American debut in 1958, John Reich, a friend of mine who had been Max Reinhardt's director for opera at Salzburg, called within an hour after her opening performance to tell me he had just heard an incredibly wonderful dramatic coloratura soprano and that Lyric would be well advised to immediately fasten down a U.S. debut for her. I quickly reported this to Carol, who said, "If she's that good, we'll eventually be hearing a lot more about her, and then we'll see." By the time we finally signed Sutherland for the title role in our 1961 *Lucia di Lammermoor* opposite Richard Tucker, her fee had grown greatly and we'd lost her U.S. debut to another opera company.

For many seasons we brought in, with rare exception, a succession of "routinier" European stage directors, although critics and audiences everywhere were then beginning to push for improved staging standards. For a decade I urged Carol to consider some American legitimate theater-stage directors of growing importance. My constant choice was always the greatly talented and successful Harold Prince, whose specialty, musical theater, I didn't think so different than opera (an opinion also prevalent throughout the opera world for some time). Finally, in 1978, my years of incessant pro-Prince propaganda at Lyric Opera brought results. He directed our successful new production of *The Girl of the Golden West* designed by Eugene Lee, which we repeated in 1990–91. (Lee and his then-wife, Franni, were the principal designers of TV's *Saturday Night Live.*) I had known Lee as a fine designer-student at the Goodman Theatre School, which I represented. In the early 1950s I publicized a legitimate stage production of the Bertolt Brecht–Kurt Weill *Three Penny Opera,* designed by Lee.

By delaying, Lyric lost Prince's U.S. opera debut to the New York City Opera. In 1982 his original and ingenious staging of *Madama Butterfly* for Lyric—designed by Clarke Dunham and Florence Klotz—was also great (we repeated it in 1991–92 and 1997–98). His delightful *Candide* was a highlight of our 1994–95 season. Prince is widely known for such Broadway musical stage productions as *Pajama Game, Damn Yankees, West Side Story, Fiorello, A Funny Thing Happened on the Way to the Forum, Fiddler on the Roof, Cabaret, Zorba, Company,* and many other musical hits, all of which were produced before he joined Lyric Opera. Later, he also did *Sweeny Todd, Evita,* and *Phantom of the Opera.* He is now the foremost proponent of the "opera is musical theater and vice versa" concept.

In 1973 I attended a Sunday matinee performance at Minneapolis's Guthrie Theatre of *The Barber of Seville,* which was presented by another of my local audience-development projects, the Center Opera Company, now called Minnesota Opera. I was astonished by a sensational and beautiful young artist, Catherine Malfitano, performing the role of Rosina.

Although I knew nothing about her background, I hurried backstage afterward and introduced myself to her and her parents. The next day, back at our Chicago Lyric office, I told Carol that the youngster was a real find and we ought to sign her right away. Carol told me to calm down and said that if she was all that good she'd soon have some strong credits. It wasn't long before the celebrated French regisseur Jean-Pierre Ponnelle cast Malfitano as Susannah for our 1975 *Marriage of Figaro* production. Of course, by this time, her fee had risen considerably. She quickly became a major star with our company (she has had twenty-some roles since 1975) and is acknowledged as one of the premier singing actresses of the era, an international *liebling* with a vast opera repertoire, lauded in Chicago, New York, Salzburg, London, Vienna, Florence, San Francisco, Berlin, Tokyo, Milan, Brussels, Barcelona, Washington, D.C., Los Angeles, Geneva, Houston, Munich, and elsewhere. In the fall of 2003 she had great success in the title role of Lyric's *Regina*.

Carol Fox, an alumna of the prestigious Chicago Girls Latin School, was raised in an era when the press devoted entire sections to "high society." Carol revered those second- and third-generation inheritors of wealth and much preferred to seek financial support for Lyric Opera from them than to approach the nouveau riche. Her father, George Fox, an office furniture manufacturer, owned a fine boat on which she became a proficient sailor. After I met Carol I observed how much she cherished her friendships with the McCormicks, the Wrigleys, and other local dynastic first families. Over the years, however, society press had begun to shift attention to the new generation of "achievers," people mainly of humble origin but who had made lots of money.

It took Carol some time to adjust to such inevitable sociological changes, but eventually she reconciled herself to accepting contributions from parvenus. On one occasion I arranged for a horse strong enough to carry the weight of Luciano Pavarotti and asked friends in the very horsey suburb of Barrington to supply the required mount. Carol's friend Brooks McCormick, however, owned a major stable, and he was a pillar of society whose wife, Hope, was a leader of our Women's Board. Carol was upset when she learned what I had done, so I quickly disengaged from my friends' assistance and Luciano did his twixt-performance cantering under the McCormick colors.

Carol, when she became the prime mover in establishing Lyric Theatre of Chicago, was an active member of the Junior League of Chicago. In 1953, when she organized her and Larry Kelly's friends to raise funds and sell tickets for the two February 1954 "calling card" *Don Giovanni* performances, other League members were involved in various social welfare activities and also were beginning to assist the Women's Board of the Art Institute in creating junior museum and docent programs. They had focused on children's theater, so Carol felt that founding an opera company for the community would be a legitimate Junior League activity and just the right vehicle for her Junior League enthusiasm.

She saw herself as the company's volunteer leader and paid all her own expenses. As we approached the first Lyric season, November 1, 1954, there were considerable costs for entertaining and transportation, and I urged her to seek reimbursement from our organization, which she finally agreed to do. She drew no salary, however, for the two-year life of Lyric Theatre. When the new Lyric Opera of Chicago entity emerged in 1956, and it was undoubtedly a full-time occupation, Carol asked for and received compensation as general manager. She remained in that paid position and was given regular pay raises (I advised her in salary negotiations with her new board of directors) for the next quarter century, until she retired in the first week of 1981 after several years of debilitating illnesses.

Although she had recruited Kelly and Rescigno, there was never any doubt that the young Carol Fox was the organization's driving force. Her accomplishments should be judged in the context of the consistent failure of some half-dozen previous Chicago opera companies. By the early 1950s, local wisdom held that Chicago couldn't, and wouldn't ever again, support a major opera company. Carol, however, didn't know the job she set for herself couldn't be done, so she went ahead and did it!

In the summer of 1958 Carol asked Dina and me to accompany her and her mother to the Empire State Music Festival in Ellenville, New York, where our Lyric Opera principal bass, the celebrated Nicola Rossi-Lemeni, would appear in the American premiere of Ildebrando Pizetti's *Assassination in the Cathedral.* We would travel in Carol's Cadillac. She was a first-rate driver, and her mother also drove although neither Dina nor I knew how.

It took two full days to reach the festival, way up in the Catskills. On the first day of the trip, we stopped for dinner at a roadside Italian restaurant near Lancaster, Pennsylvania, and an excited young man rushed to the door to greet us. His name was Raymond Pacinelli, and he had sung in the Lyric chorus for several seasons. His father, who owned the restaurant, was disappointed that the son hadn't become an overnight opera star and pulled him back to work in the family business. When late the following day we arrived in Ellenville at the modestly appointed hotel that we understood was the best the town afforded, we found it entirely sold out. Unfortunately, we hadn't thought we needed reservations, and various New York critics and other musical cognoscenti had also been drawn by the premiere event, thus taking up all accommodations. The ever-practical Carol suggested that I slip the desk clerk a $20 bill—which in 1958 wasn't hay. The strategy worked. In a few minutes the clerk decided that the famed conductor Erich Leinsdorf had forfeited his reservation by not arriving at the time he had agreed to. *We* got his two-bedroom suite!

The performance that evening was to take place in a huge tent atop a nearby mountain. For an hour before starting time, operagoers, men in black tie, the women jeweled and coiffed, were driven up a winding, treacherous little road. Rossi-Lemeni had provided us with choice third-row seats. Five minutes before curtain time, however, there came a tremendous thunderclap, and lightening bolts lit the suddenly darkened skies. Just as the curtain rose an electric storm of incredible force hit! The heavy battery of spotlights attached to a temporary rigging just above our heads groaned and threatened to break loose. The curtain rang down, and people ran from the tent as fast as they could! Carol, fastest of all, pulling her mother by the hand, ran like an Olympic track star. Even though we were seated way up front, *she* reached the entrance at the back before anybody else! In minutes the event became a disaster! Outside the tent, torrential rain quickly turned the ground to deep, oozing mud. The women's hairdos were quickly ruined, as were their gowns and shoes. The cabs that brought us up couldn't get back up the mountain for another several hours. Our bedraggled group didn't get back to the hotel until the wee hours. Early the next morning the rain was over, the sun was out, and I went down to the lobby to buy a newspaper. People were sleeping in armchairs and on couches. As I tiptoed past them, I saw—deep in slumber on a divan—my old friend Erich Leinsdorf, with whom I had worked fourteen years earlier with his re-studied Chicago production of *Carmen*. Yes, I did feel guilty at having usurped his comfortable suite.

In some respects one would have to acknowledge that Carol Fox was eccentric. One could sympathize with her not responding to a harsh letter critical of her management decisions. Such letters went right into her wastebasket. Yet she also immediately threw away letters of commendation! In either case she felt that recognizing the correspondent would be granting that person importance. In the same way, she often wouldn't acknowledge a greeting on the street. For her, there was inherent conflict in every contact with another person—someone wins and someone loses—and she refused to be the loser. When a distinguished newspaperman, impressed with Lyric Opera's growing stature, wrote her an admiring letter, Ardis Krainik and I had to retrieve it from her wastebasket, and I dashed off an appreciative reply. Ardis—who could forge Carol's signature perfectly—did so. The letter went off, and several days later the journalist expressed pleasure about it to me when I saw him in his newspaper's city room.

In the final years and months of her life Carol's eccentricities were greatly exacerbated by the physical and emotional strains she was undergoing, and often a complete loss of inhibition resulted. She had always been outspoken, but she may have thought rather than said some things. Now, however, she said things she never would previously have said, which undoubtedly accounted for her loss of support from those who didn't understand the extent of her afflictions nor forgive their unacceptable effects.

As soon as I joined the nascent Lyric in 1953–54, I began to accompany Carol to fund-raisers, some of which were in the homes of Lyric sympathizers or the lobbies of their apartment buildings. On such occasions, both of us spoke and solicited contributions. Sometimes we were invited to dinner parties together, and Carol, with considerable sensitivity, would contact hostesses beforehand to make certain that if they were serving shrimp or other seafood hors d'oeuvres—which she knew I did not eat—I would get fruit instead.

Although Carol was raised as an Episcopalian she was not religious-minded. Ever the pragmatist, she couldn't understand, for instance, why Jews didn't all convert to Christianity. When her parents opposed her marriage to a Catholic she was taken aback by the vehemence of their objections. During that difficult period we had lunch together almost daily, and she was often in tears. Her young man, a very serious medical research scientist, C. Larkin Flanagan, was—unlike her—*very* religious-minded and an ardent Roman Catholic. Eventually, she took instruction, converted to his faith, and soon we were attending their wedding in Holy Name Cathedral.

Carol's high-voltage temperament was widely known, and I was often asked how I was able to get along with her so well and for so long. Usually, I was nimble and skillful in avoiding conflict, but if an important issue came up—especially if the company's or her good was at stake—I would be stubborn. And if I was stubborn enough she would usually conclude that maybe I was right. Most important, she never doubted—or had reason to doubt—that I was on her side. Sometimes, exasperated by my "intransigence," she would begin to cry, which made me feel terrible. I'd tell her that she was hitting below the belt. Another reason for my generally good relations with Carol is that I was often away in other cities or other countries, building subscription audiences. Other Lyric executives who were always in Chicago could be singed by her flame. Moreover, she had begun to meet with her counterparts at the many major American arts organizations that I advised, and she took pride in my home base being Lyric Opera of Chicago.

When in 1973 Lyric Opera commissioned Krzysztof Penderecki for its controversial American Bicentennial opera of 1976, which eventually became *Paradise Lost* (chapter 31), Carol was in relatively good health. By the time the ambitious project came to fruition—two years late—in 1978, however, her health had taken several turns for the worse. Among her increasing catalog of illnesses, she was ravaged by severe osteoporosis and had twice suffered badly broken bones. The series of disastrous *Paradise Lost* production problems and its spiraling costs also contributed to her physical and emotional decline. By the time *Paradise Lost* had its unsuccessful world premiere in Chicago and was about to be presented in Milan (La Scala had been a partner to our production) in early January 1979, Carol was operating on a multiplicity of medicine and nerve. With an extraordinary effort of will, however, she made the trip, bound to her crutches and wheelchair. She was also on hand for a mini version of the

Penderecki work performed at the Vatican, where she was greeted by Pope John Paul II.

The year 1979 brought Lyric's twenty-fifth anniversary season, and Carol, although in constant pain, rallied for the great gala concert tribute to her quarter century of creating a world-class opera company in Chicago. Tito Gobbi and Sam Wanamaker were emcees, and the participating singers were Judith Blegen, José Carreras, Carlo Cossutta, Geraint Evans, Mirella Freni, Nicolai Ghiaurov, Alfredo Kraus, Frank Little, Sherrill Milnes, Luciano Pavarotti, Leontyne Price, Margaret Price, Katia Ricciarelli, Richard Stilwell, and Jon Vickers. The conductors' roster, headed by Lyric's artistic director Bruno Bartoletti, included Riccardo Chailly, Krzysztof Penderecki, Georges Pretre, John Pritchard, and Nicola Rescigno.

During that season, we planned to issue a book, *Lyric Opera of Chicago*, to mark the anniversary, a project Carol had made a priority for me. I spent much of two full years on it, even delaying some of my Ford Foundation–sponsored projects in order to give more time to the book. The volume was of a high literary quality. I enlisted my dear friends, author Saul Bellow and arts critic Claudia Cassidy, to write, respectively, the book's introduction and narrative. Then, I recruited Alfred A. Knopf's noted designer R. D. Scudellari to devise the overall scheme of the volume's presentation.

We were very proud of the book, which offered magnificent photographs, both in color and in black and white. The R. R. Donnelly Corporation, whose owners were friends of Carol, printed our book with loving care. The high costs in effort and money were justified, we felt, because we would send the book to the entire international musical press and to opera impresarioes everywhere. Some costs would come back through sales to Lyric subscribers and through bookstores.

The book was to be released to coincide with the September opening of the twenty-fifth anniversary season. Carol's increasing illnesses, however, and her resulting inability to make timely decisions, caused us to miss the entire first half of the season's lobby—and other—sales. Worst of all, Carol panicked in the face of mounting production deficits and suddenly declared that we couldn't afford to send the long-planned-for *complimentary* copies for worldwide reviews, thus negating the principal reason for doing the book! If the press—the world over—wanted it, they'd have to buy it. It was the low point in my morale during the forty years I had given to Lyric Opera.

During Carol's final, illness-ridden tenure at Lyric's helm, our problems were not with her making *bad* decisions. More than that, we paid a high price for her frequent inability to make *any* decisions in time. Being late authorizing sets to be built in low-cost European studios meant that construction crews had to be paid double and air freight had to be used for shipments rather than low-cost ship transportation. Each day of continuing procrastination proved extremely expensive.

Our financial situation became more desperate as we approached the 1980 season, which Carol made us cut down to only five operas, a decision that was not well thought through. By the time we reached the end of that season we had spent every penny of our working capital and all our reserves: the approximately $1 million left from our endowment fund, the $400,000 the bank had advanced (taking our warehouse as security), and the $1 million Ford Foundation grant from which I had pledged that we would take only the interest. Because I was still involved with a twenty-year-long Ford Foundation agreement to assist America's professional performing arts organizations, I was greatly embarrassed. Limping badly, we ended the 1980 Lyric season in mid-December, and the outlook was bleak.

Carol had fallen out with her board leadership. Fatally ill, she unhappily retired under board pressure on January 2, 1981. She reached me the evening before at the Eugene O'Neill Center in Waterford, Connecticut, where I was conducting a promotional seminar. I got back to Chicago and her apartment by 10 the following morning. Her distress was obvious. I wrote the release about her "retirement" while sitting at her bedside and checked it through with the board's attorney by telephone. Early that afternoon I made the rounds of the newspapers, and also sent the release to radio and television stations through the City News Bureau. Despite our empty treasury, the board somehow came up with a generous financial settlement of Carol's contract. A few days later, Ardis Krainik, at her side for so many years, was named the new general director, something not easily accomplished because, through my guidance, she had already committed herself to becoming general manager of the Australian Opera in Sydney (chapter 22).

Carol, broken in health but not in spirit, hoped to find another position and asked me to prepare a full resume for her, which I did. I had introduced her years before to Saul Bellow, who now, at her behest, contacted the National Endowment for the Arts on her behalf. She was bitter at *everybody* on Lyric's staff excepting myself, and for the remaining half year of her life we were in almost daily touch. I prepared all sorts of materials she requested concerning her Lyric career, theoretically to be used in pursuing future employment in the arts. On July 12, only nine days before her death, I received a brave, playful letter from her: "Feeling much better. Come by, 'Mr. Hectic,' I would enjoy any moment of fun, oh Marx Brother! [a reference to my imitations of Groucho]. Love."

Although Carol died of a heart attack, a newspaper listed her ailments as asthma, emphysema, diabetes, sciatica, cancer, and osteoporosis. I received a call from her former husband, C. Larkin Flanagan, asking me to be chief usher at the funeral on Friday, July 24, in St. James Episcopal Church. Almost four hundred mourners, including Archbishop John Cardinal Cody attended. Robert C. Marsh, the *Chicago Sun-Times* music critic, wrote, "She was a great lady, elegant, poised, confident, a skilled politician, and an adversary to be reckoned with." The *Tribune*'s John von Rhein reminded Chicagoans that she was "the tough and feisty lady who brought world-class opera back to Chicago. Almost overnight she built Lyric into one of America's three most important opera companies." Donal Henahan of the *New York Times* recalled Carol as "one of the most imperious, single-minded people I have ever known in all my years as a music critic. . . . Domineering? She entered the room like a gunboat, bristling for a fight. She knew how to fight, too!" Claudia Cassidy told WFMT listeners on the Sunday following Carol's funeral, "I would not need a crystal ball to know that she died of a broken heart."

Throughout the sixteen years of her own Lyric leadership (1981–97) Ardis Krainik always acknowledged all that she had learned from Carol, but Lyric's board was slow to honor the company's founder and first general manager. When in 1997 the board named the renovated main auditorium of the Civic Opera House the Ardis Krainik Theatre, it was gratifying that soon afterward a fine bust of Carol, for which I had long lobbied, was unveiled in the grand foyer. I was particularly pleased that her daughter, Victoria, with whom our management had a strained relationship over the years, reconciled with us. On Victoria's initiative, the city named the block of Wacker Drive between Madison and Washington Streets Carol Fox Drive in 2000, and I joined with Lyric's general director William Mason in hailing that event at the beautiful dedicatory ceremonies in the house's main-floor foyer.

Lyric Opera of Chicago is widely held to be one of the world's most important opera companies, both in the United States and abroad. European arts leaders have long been amazed at Lyric's artistic achievements and economic stability in the absence of any significant governmental subsidies. The prestigious *Frankfurter Allgemeine Zeitung* has observed in wonder, "Lyric is the Olympus of Opera." It is clear that Carol Fox provided the main force behind Lyric's birth—in an unpromising atmosphere—and the early momentum that led to its long-term success.

Index

DANNY NEWMAN, born in Chicago's Douglas Park area in 1919, has worked as a theatrical press agent since he was fourteen. Among the many aspects of his extraordinary life he is the "father" of modern subscription sales for the arts and served as the publicist for Lyric Opera of Chicago from its inception in 1954. He has also been an international consultant to the Ford Foundation's Division of Humanities and the Arts and is the author of a successful book, *Subscribe Now! Building Arts Audiences through Dynamic Subscription Promotion,* which teaches not-for-profit groups to create and maintain large audiences.

Music in American Life

Fiddlin' Georgia Crazy: Fiddlin' John Carson, His Real World, and the World
of His Songs   *Gene Wiggins*

America's Music: From the Pilgrims to the Present (rev. 3d ed.)
Gilbert Chase

Secular Music in Colonial Annapolis: The Tuesday Club, 1745–56
John Barry Talley

Bibliographical Handbook of American Music   *D. W. Krummel*

Goin' to Kansas City   *Nathan W. Pearson, Jr.*

"Susanna," "Jeanie," and "The Old Folks at Home": The Songs of
Stephen C. Foster from His Time to Ours (2d ed.)   *William W. Austin*

Songprints: The Musical Experience of Five Shoshone Women
Judith Vander

"Happy in the Service of the Lord": Afro-American Gospel Quartets in
Memphis   *Kip Lornell*

Paul Hindemith in the United States   *Luther Noss*

"My Song Is My Weapon": People's Songs, American Communism, and the
Politics of Culture, 1930–50   *Robbie Lieberman*

Chosen Voices: The Story of the American Cantorate   *Mark Slobin*

Theodore Thomas: America's Conductor and Builder of Orchestras,
1835–1905   *Ezra Schabas*

"The Whorehouse Bells Were Ringing" and Other Songs Cowboys
Sing   *Guy Logsdon*

Crazeology: The Autobiography of a Chicago Jazzman   *Bud Freeman,
as Told to Robert Wolf*

Discoursing Sweet Music: Brass Bands and Community Life in Turn-of-the-
Century Pennsylvania   *Kenneth Kreitner*

Mormonism and Music: A History   *Michael Hicks*

Voices of the Jazz Age: Profiles of Eight Vintage Jazzmen   *Chip Deffaa*

Pickin' on Peachtree: A History of Country Music in Atlanta, Georgia
Wayne W. Daniel

Bitter Music: Collected Journals, Essays, Introductions, and Librettos
Harry Partch; edited by Thomas McGeary

Ethnic Music on Records: A Discography of Ethnic Recordings Produced
in the United States, 1893 to 1942   *Richard K. Spottswood*

Downhome Blues Lyrics: An Anthology from the Post-World War II Era
Jeff Todd Titon

Ellington: The Early Years   *Mark Tucker*

Chicago Soul   *Robert Pruter*

That Half-Barbaric Twang: The Banjo in American Popular Culture
Karen Linn

Hot Man: The Life of Art Hodes   *Art Hodes and Chadwick Hansen*

The Erotic Muse: American Bawdy Songs (2d ed.)   *Ed Cray*

Barrio Rhythm: Mexican American Music in Los Angeles   *Steven Loza*

The Creation of Jazz: Music, Race, and Culture in Urban America
Burton W. Peretti

Charles Martin Loeffler: A Life Apart in Music   *Ellen Knight*

Club Date Musicians: Playing the New York Party Circuit
Bruce A. MacLeod

Opera on the Road: Traveling Opera Troupes in the United States, 1825–60
Katherine K. Preston

The Stonemans: An Appalachian Family and the Music That Shaped Their
Lives   *Ivan M. Tribe*

Transforming Tradition: Folk Music Revivals Examined   *Edited by*
Neil V. Rosenberg

The Crooked Stovepipe: Athapaskan Fiddle Music and Square Dancing
in Northeast Alaska and Northwest Canada   *Craig Mishler*

Traveling the High Way Home: Ralph Stanley and the World of Traditional
Bluegrass Music   *John Wright*

Carl Ruggles: Composer, Painter, and Storyteller   *Marilyn Ziffrin*

Never without a Song: The Years and Songs of Jennie Devlin, 1865–1952
Katharine D. Newman

The Hank Snow Story   *Hank Snow, with Jack Ownbey and Bob Burris*

Milton Brown and the Founding of Western Swing   *Cary Ginell, with*
special assistance from Roy Lee Brown

Santiago de Murcia's "Códice Saldívar No. 4": A Treasury of Secular Guitar
Music from Baroque Mexico   *Craig H. Russell*

The Sound of the Dove: Singing in Appalachian Primitive Baptist Churches
Beverly Bush Patterson

Heartland Excursions: Ethnomusicological Reflections on Schools of Music
Bruno Nettl

Doowop: The Chicago Scene   *Robert Pruter*

Blue Rhythms: Six Lives in Rhythm and Blues   *Chip Deffaa*

Shoshone Ghost Dance Religion: Poetry Songs and Great Basin Context
Judith Vander

Go Cat Go! Rockabilly Music and Its Makers   *Craig Morrison*

'Twas Only an Irishman's Dream: The Image of Ireland and the Irish in
American Popular Song Lyrics, 1800–1920   *William H. A. Williams*

Democracy at the Opera: Music, Theater, and Culture in New York City,
1815–60   *Karen Ahlquist*

Fred Waring and the Pennsylvanians   *Virginia Waring*

Woody, Cisco, and Me: Seamen Three in the Merchant Marine   *Jim Longhi*

Behind the Burnt Cork Mask: Early Blackface Minstrelsy and Antebellum
American Popular Culture   *William J. Mahar*

Going to Cincinnati: A History of the Blues in the Queen City
Steven C. Tracy

Pistol Packin' Mama: Aunt Molly Jackson and the Politics of Folksong
Shelly Romalis

The University of Illinois Press
is a founding member of the
Association of American University Presses.

_____

Composed in 11.5/14.9 Minion
with Myriad Italic display
by Barbara Evans
at the University of Illinois Press
Designed by Dennis Roberts
Manufactured by Thomson-Shore, Inc.

University of Illinois Press
1325 South Oak Street
Champaign, IL 61820-6903
www.press.uillinois.edu